Second Edition

COMMUNICATING WITH GRAMMAR

1

Skills for Life

Alice Johnston-Newman
Julita Milewski

OXFORD
UNIVERSITY PRESS

OXFORD
UNIVERSITY PRESS

Oxford University Press is a department of the University of Oxford.
It furthers the University's objective of excellence in research, scholarship,
and education by publishing worldwide. Oxford is a registered trade mark of
Oxford University Press in the UK and in certain other countries.

Published in Canada by
Oxford University Press
8 Sampson Mews, Suite 204,
Don Mills, Ontario M3C 0H5 Canada

www.oupcanada.com

Library and Archives Canada Cataloguing in Publication

Title: Communicating with grammar. 1 / Alice Johnston-Newman, Julita Milewski.
Names: Johnston-Newman, Alice, author. | Milewski, Julita, author.
Description: Second edition. | First edition published under title: Communicating with grammar 1. Skills for life.
Identifiers: Canadiana 20200257277 | ISBN 9780199038480 (softcover)
Subjects: LCSH: English language—Grammar. | LCSH: English language—Grammar—Problems, exercises, etc. |
CSH: English language—Textbooks for second language learners. | LCGFT: Textbooks.
Classification: LCC PE1128. J66 2021 | DDC 428.2/4—dc23

Cover image: Chris Cheadle / Alamy Stock Photo

Cover design: Laurie McGregor

Interior design: Laurie McGregor

Oxford University Press is committed to our environment.
Wherever possible, our books are printed on paper which comes from responsible sources.

Printed and bound in the United States of America

1 2 3 4 — 24 23 22 21

About the Authors

Alice Johnston-Newman, BA, MA, CTESL, is a language teacher, writer, and translator with more than 35 years' experience teaching English as a first and second language to Canadians, new Canadians, and international students. She recently retired as a professor at Collège La Cité in Ottawa and formerly taught at Algonquin College, at Carleton University, and abroad. During her professional career, she has created and adapted teaching material and student workbooks for ESL, enriched level, as well as specialized, career-oriented English courses. She also collaborated with two of the other *Communicating with Grammar* authors in the publication of *Famous Canadian Authors: Developing English Skills* (Pearson, 2008), a reading and vocabulary-building text for intermediate and advanced ESL learners.

Julita Milewski, BA, MEd, has been an ESL teacher for the last 20 years. Her desire to teach ESL started as she herself was learning English as a second language when she first immigrated to Canada as a teenager. Her teaching experience includes working with adolescent and adult learners, international students, and immigrants. She has taught at the University of Ottawa, Carleton University, and various private language schools. She is currently an ESL professor at Collège La Cité in Ottawa.

Series Team

The whole author team created the approach, the topics covered, and the chapter structure for the three-level series *Communicating with Grammar: Skills for Life*. Though each level has its specific lead author or authors, the team worked collaboratively in the development of these publications.

Mohammad Hashemi, BA, MA, is a teacher, editor, translator, and author. He has been coordinating and teaching English for over 30 years, formerly at Carleton University and Algonquin College. He currently teaches at Collège La Cité in Ottawa, Ontario. For more information about Mohammad, visit his website at www.mohammadhashemi.com.

Silvija Kalnins, BA, CTESL, has been teaching and coordinating English for the past 17 years at Collège La Cité. This is her third career. As the eldest daughter of Latvian immigrants, she has experienced first-hand the difficulties of English language acquisition, which has sensitized her to the needs and challenges that her students face.

Jaklin Zayat, BA (Modern Languages), MEd, has been teaching ESL and academic writing for over 30 years. She speaks five languages and is recognized for her knowledge of the construction of many other languages. She currently teaches at Collège La Cité and the University of Ottawa. A co-author of *Famous Canadian Authors*, she also enjoys writing stories currently accessible on her web page, jaklin.ca.

Acknowledgments

From the Authors

We would like to thank our colleagues for their help and feedback during the project of writing the first edition of the book and the revision for this new edition.

We especially want to thank our families and friends for their enormous support, understanding, and encouragement from the project's start to its very completion. Special thanks also go to the excellent editorial and publishing team at OUP Canada for their professional advice and greatly appreciated assistance during the writing of this new edition.

Finally, we want to acknowledge each other—we have enjoyed a mutually supportive, creative experience as a team.

Reviewers

Oxford University Press Canada would like to express appreciation to the instructors and coordinators who graciously offered feedback on *Communicating with Grammar* at various stages of the developmental process. Their feedback was instrumental in helping to shape and refine the series.

Anita Chaudhuri *Mount Royal University*

Laura DiTrolio *Fanshawe College*

Lisa Dubrick *Western University*

Karen Fofonoff *University of Calgary*

Brandie Glasgow-Spanos *St. Ann Adult Learning Centre*

Therese Gormley Hirmer *Humber College*

Patti Holter *Collège Lionel-Groulx*

Cheryl Howrigan *Vancouver Community College*

Olivera Jovovic *Kwantlen Polytechnic University*

Angela Losito *Université de Sherbrooke*

Angela Meyer Sterzik *Fanshawe College*

Marlaina Riggio *Collège La Cité*

Cheri Rohloff *University of Winnipeg*

Chris Smrke *English School of Canada*

Elizabeth Spalding *Kwantlen Polytechnic University*

How to Use the Book

Communicating with Grammar is an engaging three-level integrated skills series for mastering English grammar. Offering grammar instruction using the four skills—reading, writing, listening, and speaking—*Communicating with Grammar* takes students from understanding grammar concepts to successful practice and communication.

Student Text

Overview

We use the simple present verb tense to express facts and generalizations, as well as actions that happen on a regular basis. Such actions include routines, habits, and daily activities.

Use	Form	Keywords	Example Sentences
facts or generalizations	most verbs: I / you / we / they + **verb** she / he / it + **verb** + -s / -es	every day / Monday / Tuesday every weekend every year every summer every vacation / holiday always usually	I **read** books. The earth **circles** the sun. She **works** every weekend. I **go** on vacation every summer. They usually **leave** at five o'clock.
routines habits daily activities		often sometimes rarely never once a day / week / year twice per day / week / year number of times per day / week / year	
	verb *be*: I **am** she / he / it **is** you / we / they **are**		I **am** always honest. You **are** a student. It **is** difficult. They **are** from France.
	verb *have*: I / you / we / they **have** she / he / it **has**		I **have** a dessert once a week. We **have** a house. He **has** a car.

Overview

Each chapter opens with an ***Overview*** that provides an explanation of the target grammar. ***Grammar charts*** present the structure in a clear and easy-to-understand format. The grammar charts use ***consistent colours, bolding, and format*** throughout the book to help students quickly find essential information.

Warm-Up

Warm-Up activities engage students and provide opportunities to start thinking about and using the target grammar in context.

Warm-Up

Read the following passage, and <u>underline</u> the verbs in the simple present tense.

I have a sister. Her name is Izabela. She is older than I am. I live in Ottawa, but she lives in Toronto. She works as a sales representative. She likes her job. She has a son. He is 14 years old. He plays drums, takes martial arts classes, and studies hard. He also likes to play video games. My sister and I often call each other. We usually talk about our family. I really love my sister. Do you have any brothers or sisters? Are you in contact with them?

Write the verbs from the passage for the following subjects:

I, we: _____

she, he: _____

you: _____

Can you see any patterns? _____

The chapter's target grammar is divided into logical and manageable parts; each applies a *learn–practice–use in context* approach.

Formation

Positive	Negative	Yes/No Question
Subject + Verb (+ object / complement)	Subject + Auxiliary + Negative + Verb (+ object / complement)	Auxiliary + Subject + Verb (+ object / complement)
I **wake** up at 7:00 AM every day.	I **do not wake** up at 7:00 AM every day.	Do you **wake** up at 7:00 AM every day?
You **watch** TV in the evening.	You **do not watch** TV in the evening.	Do you **watch** TV in the evening?
He **likes** Honda cars.	He **does not like** Honda cars.	Does he **like** Honda cars?
She **reads** a lot.	She **does not read** a lot.	Does she **read** a lot?
It **costs** five dollars.	It **does not cost** five dollars.	Does it **cost** five dollars?
We **travel** to Yukon every summer.	We **do not travel** to Yukon every summer.	Do we **travel** to Yukon every summer?
They **work** on weekends.	They **do not work** on weekends.	Do they **work** on weekends?

For a detailed explanation of how to form and use questions and negatives, refer to Chapter 11.

Question Words for Wh- Questions

Question words ask about a specific piece of information in a sentence. We use these words when making Wh- questions.

The Wh- question formation is the same as for Yes/No questions. We just put in a question word before we add the rest of the question.

Learn

The grammar instruction starts with a *Formation* section that offers a clear explanation of the grammar topic, often in a table or chart, and illustrates the mechanics.

Practice

Exercises follow the grammar explanation. Students practice the language structures and address common difficulties faced by learners. The many different exercises types include sentence completion, sentence construction, matching, ordering, error correction, transformation, multiple choice, fill in the blanks, and more.

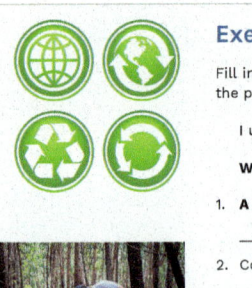

Exercise 1

Fill in the blanks with the correct question words. Each question word needs to correspond with the portion of the sentence in **bold**.

I use reusable bags **because I want to be environmentally friendly.** →

Why do you use reusable bags?

1. **A lot of** people try to carpool to work these days.

   _____ people try to carpool to work these days?

2. Common recyclable materials include **glass, metal, plastic, and paper**.

   _____ do recyclable materials include?

3. **My friend** reuses clean yogurt containers to plant flower seeds.

   _____ reuses clean yogurt containers to plant flower seeds?

4. We help to clean up a local park **every spring**.

   _____ do we help to clean up a local park?

5. My son learns **at school and at home** that it is important to care about our environment.

   _____ does my son learn that it is important to care about our environment?

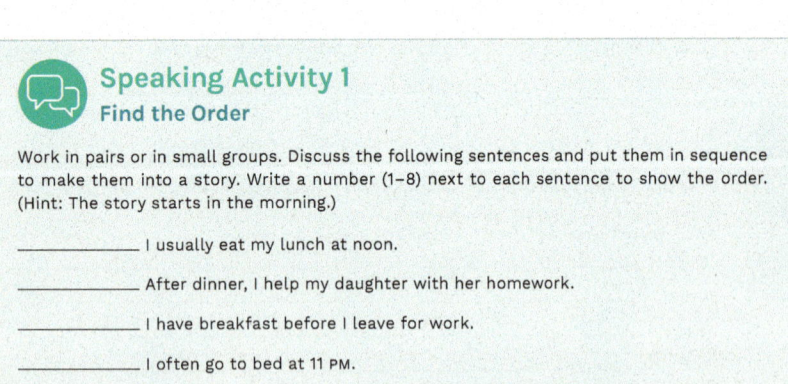

Speaking Activity 1
Find the Order

Work in pairs or in small groups. Discuss the following sentences and put them in sequence to make them into a story. Write a number (1–8) next to each sentence to show the order. (Hint: The story starts in the morning.)

_____ I usually eat my lunch at noon.

_____ After dinner, I help my daughter with her homework.

_____ I have breakfast before I leave for work.

_____ I often go to bed at 11 PM.

Use in Context

Students apply the new grammar in a practical manner through interactive *Speaking Activities*. These engaging tasks, which include class, pair, and group activities, let learners communicate in an authentic way while using the grammar they have learned.

Bringing It All Together

The **_Bringing It All Together_** section gives students an opportunity to bring together all the chapter's grammar parts and apply them in an authentic context.

Speaking Activity 6
Game—What's the Profession?

Work in pairs or small groups. Think of a profession, but don't tell your partner or group what it is. Prepare three to four sentences about what a person working in this profession usually does. Your partner or group will try to guess what the profession is. Look at the example to help you.

> This person usually inspects vehicles. He or she often changes oil and replaces car brakes. In general, this person fixes cars. (Answer: a car mechanic)

From Grammar to Speaking

This section provides many more **_Speaking Activities_** that challenge students to incorporate the chapter's grammar.

From Grammar to Reading

The **_Reading_** section contains a reading passage and comprehension questions that require students to apply the chapter's grammar points. Words from the Academic Word List (AWL) are highlighted in blue in the reading text to help students enrich their vocabulary.

As you read, pay attention to these vocabulary words in the passage: **_involved, task, contribute, ensure, participation, process, traditions,_** and **_interact._**

Weekend Breakfast with Family

The weekend is usually filled with sports, play dates, and errands, but it is also a great opportunity for the entire family to spend time together. A great way to do this is to start with a balanced family breakfast. A balanced breakfast at the beginning of the day is important. It often prepares you and your family for whatever your weekend has in store. Here are some helpful tips for a weekend family breakfast:

Participation

One of the best ways to make breakfast a family affair is to get everyone involved. All family members have a task to do and contribute to making breakfast. To ensure everyone's participation, a fun recipe is to make banana rollups. In this process, one family member spreads Nutella on a slice of whole grain pita, another person tops it off with sliced bananas, and the third rolls it up.

Family Traditions

A weekly family breakfast gives everyone something to look forward to and turns breakfast into a social activity instead of just a meal. It is a nice way to make it one of your family traditions, to interact, and to spend valuable quality time together.

Listening

Audio 07 🔊

Early Classes = Sleepy Teens!

Listen to the audio, which is a podcast about teenagers and sleep. Then answe

Comprehension

Answer the following True/False questions. Circle the correct response.

T / F 1. Half of American teenagers get enough sleep on school nights.
T / F 2. Teenagers sleep 16 to 19 minutes less than they need.
T / F 3. Many schools start classes as early as 6:00 A.M.
T / F 4. Teens usually go to bed early.
T / F 5. They are tired in morning classes.
T / F 6. Michael Breus is a high school teacher.
T / F 7. Michael Breus has sleep problems.
T / F 8. Teenagers need 8 to 10 hours of sleep per night.

From Grammar to Listening

The audio clips and comprehension questions in the **_Listening_** section reinforce the target grammatical structures.

Writing

Choose one of the following topics. Write a short composition (maximum 150 words) about the topic.
- What do you usually do during school breaks or winter or summer vacations?
- How do you usually celebrate your birthday or other family events?

From Grammar to Writing

In the **_Writing_** section, students have another productive opportunity to apply the grammar, this time in a longer piece of writing.

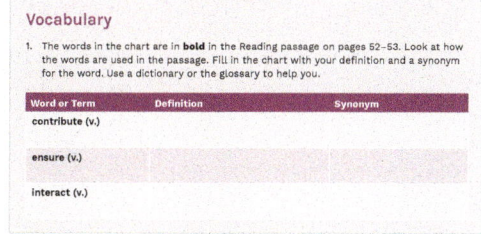

Vocabulary

1. The words in the chart are in **bold** in the Reading passage on pages 52–53. Look at how the words are used in the passage. Fill in the chart with your definition and a synonym for the word. Use a dictionary or the glossary to help you.

Word or Term	Definition	Synonym
contribute (v.)		
ensure (v.)		
interact (v.)		

Vocabulary

The **_Vocabulary_** section provides extra exposure to academic words (AWL) from the Reading and Listening sections.

Chapter Review

Summary

- We use the simple present for facts, generalizations, and actions that take place on a regular basis.
- With the simple present tense, we use certain keywords or phrases, such as *every day, every summer,* or *twice a month,* as well as frequency adverbs, such as *always, often, sometimes,* and *never.*
- With all verbs except *be,* there are two forms in the simple present. For the pronouns *I, you, we,* and *they,* use the base form of the verb. For *he, she,* and *it,* add *-s* or *-es.*
- The verb *be* is irregular in the simple present and is different for every subject. It has three forms: *am (I am), are (you are, we are, they are),* and *is (he is, she is, it is).*
- The verb *have* is also irregular, and it has two forms: *have (I have, you have, we have, they have)* and *has (he has, she has, it has).*

Chapter Review

Each chapter wraps up with a review section that provides a useful **Summary** of the grammar studied in the chapter; students can check their learning through convenient chapter grammar references. Then traditional **Exercises** give additional straightforward practice for students to work on independently in class or for homework

Section Review

The self-assessments at regular intervals throughout the book give students extra opportunities to review and reinforce the grammar points they have studied. These Part Reviews are valuable check-point that enables students to find areas that need more attention, go back to the appropriate chapter and review the material.

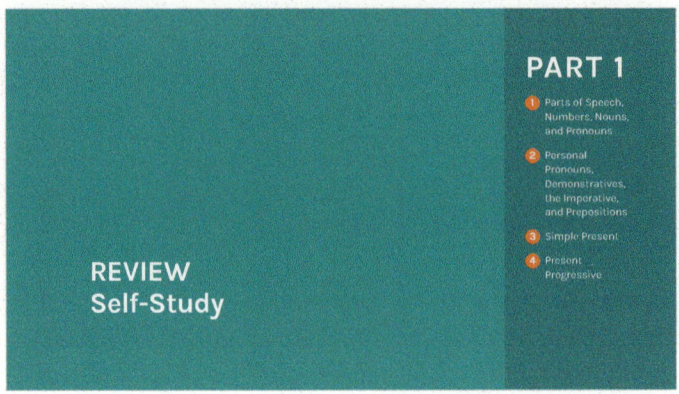

Teacher's Resource Website

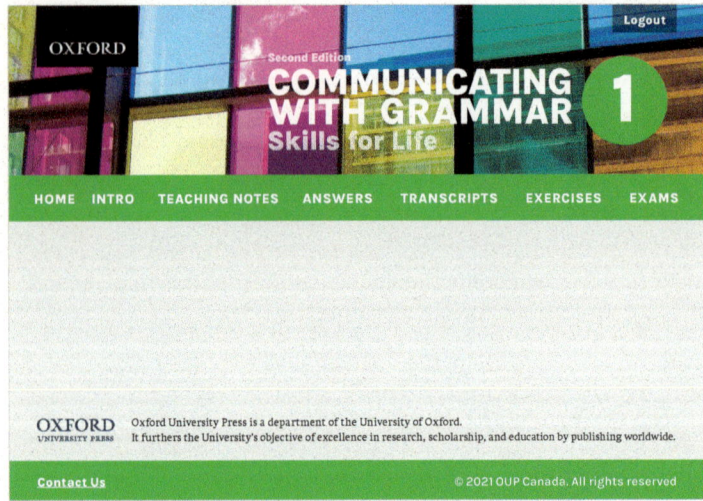

- Class **audio** is available for each level in the series. It contains authentic and constructed listening clips, appropriate for the level and grammar topic.

The online **Teacher Resource** contains

- teaching notes and aids
- additional communicative activities and exercises to be used as practice or as tests
- audio transcripts
- answer key for the Grammar and Vocabulary exercises and Reading and Listening comprehension questions.

SCOPE and SEQUENCE

	Grammar	Skills	Academic Words
Chapter 1 Parts of Speech, Numbers, Nouns, and Pronouns	Parts of speech Numbers Cardinal and ordinal numbers Dates Telling time Countable and non-countable nouns Proper nouns Plural forms Articles and determiners Definite and indefinite articles *There is, there are*	**Speaking** 1. Let's Identify 2. What Time Is It? 3. Countable or Non-Countable? 4. Editing 5. Role-Play 6. Spelling Bee **Reading** "Starting College" **Listening** Audio 01: Conversations Audio 02: Plural Nouns Audio 03: "A New Apartment" **Writing** About Me **Vocabulary**	feature finally locate register requires select specific strategy
Chapter 2 Personal Pronouns, Demonstratives, the Imperative, and Prepositions	Subject and object pronouns Possessive adjectives and pronouns Reflexive pronouns Demonstrative adjectives Demonstrative pronouns The imperative Prepositions of place	**Speaking** 1. What Is This? 2. Giving Directions 3. How Do You...? Mini Oral Presentation 4. People, Places, and Things **Reading** "DIY" **Listening** Audio 04: Family Tree Audio 05: Following Directions Audio 06: "Before the Canoe Trip" **Writing** Leisure Activities **Vocabulary**	assess available create focused potentially rely on sites sources
Chapter 3 Simple Present	Use of the simple present Conjugating regular verbs Question words Frequency adverbs Spelling rules for third-person singular verbs The verb *be* The verb *have*	**Speaking** 1. Find the Order 2. Mini Oral Presentation 3. Partner Interview 4. Find Someone Who... 5. Surveys 6. Game: What's the Profession? **Reading** "Weekend Breakfast with Family" **Listening** Audio 07: "Early Classes = Sleepy Teens!" **Writing** Short composition **Vocabulary**	contribute ensure interact involved participation process task traditions

	Grammar	Skills	Academic Words
Chapter 4 Present Progressive	Use of the present progressive Conjugating regular verbs Spelling rules for verbs with *-ing* ending Present progressive versus simple present Non-progressive verbs	**Speaking** 1. Spelling Bee 2. What's in the Photo? 3. Game: What Am I Doing? 4. Audio 08: "What's That Noise?" 5. Game: What's Happening? 6. Role-Play **Reading** "What's Keeping Kids from Being More Active?" **Listening** Audio 09: "Tom's Diner" Audio 10: Busy or Not? **Writing** Describe a photo **Vocabulary**	benefits percent physical role seek significant sufficient surveys
Chapter 5 Simple Past	Use of the simple past Spelling rules for adding the *–ed* ending Pronouncing the *-ed* ending Conjugating regular verbs Conjugating irregular verbs The verb *be*	**Speaking** 1. Find the Order 2. Exchange Information 3. Video Summary 4. Telling Stories about the Weekend 5. Spelling Bee **Reading** "Our Canada Day" **Listening** Audio 11: "Canada Day in Ottawa" **Writing** Short composition **Vocabulary**	areas evident initially items positive purchase range varied
Chapter 6 Past Progressive	Use of the past progressive Conjugating the past progressive Contractions Past progressive versus simple past Non-progressive verbs	**Speaking** 1. Describing a Picture 2. Scrambled Parts 3. Freeze Frame 4. Video Summary **Reading** "Canadian Folklore: Myths, Legends, and More" **Listening** Audio 12: "Urban Legends" **Writing** Write a legend or myth **Vocabulary**	consequently define derives environment illustrate immigrants link similar

	Grammar	Skills	Academic Words
Chapter 7 Adjectives and Adverbs	Adjectives Adverbs Comparative adjectives Superlative adjectives Comparative and superlative adverbs Equatives	**Speaking** 1. A Good Friend Is... 2. What's the Adverb? 3. Conversation 4. Role-Plays 5. Game: Guess the Action 6. Mini Oral Presentation **Reading** "Multiple Intelligences and Learning Styles" **Listening** Audio 13: "My Future Spouse" **Writing** Your personality **Vocabulary**	complex design identify impact issues negative relevant theories
Chapter 8 Word Choice, Word Pairs	Homonyms Commonly confused words Word pairs *Listen, hear, look, see, watch*	**Speaking** 1. Creative Sentences 2. Concentration Game 3. Spelling Bee 4. Scrambled Sentences **Reading** "The English Language" **Listening** Audio 14: "What a Wonderful World" **Writing** Create a story in a group **Vocabulary**	approach aspects considerable constantly domination major periods structure
Chapter 9 Simple Future—*Will* and *Be Going To*	*Will* *Be going to* Time markers	**Speaking** 1. News from the Future 2. Bingo: Find Someone Who... 3. Audio 15: Phone Messages 4. Role-Play 5. Dictation 6. Agendas and Plans **Reading** "New Year's Resolutions" **Listening** Audio 16: "What Are Your Goals?" **Writing** Future goals **Vocabulary**	achieve assistant establish evaluate financial investments legal proceed

	Grammar	Skills	Academic Words
Chapter 10 Modals	Modals of ability Modals of necessity or prohibition Modals of advice Modals for polite requests, permission, offers, and desires	**Speaking** 1. Q&A 2. To Do or Not to Do 3. Dear Know-It-All 4. Role-Play 5. Scrambled Parts 6. Role-Play **Reading** "Working and Studying" **Listening** Audio 17: "Interview with a College Counsellor" **Writing** Part-time jobs for students **Vocabulary**	acquire affect coordinate income individuals restricts sector shift
Chapter 11 Questions, Negatives, and Short Answers	Questions with simple tenses Questions with progressive tenses Questions with future tenses Questions using modals Wh- questions Negative sentences Short answers	**Speaking** 1. Change and Exchange 2. What Do You See? 3. Fortune Teller 4. Scrambled Parts 5. Change and Exchange 6. Scrambled Parts **Reading** "Buyer Beware" **Listening** Audio 18: "Apartment for Rent" **Writing** Interview with a famous person **Vocabulary**	analyze assume credit document estimate research security transfer
Chapter 12 Sentence Structure	Sentence structure Sentence types Sentence problems	**Speaking** 1. Game: Make a Sentence! 2. What Type of Sentence Is It? 3. Newspaper Headlines 4. Game: Join the Sentences 5. Role-Play 6. Mini Oral Presentation 7. Quotations **Reading** "Jigsaw Puzzles" **Listening** Audio 19: "The Art of Broken Vases" **Writing** Short description **Vocabulary**	appropriate community computer normally outcome partners primarily technique

Contents

Introduction

Welcome to Communicating with Grammar!

Communicating with Grammar: Skills for Life is a Canadian series for ESL and EFL students working to improve their understanding of English grammar. Offering grammar instruction using the four skills—reading, writing, listening, and speaking—the series helps students internalize concepts for use in all their communication. Students improve their command of English grammar through a broad range of activities that set them up for further study or work in an English-speaking environment.

The *Communicating with Grammar* series employs a communicative methodology. Using a "learn–practise–use in context" approach, the books deliver the essential grammar concepts via practical exercises and activities, helping learners become functional in English as quickly and efficiently as possible. The communicative activities then help students internalize the grammar in context.

Series Features

This Canadian series guides student learning by combining a communicative approach with discrete grammar instruction using traditional exercises. It provides warm-up activities, explicit grammar teaching, practical example sentences, and mechanical and interactive exercises. The exercises allow students to practise each concept; engaging communicative activities further reinforce the grammar being studied. The target grammar is embedded in the Reading, Listening, and Writing sections, facilitating further grammar use in context. Vocabulary exercises provide additional exposure to and practice with the featured academic vocabulary. Review units provide, at regular intervals, an opportunity for students to practise and solidify the key aspects of their learning. The books provide flexibility for learners who thrive on extra challenge while maintaining the intended level of the target material.

Chapter Structure

Chapters are logically organized into an overview, a series of grammar topics with practice, a cumulative section incorporating all four skill areas as well as academic vocabulary, and a summary. Grammar is a necessary component of all four skill areas, and students are encouraged to use the focal grammar topic with each skill in every chapter.

Overview

Each chapter opens with a brief explanation of the chapter's grammar topic, followed by a **Warm-Up** activity that engages students and provides an opportunity to start thinking about and using the target grammar in context.

Students are encouraged to use the new grammar concept to communicate with their classmates often in real-life situations.

Grammar

The chapter's target grammar is divided into logical and manageable parts; each applies a "learn–practice–use in context" approach.

The grammar instruction starts with a **Formation** (learn) section that offers a clear explanation of the grammar topic, often a table or chart, and illustrates the mechanics.

We have tried to keep the metalanguage to the minimum to keep the focus on meaning in context. Depending on the background and level of the students and your teaching style, the existing metalanguage can be skipped, just referred to occasionally, or used as is. If you decide to skip the metalanguage, it might still be a good idea to remind students that they can gain access to extensive extra quizzes and practice material by typing the grammar terminology and the words *quiz* or *practice* on a search engine (e.g., *perfect gerunds quiz*).

Exercises (practice) follow the grammar explanation. A series of traditional drills gives students exposure to the language structures and addresses common difficulties faced by learners. The exercises include sentence completion, sentence construction, matching, ordering, error correction, transformation, multiple choice, fill in the blanks, and more.

Students apply the new grammar topic in a practical manner through interactive **Speaking Activities**. These engaging tasks, which include class, pair, and group activities, let learners communicate in an authentic way by using the grammar they have learned.

Bringing It All Together

This key section provides an opportunity for students to bring together all the chapter's grammar parts and apply them in an authentic context. It includes a number of additional **Speaking Activities** that challenge students to incorporate the chapter's grammar. The **Reading** section contains a reading passage and comprehension questions requiring students to apply the chapter's grammar points. The audio clips and comprehension questions in the **Listening** section also reinforce the target grammatical structures. In the **Writing** section, students have another productive opportunity to apply the grammar, this time in a longer piece of writing. The **Vocabulary** section provides extra exposure to academic words (AWL) from the Reading and Listening sections.

Chapter Review

Each chapter's review section opens with a helpful **Summary** of the grammar taught in the chapter; students can check their learning through convenient chapter grammar references. Then traditional **Exercises** give additional straightforward practice for students to work on independently in class or for homework.

Appendices and Glossary

To supplement and support students' learning, each book ends with quick-reference appendices, providing additional information on grammar points or usage and a glossary of key vocabulary from the chapters' Readings. Target words that students encounter in the Reading and Listening sections—vocabulary found on the Academic Word List (AWL)—are identified in the glossary as well.

Three Levels

Level 1 is designed for students with basic English who need to build a solid foundation of the major verb tenses and sentence structure. Students learn to formulate accurate sentences and questions through the grammar lessons and exercises. They expand their English vocabulary through the Reading and Listening components. The Vocabulary section provides additional exposure to academic words from the Reading and Listening sections. This level also focuses on targeting common basic grammatical errors students may need to learn how to correct.

Level 2 is designed for students who have completed Level 1 or know enough grammar and have a basic understanding of the four skills to formulate questions in English and construct more complex sentences. Entering this level, students can usually communicate their intentions to others but still make frequent errors in structure, tense, and usage that may slow comprehension. Level 2 focuses on improving grammar in the four skill areas so students acquire more fluency, a larger vocabulary, and the ability to express themselves using more complex sentence structures.

Level 3 is the bridging level to fluency in English usage. This level completes all the perfect verb tenses and addresses active and passive voice and reported speech. The study of clauses develops students' ability to construct more complex sentences. Reading and Listening components are from authentic sources, preparing students for real-world communication. At the completion of this level, students will have the confidence to communicate with native speakers academically or professionally.

Additional Series Components

- Class **audio** is available for each level in the series. It contains either authentic or constructed listening clips, depending on the level and grammar topic.
- The **online Teacher Resource** contains teaching notes and aids, additional communicative activities and exercises to be used as practice or as tests, audio transcripts, and an answer key for the Grammar and Vocabulary exercises and the Reading and Listening comprehension questions.

1 Parts of Speech, Numbers, Nouns, and Pronouns

Overview

- There are some basic things to know about a language in order to learn it more easily.

- Understanding the parts of speech, numbers, nouns, articles, and *there is / there are* helps you start using the English language more quickly and easily.

Parts of Speech

Learning the parts of speech helps you understand and use the parts of a sentence correctly.

Warm-Up

Work in pairs. Read the following sentences. Pay special attention to the **bold** word in each sentence. Does the word present

- an action?
- a person or a thing?
- more information about another word?
- a location?
- a link between two ideas in the sentence?

EXAMPLE Frank **drives** a bus. *drives* = action

1. They sing in a **choir.** _ a group of sing
2. The man is **in** the car.
3. Mary **plays** the guitar.
4. I have a brother **and** a sister.
5. The sun is very **warm** today.
6. Kiera dances **beautifully**. warb

Formation

Part of Speech	Use	Examples
verb (v.)	• expresses an action or a state	John **walks** to school. John **is** tall.
noun (n.)	• names a person, place, or thing	**John** walks to **school**.
article (art.)	• limits a noun	**a** book
	• *a* and *an* are singular and not specific. Use *a* before consonant sounds and *an* before vowel sounds.	**an** apple **the** books on **the** table
	• *the* is specific and can be singular or plural	
adjective (adj.)	• modifies or qualifies a noun or pronoun	the **black** cat John is **tall**. **This** book is **new**.
adverb (adv.)	• modifies or qualifies a verb, an adjective, or an adverb	John walks **quickly**. John is **really** tall. John walks **very quickly**.
pronoun (pron.)	• replaces a noun	*I, you, he, she, it, we, they*: **I** see a book. *me, you, him, her, it, us, them*: She knows **them**.

Part of Speech	Use	Examples
preposition (prep.)	• shows a link between words for place, time, direction, origin, etc.	*at, on, in, to, from, for, above*: The book is **on** the table.
conjunction (conj.)	• creates a link between parts of a sentence • Note: There are coordinating conjunctions and subordinating conjunctions.	coordinating conjunctions: *and, but, so, or*: The students **and** the teacher are in the room. subordinating conjunctions: *before, after, when, because*: She takes the bus **when** it is cold.

Speaking Activity 1
Let's Identify

Work in pairs to identify the part of speech of each word in the following sentences. Compare your answers with another pair's answers.

کیا کیسے

لوازش مند والا

میں اور وہ جو صحیح ہم کواٹھانے والا

سے

EXAMPLE
     noun   art.   prep.
Maya rides a bike to school.
     verb noun noun

1. The students study in the library after class.

the	article
students	noun
study	verb
in	Prep
the	Art
library	noun
after	Prep
class	noun

2. Frank and I are best friends.

Frank	noun
and	Pronoun
I	Pron
are	Pverb
best	Verb
friends	noun

3. He lives in a very small apartment.

he	Pron
lives	verb
in	Prep
a	Art
very	Adverb
small	Adjec
apartment	noun

4. That teacher reads slowly and clearly.

that	Pronoun
teacher	noun
reads	verb
slowly	Adverb
and	Prep
clearly	verb

Numbers

Numbers help us get and give necessary information about ourselves and our lives. We use them to give personal information, to tell the time, to find out the cost of something, and so on.

Warm-Up

In the following word search puzzle, find and circle the numbers in the list below. The words only go left to right → and top to bottom ↓. The number *one* is already circled for you.

T	T	T	H	R	E	E	I	G	H	T	W	O	E
E	S	I	X	E	F	O	R	T	Y	-	S	I	X
L	N	E	T	S	I	X	T	Y	-	T	W	O	E
E	I	I	E	I	F	E	H	I	N	H	F	V	T
V	N	G	N	X	T	I	I	E	Y	I	O	N	F
E	E	H	S	T	Y	G	R	T	F	R	U	I	I
N	T	T	E	E	-	H	T	W	O	T	R	N	F
S	Y	Y	V	E	F	T	E	E	R	Y	T	E	T
E	-	T	E	N	I	E	E	N	T	-	E	T	E
V	N	W	N	S	V	E	N	T	Y	F	E	E	E
E	I	E	T	W	E	N	T	Y	-	O	N	E	N
N	N	L	E	T	H	I	R	T	Y	U	T	N	I
S	E	V	E	N	T	Y	-	T	H	R	E	E	N
O	N	E	N	F	I	V	E	F	O	U	R	I	E

~~one~~	sixteen
two	seventeen
three	eighteen
four	nineteen
five	twenty
six	twenty-one
seven	thirty
eight	thirty-four
nine	forty
ten	forty-six
eleven	fifty-five
twelve	sixty-two
thirteen	seventy-three
fourteen	eighty
fifteen	ninety-nine

Formation

Cardinal numbers show quantity; we count with them. Ordinal numbers show the order of things, not the quantity.

Cardinal Numbers		Ordinal Numbers	
1	one	1st	first
2	two	2nd	second
3	three	3rd	third
4	four	4th	fourth
5	five	5th	fifth
6	six	6th	sixth
7	seven	7th	seventh
8	eight	8th	eighth
9	nine	9th	ninth
10	ten	10th	tenth
11	eleven	11th	eleventh
12	twelve	12th	twelfth
13	thirteen	13th	thirteenth

Cardinal Numbers		Ordinal Numbers	
14	fourteen	14th	fourteenth
15	fifteen	15th	fifteenth
16	sixteen	16th	sixteenth
17	seventeen	17th	seventeenth
18	eighteen	18th	eighteenth
19	nineteen	19th	nineteenth
20	twenty	20th	twentieth
21	twenty-one	21st	twenty-first
22	twenty-two	22nd	twenty-second
30	thirty	30th	thirtieth
40	forty	40th	fortieth
50	fifty	50th	fiftieth
60	sixty	60th	sixtieth
70	seventy	70th	seventieth
80	eighty	80th	eightieth
90	ninety	90th	ninetieth
100	one hundred	100th	one hundredth
101	one hundred and one	101st	one hundred and first
110	one hundred and ten	110th	one hundred and tenth
200	two hundred	200th	two hundredth
300	three hundred	300th	three hundredth
1000	one thousand	1000th	one thousandth
1500	one thousand five hundred or fifteen hundred	1500th	one thousand five hundredth or fifteen hundredth
3300	three thousand three hundred or thirty-three hundred	3300th	three thousand three hundredth or thirty-three hundredth
10 000	ten thousand	10 000th	ten thousandth
1 000 000	one million	1 000 000th	one millionth

Number Patterns

All languages have patterns. Learn the patterns, and the language becomes easier to learn and use.

- *One*, *two*, and *three* and their combinations have their own patterns for the ordinal numbers; all the other numbers just add *-th*.
- Spelling: When the number ends in a consonant and *y*, change the *y* to *i* before adding the ending *-eth*. We add the *e* to make the ending easier to pronounce.
- We commonly group numbers in pairs when we say them for money, years, and telephone numbers.
  - We usually say *1983* as "nineteen eighty-three."
  - We can say *742-2690* as the individual numbers, but we often group the last four numbers in pairs: "seven four two, twenty-six ninety."

Months of the Year

January
February
March
April
May
June
July
August
September
October
November
December

Dates

Numbers are also part of the formation of dates. There are a few ways to express dates. How we say them and write them differ also.

Written Dates	Spoken Dates
February 10, 2021	February the tenth, 2021
the 10th of February, 2021	the tenth of February, 2021
02/10/21 (02-10-21)	the tenth of February, 2021 the tenth of the second month of 2021
21/02/10, 2021/02/10 (21-02-10, 2021-02-10)	February the tenth, 2021

The first two written dates are more formal, and we use them in correspondence. We use the numerical versions on application forms, for example.

Exercise 1

Audio 01 🔊

Listen to the audio, which includes three phone conversations. Then answer the questions.

Conversation 1

1. What is Ms. London's phone number?
   a) 545-6215
   b) 545-6250
   c) 445-6250

2. What is the work order number?
   a) B1423S19
   b) B4023S19
   c) B1423S90

3. How much is the repair bill?
   a) $70.87
   b) $77.87
   c) $72.87

Conversation 2

1. How much cash do the speakers have? _____
2. What is the phone number of the pizza place? _____
3. What is the total cost of the pizza? _____
4. What is the street number of their address? _____
5. What is their phone number? _____

Conversation 3

1. What is Mr. Powers's bank card number? _____
2. Write his date of birth. _____
3. What is the date of his anniversary? _____

Telling Time

We also use numbers for telling the time. There are two ways to say the time: traditional (T) and digital (D).

For the first 30 minutes of the hour, we say "past" or "after" the hour.

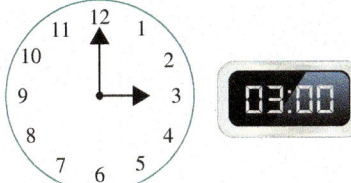

T: It is three o'clock.
D: 3:00: It is three.

T: It is ten past seven.
D: 7:10: It is seven ten.

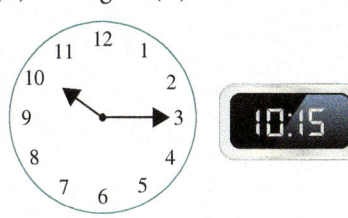

T: It is a quarter after ten.
D: 10:15: It is ten fifteen.

For the second 30 minutes or half hour, we say "to" the next hour.

T: It is half past twelve.
D: 12:30: It is twelve thirty.

T: It is twenty-five to nine.
D: 8:35: It is eight thirty-five.

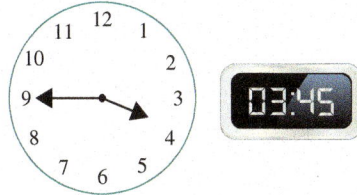

T: It is a quarter to four.
D: 3:45: It is three forty-five.

For specific times, use *at*.

I go to work at 9:00 (at nine o'clock) in the morning.

For periods of time, use *in*, except with *night*.

We visit friends in the evening. John works at night.

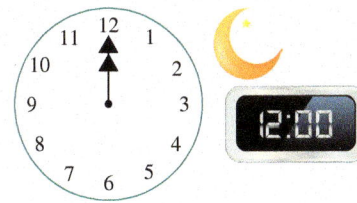

It is midnight.
12:00 am.
It is twelve at night.

It is noon.
12:00 pm.
It is twelve in the afternoon.

Exercise 2

Write the following times in both forms.

11:24 Traditional It is twenty-four past eleven.
      Digital It is eleven twenty-four.

1. **6:30** Traditional: _____ Digital: _____

2. **1:40** Traditional: _____ Digital: _____

3. **8:15** Traditional: _____ Digital: _____

4. **2:45** Traditional: _____ Digital: _____

5. **12:50** Traditional: _____ Digital: _____

Countable, Non-Countable, and Plural Nouns

English has two main kinds of nouns: countable and non-countable. Countable nouns have plural forms; non-countable nouns have no plural forms.

Warm-Up

Work in pairs. Read the following passage and underline all the nouns. Are the nouns in the passage things or items that you can count? Are they ideas or categories of things? Write the nouns in the correct columns below.

The students in this class enjoy playing games. The teacher thinks these activities help the students learn English more quickly. Every day, they spend some time doing activities that use the language. They have fun. They also practise the lessons, reinforce their knowledge, and gain confidence.

Things or People You Can Count		Abstract Ideas or Categories
1. students	6. students	1. English
2. classes	7. days	2. time
3. games	8. activities	3. fun
4. teachers	9. languages	4. knowledge
5. activities	10. lessons	5. confidence

Formation

Countable nouns have plural forms; we can count them.

   one boy → two boys   one book → two books   one table → two tables

Non-countable nouns have no plural forms; we cannot count them (*air, sand, water, time, money*). However, we can divide them into the categories shown in the following chart.

Categories of Non-Countable Nouns				
Categories of Items	Abstract Ideas and Mass Nouns	Certain Food and Drink Categories	Names of Languages and Proper Names	Academic Subjects
clothing	advice	bread	Chinese	biology
equipment	beauty	butter	English	history
furniture	evidence	cheese	French	mathematics
homework	experience	coffee	Spanish	physics
jewellery	fun	meat	Mary	politics
luggage or baggage	health	milk	Frank	science
machinery	information	pasta		
mail	knowledge	poultry		
money	love	sugar		
music	luck	tea		
news	research	water		
software	sand	wine		
tourism	soil			
work	time			
	violence			
	weather			

Abstract nouns are concepts, feelings, or things we can't touch.

> love, knowledge, evidence

Mass nouns are substances that we can touch but cannot count.

> sand, smoke, butter

Proper nouns are the names or titles of people and things. Proper nouns always start with a capital letter.

> Lake Ontario is a very large lake.

Lake Ontario is a proper noun because it is the name of a specific lake. The second *lake* in the sentence is a common noun because it refers to a body of water in general.

Non-countable nouns are always singular even if they end in an -*s*.

> news, politics, physics

> The **news** is on TV at 6:00 PM.

> **Politics** is a popular topic of discussion.

> **Physics** is my favourite science subject.

A few non-countable nouns can also be countable nouns, but their meanings usually change when used this way.

> I have a lot of **work** to do.

> The museum has many beautiful **works** of art.

Nouns—Plural Forms

Nouns Ending in	Plural Spelling	Examples
most consonants and silent **e**	+ **-s**	bands, cats, dogs, books, computers
		houses, suitcases, blouses
a consonant + **y**	change **y** to **i** + **-es**	city ➔ cities
		baby ➔ babies
a vowel + **y**	+ **-s**	boys, plays, bays
a consonant + **o**	+ **-es**	hero ➔ heroes
		echo ➔ echoes
		(except musical terms and shortened words + **-s** ➔ pianos, photos)
other vowels (not **o**)	+ **-s**	bananas, skis
two vowels	+ **-s**	radios, videos
s, x, z, ch, sh	+ **-es**	buses, boxes, buzzes, watches, bushes
		(to make them easier to pronounce)
f or **fe**	+ **-s**	chefs, chiefs
	change **f** to **v** + **-es**	wife ➔ wives
		life ➔ lives
		leaf ➔ leaves
		(There is no regular pattern.)

Irregular Plurals

Some plural forms remain from Old English and do not follow the rules in the previous chart.

Singular	child	foot	goose	man	mouse	person	tooth	woman
Plural	children	feet	geese	men	mice	people	teeth	women

Some nouns have the same form for the singular and plural but are still countable nouns. The most common are *sheep, fish, deer, salmon, moose, trout.*

> I saw a sheep in the garden. He has 100 sheep.

Exercise 3

Write four plural countable nouns related to each non-countable noun category.

mail: letters, parcels, bills, flyers

1. food _____

2. equipment _____

3. furniture _____

4. jewellery _____

5. money _____

Exercise 4

Write the plural forms of the nouns. If the noun does not have a plural form, put X in the blank.

1. horse	_____	11. information	_____
2. tomato	_____	12. truck	_____
3. woman	_____	13. life	_____
4. money	_____	14. radio	_____
5. city	_____	15. bicycle	_____
6. child	_____	16. toy	_____
7. homework	_____	17. deer	_____
8. piano	_____	18. foot	_____
9. house	_____	19. mouse	_____
10. fax	_____	20. ash	_____

Pronouncing the -s Ending

To make pronunciation easier, remember that there are three ways to pronounce the *-s* ending of plural nouns. Whether we say the / s /, the / z /, or the / iz / sound depends on the final sound of the singular noun. Remember: it is the **sound** that matters, not the written letter.

Use the Sound	When the Final Sound of the Singular Noun Is	Examples
/s/	one of these voiceless consonant sounds: **f, k, p, t, th** (as in *with*)	chef ➜ chefs (chef/s/) book ➜ books (book/s/) mop ➜ mops (mop/s/) cat ➜ cats (cat/s/) bath ➜ baths (bath/s/)
/z/	a **vowel sound** or one of these voiced consonant sounds: **b, d, g, j, l, m, n, ng, r, v, th** (as in *then*)	tomato ➜ tomatoes (tomato/z/) banana ➜ bananas (banana/z/) cab ➜ cabs (cab/z/) dog ➜ dogs (dog/z/) doll ➜ dolls (doll/z/) ring ➜ rings (ring/z/)
/iz/	one of these consonant sounds: **s, x, ch, sh, z, zh**	bus ➜ buses (bus/iz/) box ➜ boxes (box/iz/) watch ➜ watches (watch/iz/) bush ➜ bushes (bush/iz/) buzz ➜ buzzes (buzz/iz/) edge ➜ edges (edge/iz/)

Exercise 5

Audio 02 🔊

Listen to the audio. Write each plural noun you hear in the correct column, based on the pronunciation of the -s ending.

/ s /	/ z /	/ iz /

Speaking Activity 3
Countable or Non-Countable?

Work in teams. Your teacher will provide a worksheet with 20 nouns. Discuss and then write the nouns in the correct column: countable or non-countable. If the noun is countable, write the plural form as well. The team that finishes first with the correct answers wins. Practise saying the plural nouns out loud with other team members.

Articles and Determiners

Articles and other determiners introduce nouns and tell us if the nouns are singular or plural; indefinite, definite (or specific), or general; and countable or non-countable.

Warm-Up

Work in pairs. Read the following passage and <u>underline</u> all the nouns. What do you notice about the words that come immediately before the nouns?

Francisco is a student. He studies English at the college. There are many students in the class. Some students want to take courses at the college when they finish the English course. Francisco wants to go to a university to study medicine. He wants to become a doctor. That takes much time and effort.

Formation

Article or Determiner	Definite / Indefinite	Singular / Plural	Countable / Non-Countable	Examples
a (before a consonant sound)	indefinite	singular	countable nouns	**a** cat
an (before a vowel sound)	indefinite	singular	countable nouns	**an** umbrella
the	definite (specific)	singular or plural	countable and non-countable nouns	**the** cat **the** cats **the** furniture
some	indefinite	plural	countable and non-countable nouns	I have **some** books. I have **some** money.
Ø (no article)	general	plural	countable and non-countable nouns	Cats are smart. Knowledge is power.

Definite and Indefinite Articles

The indefinite articles *a* and *an* introduce a singular, countable noun that we don't know anything about yet. The definite article *the* introduces a specific noun, something that is known.

> There is **a** dog in the yard.
> (There is no specific information about the dog.)

> **The** dog is looking for its ball.
> (The dog is now a specific dog.)

The first time something is mentioned, use *a* or *an*; the second time, use *the*. Do not use articles with

- languages   He speaks Russian.
- sports   I like hockey.
- names of countries, provinces or territories, or states that are singular   We live in Canada.

Exception: Use *the* with plural or qualified names of countries, provinces or territories, or states:

> the United States, the Philippines, the Republic of China, the Northwest Territories

Other Determiners

Type of noun	Determiner	Example sentences
countable	many	It takes **many** years to become a doctor.
	a few	I have **a few** dollars.
	a lot of	It takes **a lot of** years to become a doctor.
non-countable	much	I don't have **much** time.
	a little	I have **a little** money.
	a lot of	I don't have **a lot of** time.

Exercise 6

Fill in the blanks with *a, an, the, some,* or Ø (nothing).

1. Two of __the__ students in my class come from __the__ France.

2. John is __a__ good hockey player. He plays __a__ hockey for __the__ college team.

3. It is nice to have __a__ break between __the__ classes. We have __a__ hour to relax.

4. I need to buy __a__ furniture for my new apartment. I need __a__ desk, table,

   and __a__ chairs. I also need __an__ alarm clock.

5. Amanda is really interested in __a__ politics. She watches __the__ news every day.

Exercise 7

Circle the letter of the correct word or phrase to complete the sentences.

1. How _____ homework do you have tonight?

   a) a little   b) many   c) **much**

2. The museum has _____ interesting exhibits.

   a) much   b) **many**   c) a little

3. I have _____ exercises to finish for homework.

   a) a little   b) **a few**   c) much

4. Susan has _____ photos of her family.

   a) a few of   b) **a lot of**   c) much

5. How _____ does this shirt cost?

   a) **much**   b) many   c) a little

6. We need to hurry. I only have _____ time before my next class.

   a) a few   b) much   c) **a little**

There Is, There Are

The structure *there + be* introduces information. *There is* introduces singular and non-countable nouns. *There are* introduces plural nouns.

Use	Form	Keywords	Example Sentences
to introduce singular or non-countable nouns	there is	a, an, the, some, much, a little, one	**There is** a book on the table.
			There is some money in my wallet.
			There is a little time before class.
to introduce plural nouns	there are	the, some, many, few, two, three, etc.	**There are** some books on the table.
			There are many students in the class.

Warm-Up

There is...	There are...
a teacher	12 students

On a separate sheet of paper, make a chart like the one in the margin. Look around the classroom and list the things and people you see. Write each item in the correct column. Compare your list with your classmates' lists.

Formation

Positive	Negative	Yes/No Question
There + is + noun / noun phrase *There + are +* noun / noun phrase	*There + is + not +* noun / noun phrase *There + are + not +* noun / noun phrase	*Is + there +* noun / noun phrase *Are + there +* noun / noun phrase
There is a book on the table.	**There is not** a book on the table.	**Is there** a book on the table?
There is some money in my wallet.	**There is not** any money in my wallet.	**Is there** any money in my wallet?
There are some books on the table.	**There are not** any books on the table.	**Are there** any books on the table?
There are many students in the class.	**There are not** many students in the class.	**Are there** many students in the class?

Look at the noun that follows the structure *there is/are*. If it is singular, use *is*. If it is plural, use *are*.
The indefinite article *some* usually changes to *any* in negative and question formations.

Exercise 8

Fill in the blanks with *is* or *are*.

1. There _____ many people in the restaurant.

2. _____ there some information about the art exhibit online?

3. There _____ a birthday party tonight for Mariko.

4. There _____ a lot of good movies playing this week.

5. _____ there an assignment to do for our English class for tomorrow?

6. There _____ a little tea in my cup.

Speaking Activity 4
Editing

Work in pairs. Together, find and correct the five errors with the structure *there is / there are* in the following passage. (Hint: Sometimes it helps to read out loud when looking for errors.)

Hi Paul,

How's college? I'm really enjoying my school. There are many social activities so you can get to know other students. There are many clubs and sports teams too. Is there many things to do at your school? How are your courses? Are you enjoying them?

I really like mine, but I am really busy and stressed. There are eight courses to take each semester. Most of them are okay, but there is a couple of courses that are really heavy. For example, there is a lot of homework for the communications course. There is at least five projects to do before the end of the semester. There are so much to do. I don't know if there are enough time to do all that work and the work in my other courses.

I hope your courses are going well. Talk to you soon.

Jan

Speaking Activity 5
Role-Play

Work in pairs. Take turns role-playing the situations. Then perform them for the class.

Situation A: Call the dentist's office to make an appointment because you have a toothache. The receptionist will tell you when you can come. Write down the date and the time of the appointment.

Situation B: Ask the clerk in a store for the price of printer ink. Tell the clerk the make of the printer or the number of the ink cartridge.

Situation C: You want to arrange to meet your friend for a coffee. Leave a message. Mention the time, the place, and your phone number.

Situation D: You want to get more information about a used car (or something else) that's for sale. Call the number and ask questions.

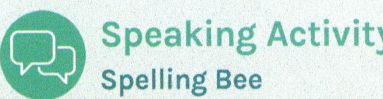

Speaking Activity 6
Spelling Bee

Work in teams. Your teacher will read a noun. A member of Team 1 spells the plural form of the noun out loud and writes it on the board. If the spelling is correct, that team scores a point. If not, Team 2 gets a chance to spell it correctly and steal a point. Your teacher will then read another noun for Team 2. The team with the most points wins.

Reading

Read the email and answer the questions that follow.

As you read, pay attention to these vocabulary words in the passage: *register*, *requires*, *specific*, *select*, *locate*, and *strategy*.

Starting College

Hi Sam,

I just want to let you know that I'm beginning to get used to college. It's a bit crazy at first, and it's definitely a lot different from high school.

When you first start your studies at college, there is a lot of information to take in. They give you so much stuff to read. Before you start your classes, there is so much to do and so many lineups to wait in. First, you need to **register** and pay your fees. Each program **requires** you to take **specific** courses. Then you get to **select** your optional courses. The next step is to print out your class schedule. It's a good idea to become familiar with the campus. It's really important to **locate** all your classrooms before your classes start. I try not to get lost, but it's confusing sometimes.

I start my classes tomorrow morning at 8:00 and I don't finish until 7:00 in the evening. Plus, I need to buy my textbooks tomorrow. I'm really busy, kind of nervous, but really excited all at the same time. My **strategy** is to take it one day at a time.

Talk to you later.
Joe

Comprehension

Answer the following True/False questions. (Circle) the correct response.

T / F 1. Joe thinks college isn't the same as high school.

T / F 2. You can pay for school after your classes start.

T / F 3. All your courses can be optional.

T / F 4. On the first day of Joe's classes, he is at the college for 11 hours.

T / F 5. Joe is not happy at all about starting college.

Listening

Audio 03

A New Apartment

Listen to the audio, which is a phone conversation between two friends. Then answer the following questions. Try to write complete sentences.

Comprehension

Answer the questions. Try to write complete sentences.

1. Who has a new apartment?

   _____

2. What floor is his apartment on?

   _____

3. How many boxes are not unpacked?

   _____

4. What do Dave and Martin plan to do?

   _____

5. What is Martin going to bring?

   _____

6. What is Dave's address?

   _____ O'Connor, Apt. _____

As you listen, pay attention to the vocabulary words *finally* and *feature* and the context in which they are used.

7. What is his new phone number?

_____

8. What time is it now?

_____

9. When does Martin expect to arrive?

_____

10. Is Martin going to drive or take the bus?

_____

Writing

Answer the following questions to write a short composition about yourself.

- What is your name?
- Where are you from?
- How old are you? When is your birthday?
- Do you have any brothers or sisters? How many?
- When do you usually get up in the morning?
- When do you come to school every day?
- When do you go home after your classes?
- How much time do you spend every day doing your homework?
- At what time do you usually go to sleep?
- Are there any activities you like to do on the weekend?

Vocabulary

1. Read the following sentences. The words in **bold** are from the Reading and Listening activities. Use the context to help you understand what the words in bold mean.
   a) My client **requires** a flight from Calgary to Vancouver for this **specific** date, May 3.
   b) We want to **locate** a local fitness gym that doesn't cost too much.
   c) When you buy a new car, you can **select** extra options. One popular **feature** for Canadians is heated seats.
   d) **Finally**, the last thing to do to **register** for the service is to give your name and address to the organization.
   e) My plan is to review my notes for the test for at least two hours tonight. What is your **strategy**?

2. Fill in the blanks with your definition and a synonym for the word. Use a dictionary or the glossary to help you.

Word or Term	Definition	Synonym
feature (n.)		
finally (adv.)		
locate (v.)		

Word or Term	Definition	Synonym
register (v.)		
requires (v.)		
select (v.)		
specific (adj.)		
strategy (n.)		

3. Fill in the blanks with the vocabulary words listed in the chart.

a) _____, I have a new plan for the future. This is my new _____.

b) I want to _____ for two social media and communications courses. Do you know which _____ courses you want to _____ as your options?

c) Juan wants to _____ an apartment to rent close to the college and work. Another important _____ he _____ is a parking space.

Chapter Review

Summary

- Each word is a part of speech and has a specific function or use. Understanding how the parts of speech work together helps you create and use correct sentences more easily.
- Numbers give specific information about the time of day; personal information, such as dates and ages; and the quantity or costs of things.
- There are two ways to express the time: traditional and digital. Use the preposition *at* with a specific time, and use *in* with a period of time, except with *night*.
- English has two kinds of nouns: countable and non-countable. Countable nouns have plural forms. Non-countable nouns are always singular.
- There are spelling rules for writing the plural forms. We add *-s* or *-es* to most nouns. Check the rules for words ending in *y*, *o*, *f*, *fe*, *s*, *sh*, *ch*, *x*, or *z*.
- Some nouns, like *sheep*, have the same singular and plural forms.
- There are also some irregular plural nouns that you must learn and memorize.
- We use the word *much* to show quantity with non-countable nouns and *many* with countable nouns.
- Articles introduce nouns. Nouns can be indefinite (*a*, *an*, *some*), definite (*the*), or general (no article). We use *a* and *an* only with singular, countable nouns; we use *the* and *some* with countable and non-countable nouns.
- The structure *there + be* introduces information. *There is* introduces singular and non-countable nouns; *there are* introduces plural nouns.

Exercise 9

Fill in the blanks with the times you do the following things. Write the time in words and (circle) *at* or *in* to complete your answers.

Every day, I get up (**at** / **in**) <u>six thirty (half past six)</u> (time) (**at** / **in**) the morning. I take a shower and get dressed by **1** _____ (time). I usually leave for school (**at** / **in**)

2 _____ (time). My class starts (**at** / **in**) **3** _____ (time). I have

lunch (**at** / **in**) **4** _____ (time). (**At** / **In**) the afternoon, I go to class and study.

I go home (**at** / **in**) **5** _____ (time). I eat supper (**at** / **in**) **6** _____

(time). I watch TV for a little while (**at** / **in**) the evening. I usually go to bed (**at** / **in**)

7 _____ (time). Sometimes, I stay up late (**at** / **in**) night to study or to call my

friends.

Exercise 10

There are five plural noun errors in the following paragraph. Find and correct them.

There are so many activitys for people of all ages to do in the city. There are restaurantes,

movies, and theatres. Everyone enjoys the parks too. I like to take a walk in the park on

Sundays. I watch parent playing with their childrens and people throwing Frisbees for their

dogs. If it rains, I often go to the library to read books about the local history. It's fun to

learn more informations about the place where you live.

Exercise 11

Fill in the blanks with *much*, *many*, *a little*, or *a few*.

1. How ___*much*___ time do we have before supper is ready? I just need ___*few*___

   minutes to finish this exercise. The teacher gave us so ___*many*___ exercises to do.

2. We're having spaghetti and a salad. How ___*much*___ pasta would you like? Do you

   want a lot or just ___*little*___ sauce?

Exercise 12

There are five article errors in the following paragraph. Find and correct them.

The Mexico is great! I enjoy shopping when I'm on the holidays. I want to buy a dress. A blue one is nice, but it's the wrong size. I want to ask for a help, but I don't know how to say the words in Spanish. Do you think the clerk speaks the English?

Exercise 13

Write the correct choice in the blank to complete each sentence.

1. _____ there any good restaurants in your neighbourhood? **(Is / Are)**

2. There _____ a lot of homework to do for this course. **(is / are)**

3. The movie starts at 9:00. There _____ much time to get there. **(isn't / aren't)**

4. There _____ many children playing in the park today. **(is / are)**

5. _____ there any butter in the fridge? **(Is / Are)**

Personal Pronouns, Demonstratives, the Imperative, and Prepositions

Overview

- Personal pronouns replace nouns and their modifiers.

- Demonstrative adjectives introduce nouns and show how near they are to the speaker; demonstrative pronouns replace the demonstrative adjectives and the nouns.

- The imperative gives instructions, commands, warnings, and advice.

- Prepositions tell us the relationship between people, things, or actions and place, time, direction, and origin. Prepositions of place tell us the relationship between people, things, or actions and place or location.

Warm-Up

Work in pairs. Read the paragraph. First, <u>underline</u> all the verbs. (Circle) all the nouns and pronouns that appear in front of the verbs. Write the nouns and pronouns in the following chart. Write the verbs in the chart. There are four verbs that don't have a noun, a pronoun, or *to* in front of them. List them as imperative verbs. What do these verbs do?

Magdalena is one of our friends from school. She lives in a house a few blocks away from the college. Saturday is her daughter's fourth birthday. Magdalena wants to have a party. We plan to go to the party. Jerome wants to go too, but he doesn't know how to get to her house. There are two ways to get there.

Take the 97 bus from the shopping mall. Get off at Billings Avenue. Magdalena's house is three doors down from the corner at 64 Billings. Or walk up Bartlow Street from the college. Turn right on Billings Avenue. Her house is not far.

Nouns	Pronouns	Verbs	Imperative Verbs

Personal Pronouns

Personal pronouns replace nouns and their modifiers.

Warm-Up

Work in pairs. Read the first paragraph. <u>Underline</u> all the nouns. Now read the second version of the paragraph. What is different? (Circle) the words that replace the nouns you underlined.

Paragraph 1 George and his brother live in an apartment. The apartment is very small. George studies engineering at the college. His brother sometimes helps George with his homework.

Paragraph 2 They live in an apartment. It is very small. He studies engineering at the college. He sometimes helps him with it.

Formation

Subject Pronoun	Object Pronoun	Possessive Adjective (used with nouns)	Possessive Pronoun (replaces possessive adj. + noun)	Reflexive Pronoun
I	me	my (car)	mine	myself
you (singular)	you	your (hat)	yours	yourself
he	him	his (cat)	his	himself
she	her	her (card)	hers	herself
it	it	its (meaning)	its	itself
we	us	our (house)	ours	ourselves
you (plural)	you	your (friend)	yours	yourselves
they	them	their (family)	theirs	themselves

- *I* is always a capital letter.
- *You* has the same form in both singular and plural, except for the reflexive pronouns.
- *He*, *she*, and *it* are all the third-person singular; *he* is only for a male person, *she* is only for a female person, and *it* is for a thing or an animal.
- Notice that we create the reflexive pronouns from the possessive adjective form for all persons except <u>him</u>self and <u>them</u>selves. We often use the word *by* before the reflexive pronouns.

Subject pronouns control the action of the verb and appear in front of the verb in sentences.

> **John** drives to work. → **He** drives to work.

> **Judy and her friends** walk to school. → **They** walk to school.

Object pronouns replace the object of the verb or the object of a preposition.

> Sarah teaches **piano lessons** on Saturday. → Sarah teaches **them** on Saturday.

> Geraldo lives with **his wife**. → Geraldo lives with **her**.

Possessive adjectives are not pronouns. We use them with nouns to show possession.

Possessive pronouns replace possessive adjectives and the nouns.

Both possessive adjectives and possessive pronouns tell us about the owner of the noun. They show the person (*I, you, they*, etc.), the number (singular or plural), and the gender (male or female) of the owner. The person, number, or gender of the noun does not affect or change the possessive adjective or pronoun.

> **John** drives **his car** to work.
> *His* refers to *John*. Both are male and singular. *Car* is a third-person singular thing.

> **Judy** and **her friends** walk to school.
> *Her* refers to *Judy*. Both are female and singular. *Friends* is third-person plural.

> **We** have a small house. **Our house** is small. The small house is **ours**.
> *Our* and *ours* refer to *we*. Both are first-person plural. *House* is a third-person singular thing.

> **My books** are on the table. The books on the table are **mine**.
> *My* and *mine* refer to the first-person singular *I*. *Books* is third-person plural and a thing.

To show **possession with nouns**, add apostrophe + *s* ('*s*) to singular nouns and plural nouns that do not end in *s*. Add only the apostrophe (') to plural nouns ending in *s*.

The book belongs to Peter. It's **Peter's** book.

The **children's** toys are in the box.

The **dogs'** tails are wagging. They are happy.

Exercise 1

Circle the correct pronouns or possessive adjectives to complete the sentences.

1. Fernando enjoys fixing things. When something breaks, he likes to fix it **(herself / himself)**.

2. My mother and **(I / me)** like to go for a walk after dinner. Sometimes, my brother comes with **(ours / us / we)**.

3. The book on the table belongs to Maria. Please give it to **(herself / her / hers)**.

4. The brown shoes by the door are **(me / my / mine)**. **(They / Their / Them)** are my favourite shoes.

5. The house on the corner belongs to us. It is **(our / ours / ourselves)**.

6. Mohammad and his cousin live in that apartment building. **(They / Their / Theirs)** apartment is on the second floor.

7. Jennifer, you need to do your homework by **(yours / yourself / yourselves)**.

8. Sarah often plays soccer with **(her / his / hers)** brothers.

9 Our cat has a favourite place to sleep. **(He / She / It)** sleeps on **(his / her / its)** pillow on the sofa.

10. The students study **(our / their / them)** lessons by **(ourselves / yourselves / themselves)**.

Exercise 2

Replace the <u>underlined</u> words with pronouns or possessive adjectives.

Sofia shares an apartment with a friend. <u>Sofia</u> *She* takes social work at the college. <u>Sofia's</u> roommate studies <u>social work</u> at the college too. <u>Sofia and Zara</u> take the bus to school every day. <u>Sofia's and Zara's</u> class schedules are the same. Sofia has a part-time job. <u>Sofia's</u> job is in the cafeteria. Zara often studies in the library and waits for <u>Sofia</u> to finish work. Then <u>Sofia and Zara</u> take the bus home. After supper, they do <u>Sofia's and Zara's</u> homework. Sometimes they do <u>homework</u> together and sometimes they do <u>homework</u> alone.

Exercise 3

Audio 04 🔊

Look at the diagram of a family. Listen to the audio. Answer the questions.

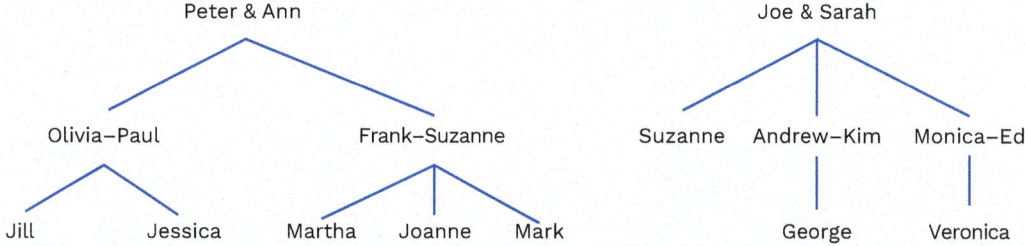

	Family Members		
	Male	**Female**	**Group**
senior generation	grandfather	grandmother	grandparents
middle generation	father	mother	parents
young generation	son	daughter	children
young generation	brother	sister	siblings
young generation	grandson	granddaughter	grandchildren
middle generation	uncle	aunt	———
young generation	nephew	niece	cousins
middle generation	husband	wife	couple

Comprehension

Answer the following questions.

1. What is my name? Your name is _____.

2. What is my sister's name? Your sister's name is _____.

3. How many cousins do I have? You have _____ cousins.

4. What is the relationship between Jill and Jessica? Jill and Jessica are _____.

5. What is my relationship to George? George is your _____.

6. Who is Frank's wife? _____ is Frank's wife.

7. Who is Veronica's grandmother? _____ is her grandmother.

8. Who is Ann's grandson? _____ is her grandson.

9. Who is Olivia's husband? _____ is her husband.

10. What is my relationship to Paul? You are his _____.

Demonstrative Adjectives and Demonstrative Pronouns

Demonstrative adjectives introduce nouns and show how near they are to the speaker.
Demonstrative pronouns replace the demonstrative adjectives and the nouns.

Warm-Up

Look at the picture. Read the description below. Identify the people and things Andrea is describing
in the picture. What do the words *this*, *that*, *these*, and *those* tell you about the location of the people
and things in relation to where Andrea is? Are they near her or far from her?

My name is Andrea. I'm sitting on the bench in the picture. This spot is great for watching
the people around me. That man is playing the guitar. Those children are playing with a
ball. These birds want me to feed them. That family is having a picnic.

Formation

Near		Far	
Adjectives	**Pronouns**	**Adjectives**	**Pronouns**
This book is new.	**This** is new.	**That book** is brown.	**That** is brown.
These books are mine.	**These** are mine.	**Those books** are not mine.	**Those** are not mine.

Exercise 4

Fill in the blanks. Use the correct demonstrative adjectives or pronouns to complete the sentences.

Are **those** your keys on the table by the door?

1. Look over there! What are _____ people doing?

2. I don't really like the shirt on the rack over there. I prefer _____ shirt.

3. Wow! _____ pizza is fantastic! Is it from Guillermo's Pizzeria?

4. There's a weird light in the park. What is _____ ?

5. Over there are the books you want. _____ are mine right here.

Exercise 5

Underline the six demonstrative adjectives or pronouns in the following paragraph. Three are incorrect; correct them.

My grandparents have so many things packed away in this storage room. Look at these old

boxes under all that stuff in the corner. Here is a book of old photos in that one. That box

has a bunch of old toys. I wonder if these doll furniture is my mother's.

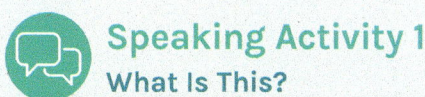

Speaking Activity 1
What Is This?

Work in small groups. Place a number of personal items, such as pens, books, cellphones, keys, and so on, on the desk. Discuss the items and write sentences using *this* and *these* to identify the objects on the desk. Then write sentences using *that* and *those* to identify the objects on another group's desk. Take turns reading the sentences out loud.

This is Frank's cellphone.
These keys are mine.

The Imperative

The imperative gives instructions, commands, warnings, and advice.

Warm-Up

Audio 05 🔊

Work in pairs. Listen to the audio, which is a phone conversation between two friends. Trace the directions you hear on the map. Include the landmarks (church, bank, and so on) mentioned in the telephone conversation. Compare your results with another pair's results.

Formation

We use the imperative to give instructions, commands, and warnings. To form the imperative, use the base form of the verb—for all verbs. There are no endings and no agreements, and nothing is irregular.

	Positive (base form of verb)	Negative (do not / don't + base form of verb)
be	Be on time for class.	Don't be late for class.
stay	Stay at home when you are sick.	Don't stay up late every night.
sit	Sit down, please.	Don't sit there.
go	Go straight down this street.	Don't go to the store today.
eat	Eat your vegetables.	Don't eat my lunch.

To make a suggestion for the first-person plural (*we*), use *let's* + the base form of the verb. *Let's* is the contracted form of *let us*.

	Positive (*let's* + base form of verb)	Negative (*let's* + *not* + base form of verb)
be	Let's be on time for class.	Let's not be late for class.
do	Let's do the dishes now.	Let's not do the dishes now.
sit	Let's sit beside those guys.	Let's not sit beside those guys.
go	Let's go to the movies tonight.	Let's not go to the movies tonight.
eat	Let's eat pizza tonight.	Let's not eat pizza tonight.

Exercise 6

Change each of the following sentences into the imperative.

You need **to bring** your books to class. → **Bring** your books to class.

1. You need to take the number 18 bus to go to the grocery store.

   _____

2. It's not a good idea to sit on that bench. It is wet from the rain.

   _____

3. You need to be at work by 5:30.

   _____

4. You need to practise your lessons.

   _____

5. It's not a good idea to talk to strangers.

   _____

Exercise 7

There are five imperative errors in the recipe. Find and correct them.

Scrambled Eggs

Heat the frying pan over medium heat. Cracks three eggs into a bowl. Add a little milk (five to ten millilitres). Season the eggs with some salt and pepper. Adds some herbs, such as marjoram or thyme, if desired. Beat the mixture with a whisk. Melts a tablespoon of butter in the frying pan. Pour the eggs into the pan. Once the eggs start to cook, turns the heat to medium low. Turn the eggs over in portions until cooked. Enjoys.

Speaking Activity 2
Giving Directions

Work in small groups. Take turns telling the others how to get from the school to the nearest bank, corner store, or grocery store. Use a local map to help you with the street names.

Prepositions of Place

Prepositions of place tell us the relationship between people, things, or actions and place or location.

Warm-Up

Work in pairs. Identify the prepositions of place—the words that introduce a location—in the paragraph. <u>Underline</u> them. Compare your answers with another pair's answers.

> I live in a nice neighbourhood. I live at 95 Park Avenue in apartment 1A on the first floor. My friend Miguel lives on the floor above me in apartment 2C. The laundry room is below my apartment, in the basement. There is a parking lot behind the building. My friend parks his car there. When I have visitors, they can park on the street. There is a convenience store across the street from my apartment building. Beside the store is a small park with lots of trees and a playground for the children in the neighbourhood. In front of the store is the bus stop. It's a great place to live.

Formation

Prepositions introduce nouns and their modifiers. Prepositions of place give information about the location of nouns and their relationship to other nouns. There are no rules for prepositions. You need to learn their meanings.

Common Prepositions of Place		
in front of	at	above
behind	on	below
beside	in	over
across from		under

In front of and *across from* can sometimes be synonyms but not always.

> The park **is across** the street from my house. The park is **in front of** my house.
> The teacher stands **in front of** the class. (not *across from*)

At, *on*, and *in* have two uses with location.

> He sits **at** his desk. (his position) He lives **at** 151 Lakeside Avenue. (very specific location)

The book is on the desk. (its position) **He lives on Lakeside Avenue.** (larger location)

Your book is in the kitchen. (location in an area) **He lives in Calgary.** (large general location)

At is used with certain expressions: *at home, at work, at school.*
Above and *over* are synonyms; *below* and *under* are synonyms.

Exercise 8

Look at the picture. Fill in the blanks with the best prepositions from the list in the Formation box. Some prepositions are used more than once.

There are three rows of desks **1** _____ the classroom. Melissa is sitting

2 _____ her desk. Her desk is the first in the row of desks **3** _____ the

windows. Eugene is sitting **4** _____ Melissa in the same row of desks. The teacher

is standing **5** _____ all the students **6** _____ his desk. He has a pointer

7 _____ his hand. He is pointing **8** _____ the exercise **9** _____

the blackboard. There is a clock **10** _____ the blackboard. There is a map on the

wall **11** _____ the blackboard. **12** _____ the map, there is a desk. The desk

has some books **13** _____ it, and there is a pile of magazines **14** _____

the desk.

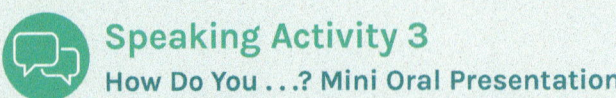

Speaking Activity 3
How Do You . . .? Mini Oral Presentation

First, prepare your presentation. Use the imperative to write instructions for a simple activity. Use sequence markers, such as *first, second, then, next*, and so on. Choose your own activity or use one of these:

- how to make your favourite meal
- how to change a tire or change the oil in a car
- how to create a particular kind of document on the computer
- how to replace a light fixture
- how to play a particular card game or sport

Next, work in small groups. Present your instructions for the activity to your group. Ask questions about the other activities that your classmates present.

Speaking Activity 4
People, Places, and Things

Work in pairs. Compete with your partner to write as many short sentences as possible about things or people in the classroom. Use *there is* or *there are* to begin the sentences and use prepositions to give the location of the things. Give yourselves two to three minutes. The person with the most sentences wins. Compare your sentences and discuss how many are about different things.

There is a book **on** my desk.

There are 15 desks **in** the classroom.

Reading

Read the passage and answer the questions that follow.

DIY

DIY is an acronym or short form for Do It Yourself. The term means that people **create**, renovate, or repair all kinds of things without the help of a professional. Some people do DIY projects to save money. Hiring a professional to fix your toilet, for example, is often expensive. Other people enjoy the creative part of DIY. Completing a DIY project gives them a good feeling of success and accomplishment.

Doing it yourself is a very popular <u>trend</u> these days. DIY activities include everything from home improvement projects to arts and crafts to cooking to recording music and more. People complete or try to complete their projects by themselves without professional help. However, they very often **rely on** information from professionals to be able to do their projects. Many professionals and amateurs make a lot of money from sharing their knowledge and skills. There are thousands of "How to" books and magazines to help with DIY projects. There is at least one television channel **focused** on do-it-yourself topics. Many other television broadcasters have their own DIY programs. The Internet is also <u>loaded</u> with DIY **sites**.

There is a lot of information **available** for anyone who wants to complete a project by himself or herself. However, with so much information available, it is sometimes difficult to know if those **sources** of information are good or not. Sometimes people who call themselves experts are not really experts at all. Before you start your project, always check more than one source, so you can **assess** and compare **potentially** different instructions and information. Then go for it and do it yourself. Good luck.

As you read, pay attention to these vocabulary words in the passage: *create*, *rely on*, *focused*, *sites*, *available*, *sources*, *assess*, and *potentially*.

Comprehension

Answer the following questions. Try to write complete sentences.

1. What does DIY mean?

    _____

2. Give two reasons that people do DIY projects.

    _____

3. Name three kinds of DIY activities.

    _____

4. Name three sources of information for DIY projects.

    _____

5. What advice does the writer give to help make sure the sources of information are good or reliable?

    _____

    _____

Analyzing the Reading Passage

Read the passage again and underline all personal pronouns (18) with a <u>single line</u>. Underline all the possessive adjectives (6) with a <u>double line</u>. Circle the imperatives (4).

Discussion

What do you think about do-it-yourself projects? Do you do any DIY projects? Do you succeed? Give some examples of your projects.

Listening

Audio 06

Before the Canoe Trip

Listen to the audio of a conversation between roommates and answer the following questions.

Comprehension

Answer the following questions. Try to write complete sentences.

1. Where are the friends going on Friday?

   _____

2. How many life jackets do they have?

   _____

3. They have two lighters. What else do they have?

   _____

4. What do they have lots of that is very important?

   _____

5. What do they need to buy tomorrow?

   _____

6. At what time do they agree to leave on Friday morning?

   _____

7. Why does one of the men call his friend crazy?

   _____

Writing

Write a short composition (maximum 150 words) about your usual leisure activities with family or friends on weekends or on holidays.

Here are some questions to guide your writing:

- Do you have picnics in the park with family or friends?
- Do you get together with friends to play music, games, cards, or sports?
- When you take a vacation, do you travel, visit family, go camping, or do something else?

   _____

   _____

   _____

   _____

Vocabulary

1. Read the following sentences. The words in **bold** are from the Reading activity. Use the context to help you understand what the words in bold mean.

   a) I need to **rely on** my brother to check on my apartment and feed my cat while I am away. I hope he is **available** next week.

   b) I want to **create** more storage space in my room. There are many online **sites** that are good **sources** of information and provide clear instructions on how to build bookcases and hanging shelves.

   c) Juanita wants to stay **focused** on her academic goals because she hopes to **potentially** get a scholarship next year.

   d) We need to **assess** the advantages and disadvantages of buying a new or a used car.

2. Match the words or expressions in the left column with their definitions in the right column.

Word or Term	Definition
1. assess (v.) ____	a) concentrating on, directly looking at, or paying attention to something very specific
2. available (adj.) ____	b) describing a possible outcome in the future; possibly; not yet but possible
3. create (v.) ____	c) the original places where you find information
4. focused (adj.) ____	d) describes something that anyone can get, find, or have; not busy
5. potentially (adv.) ____	e) to make something new from other material or objects, or to make something happen
6. rely on (phrasal verb) ____	f) to evaluate or judge the merits or value of something
7. sites (n.) ____	g) to be certain of; depend on; count on
8. sources (n.) ____	h) specific places or locations, in this case, on the Internet

3. Fill in the blanks with the vocabulary words listed in the chart.

   a) I need to carefully _____ my financial situation if I want to _____ get a new apartment.

   b) We have a fun project for this weekend. We want to _____ a new garden in the yard. We _____ local garden centres as great _____ for plants.

   c) Hello. Are there any tickets _____ for the game on Saturday?

   d) Look for some _____ on the Internet that are _____ on kitchen renovations.

Chapter Review

Summary

- Pronouns replace nouns and their modifiers.
- Demonstrative adjectives introduce nouns and show how near they are to the speaker; demonstrative pronouns replace the demonstrative adjectives and the nouns.
- Use the imperative to give instructions, commands, warnings, and advice.
- Prepositions of place tell us the relationship between people, things, or actions and place or location.

Exercise 9

Unscramble the following words and make them into sentences.

we eat / to the park / Let's / after / go → Let's go to the park after we eat.

1. does / with her friends / Marlena / her homework

   _____.

2. at home / I / in the evening / study

   _____.

3. is mine / belong to Philip / , but this book / Those books

   _____.

4. is / about pronouns / tomorrow / Our test

   _____.

5. at / left / the next corner / Turn

   _____.

Exercise 10

Circle the letter of the correct possessive adjective or pronoun to complete the sentences.

1. The students listen to _____ teacher.
   a) his   b) theirs   c) their

2. Allija tries to fix her computer by _____.
   a) her   b) herself   c) itself

3. Stephan has lunch with _____ wife on Fridays.
   a) her   b) his   c) him

4. Manolo and _____ need to study for our test.
   a) I   b) me   c) us

5. Those aren't your keys. They are _____.
   a) my   b) hers   c) our

Exercise 11

Fill in the blanks with the missing pronouns.

My boyfriend Jorge has a large family. __His__ grandparents have six children. Now

1 _____ have 21 grandchildren and 3 great-grandchildren. That's just on 2 _____

mother's side of the family. Jorge's father has three brothers and two sisters, and

3 _____ all have children. In fact, 4 _____ children are all between the ages of

17 and 20. Jorge says all the cousins have great fun when his parents have a big family

gathering for all of 5 _____ once a year.

Exercise 12

There are five errors with personal pronouns or demonstrative adjectives (*this*, *that*, *these*, and
those) in the following paragraph. Correct them.

I enjoy watching people. For example, this young girl over there looks like she is talking to

himself. She is really talking on the phone. There is a couple sitting on those park bench.

The man looks nervous. Perhaps the couple is on a first date. These kids over there are

playing with a ball. Oops! The ball is now in that pond. There are some teenagers walking

near the pond. One of they is getting the ball out of the water.

Exercise 13

Change the following instructions into the imperative.

It's a good idea to test the temperature of the water. → Test the temperature of the water.

To get to the museum, you need to go straight down this street. You need to turn right

onto First Avenue. Then you need to walk for two blocks. You turn left onto Frank Street.

You don't need to make any more turns. You need to walk to the end of Frank Street. The

museum is right in front of you.

Communicating with Grammar 1

3 Simple Present

Overview

We use the simple present verb tense to express facts and generalizations, as well as actions that happen on a regular basis. Such actions include routines, habits, and daily activities.

Use	Form	Keywords	Example Sentences
facts or generalizations	most verbs: I / you / we / they + **verb** she / he / it + **verb** + -s / -es	every day / Monday / Tuesday every weekend every year every summer every vacation / holiday always usually	I **read** books. The earth **circles** the sun. She **works** every weekend. I **go** on vacation every summer. They usually **leave** at five o'clock.
routines habits daily activities		often sometimes rarely never once a day / week / year twice per day / week / year number of times per day / week / year	
	verb *be*: I **am** she / he / it **is** you / we / they **are**		I **am** always honest. You **are** a student. It **is** difficult. They **are** from France.
	verb *have*: I / you / we / they **have** she / he / it **has**		I **have** a dessert once a week. We **have** a house. He **has** a car.

Warm-Up

Read the following passage, and <u>underline</u> the verbs in the simple present tense.

I have a sister. Her name is Izabela. She is older than I am. I live in Ottawa, but she lives in Toronto. She works as a sales representative. She likes her job. She has a son. He is 14 years old. He plays drums, takes martial arts classes, and studies hard. He also likes to play video games. My sister and I often call each other. We usually talk about our family. I really love my sister. Do you have any brothers or sisters? Are you in contact with them?

Write the verbs from the passage for the following subjects:

I, we: _____

she, he: _____

you: _____

Can you see any patterns? _____

Simple Present—Regular Verbs

All verbs except *be* have two forms in the simple present.
For *I*, *you*, *we*, and *they*, use the base form of the verb.
For *he*, *she*, and *it*, add -*s* or -*es*.

Warm-Up

Work in pairs. Read the following conversations out loud.

Conversation 1

Partner A: What time do you **usually** wake up?

Partner B: I **usually** wake up at seven in the morning.

Conversation 2

Partner A: Do you work?

Partner B: No, I go to college. I study in a hairdressing program.

Partner A: Do you like it?

Partner B: I love it!

Conversation 3

Partner A: What do you **usually** do during summer?

Partner B: I **always** visit my family in Vancouver for the first two weeks of summer. After, I come back to Ottawa, and I **usually** get a summer job.

Partner A: Do you **sometimes** spend some time with your friends?

Partner B: Yes, I see them on weekends. We **often** watch a movie or go out.

Read the warm-up conversations again. Notice the placement of the adverbs. The adverbs are the words in **bold**.

Formation

Positive	Negative	Yes/No Question
Subject + Verb (+ object / complement)	Subject + Auxiliary + Negative + Verb (+ object / complement)	Auxiliary + Subject + Verb (+ object / complement)
I **wake** up at 7:00 AM every day.	I **do not wake** up at 7:00 AM every day.	**Do** you **wake** up at 7:00 AM every day?
You **watch** TV in the evening.	You **do not watch** TV in the evening.	**Do** you **watch** TV in the evening?
He **likes** Honda cars.	He **does not like** Honda cars.	**Does** he **like** Honda cars?
She **reads** a lot.	She **does not read** a lot.	**Does** she **read** a lot?
It **costs** five dollars.	It **does not cost** five dollars.	**Does** it **cost** five dollars?
We **travel** to Yukon every summer.	We **do not travel** to Yukon every summer.	**Do** we **travel** to Yukon every summer?
They **work** on weekends.	They **do not work** on weekends.	**Do** they **work** on weekends?

For a detailed explanation of how to form and use questions and negatives, refer to Chapter 11.

Question Words for Wh- Questions

Question words ask about a specific piece of information in a sentence. We use these words when making Wh- questions.

The Wh- question formation is the same as for Yes/No questions. We just put in a question word before we add the rest of the question.

Question Word	Use	Example Sentences	Wh- Question
			Question Word +Auxiliary + Subject + Verb (+ object / complement)
who	only people	Alex loves **Milo**.	**Who** does Alex love?
what	things or actions	They build **houses**. He **hangs out with his friends** every Friday.	**What** do they build? **What** does he do every Friday?

Question Word	Use	Example Sentences	Wh- Question
where	places	She works at **McDonald's**.	**Where** does she work?
when	time	My class starts **at 9:00**.	**When** does your class start?
why	reasons	He studies a lot **because he wants good grades**.	**Why** does he study a lot?
		I paint every weekend **to relax**.	**Why** do you paint every weekend?
how	manner or degree	She goes to work **by bus**.	**How** does she go to work?
		I feel **great**!	**How** do you feel?
how much / how many	quantity	It costs **10 dollars**.	**How much** does it cost?
		We have **two** cats.	**How many** cats do you have?
how far	distance	I live **50 kilometres** from here.	**How far** do you live from here?
how long	duration	It usually takes us **half a day** to clean our house.	**How long** does it usually take us to clean our house?
how often	frequency	They meet **once** a week.	**How often** do they meet?

Exercise 1

Fill in the blanks with the correct question words. Each question word needs to correspond with the portion of the sentence in **bold**.

I use reusable bags **because I want to be environmentally friendly.** →

Why do you use reusable bags?

1. **A lot of** people try to carpool to work these days.

   _____people try to carpool to work these days?

2. Common recyclable materials include **glass, metal, plastic, and paper**.

   _____do recyclable materials include?

3. **My friend** reuses clean yogurt containers to plant flower seeds.

   _____reuses clean yogurt containers to plant flower seeds?

4. We help to clean up a local park **every spring**.

   _____do we help to clean up a local park?

5. My son learns **at school and at home** that it is important to care about our environment.

   _____does my son learn that it is important to care about our environment?

Frequency Adverbs

In the simple present, we often use frequency adverbs. These adverbs tell us how often an action takes place. With regular verbs, we place adverbs before the verb.

0%	never	I **never** lie.
	rarely/seldom	My school volleyball team **rarely** loses any games.
	occasionally	She **occasionally** eats red meat.
	sometimes	They **sometimes** do silly things.
	generally	We don't **generally** buy our groceries at a local store.
	often	Do you **often** forget what I tell you?
	usually	The bus **usually** comes on time.
100%	always	Evgeny **always** works on Saturdays.

Exercise 2

Unscramble the following words and make them into sentences or questions.

snows / in / It / Canada → It snows in Canada.

1. with / She / lives / her parents

   _____.

2. don't / buy / They / any junk food / usually

   _____.

3. your class / at eight o'clock / always / Does / start

   _____?

4. England / come / My father / doesn't / from

   _____.

5. you / ride / Do / on a motorcycle

   _____?

Spelling Rules for Verbs in the Third-Person Singular

Condition	Rule	Examples
For most verbs	add **-s**	work → works travel → travels speak → speaks
If the verb ends in **ch**, **s**, **sh**, **x**, or **z**	add **-es**	watch → watches fix → fixes pass → passes buzz → buzzes wash → washes
If the verb ends in a **single vowel**	add **-es**	go → goes do → does
If the verb ends in **two vowels**	add **-s**	tattoo → tattoos
If the base form ends in a **consonant + y**	change **y** to **i** and add **-es**	study → studies carry → carries
If the base form ends in a **vowel + y**	add **-s** (do not change the **y**)	pay → pays

For the pronunciation rules for the -s endings, see Chapter 1, page 11.

Exercise 3

Write the correct spelling of the following verbs in the third-person singular.

1. look   _____
2. want   _____
3. brush   _____
4. play   _____
5. hope   _____

6. hurry   _____
7. try   _____
8. write   _____
9. relax   _____
10. enjoy   _____

11. travel   _____
12. match   _____
13. go   _____
14. stay   _____
15. arrive   _____

Exercise 4

Answer each question with a complete sentence. Look at the examples to help you.

Do you speak other languages? Yes, I speak other languages.

Does she do her homework every night? No, she does not do her homework every night.

1. Do Simon and Derek know how to cook?

   No, _____.

2. Does your daughter like to read?

   Yes, _____.

3. Do dogs bark?

   Yes, _____.

4. Do you have a pet?

   No, _____.

5. Does he play football?

   No, _____.

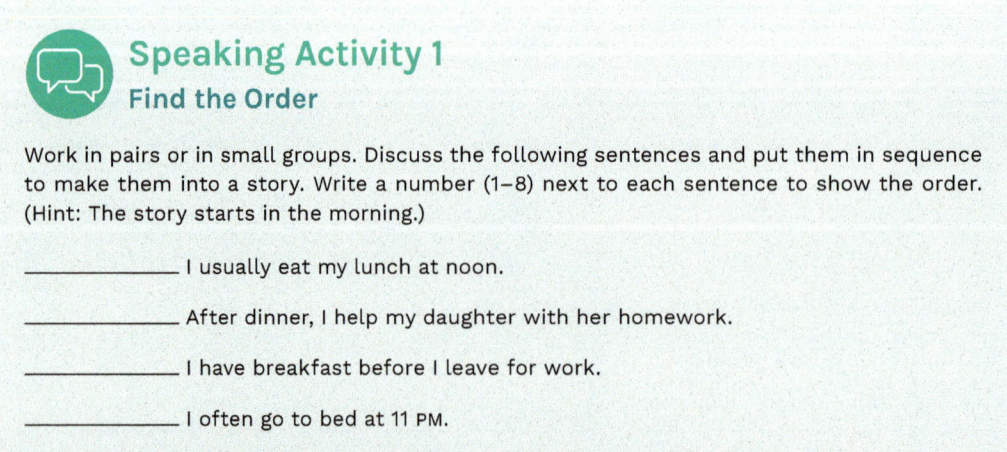

Speaking Activity 1
Find the Order

Work in pairs or in small groups. Discuss the following sentences and put them in sequence to make them into a story. Write a number (1–8) next to each sentence to show the order. (Hint: The story starts in the morning.)

_____ I usually eat my lunch at noon.

_____ After dinner, I help my daughter with her homework.

_____ I have breakfast before I leave for work.

_____ I often go to bed at 11 PM.

_____ I get up at seven o'clock in the morning.

_____ In the evening, I sometimes call my friends.

_____ When I come back from work, I cook dinner for my family.

_____ I start work at nine o'clock.

Simple Present—The Verb *Be*

The verb *be* is irregular in the simple present.

Warm-Up

Tell your partner about yourself. You can include some information from the chart below.

Category	Your Information
age	(_____ years old)
nationality / city you live in	(for example, Canadian, Mexican)
relationship status / family / siblings	(for example, single, married, a mother / a father)
personality	(for example, friendly, shy, hard-working, ambitious)
profession or professional goals	(for example, a student, a nurse, an engineer, a computer technician)
sports or hobbies	(for example, play soccer, make ceramics, play music)

Now, your partner will tell you about himself or herself. Write notes in the chart about the information he or she gives you.

Category	Partner's Information
age	
nationality / city he or she lives in	
relationship status / family / siblings	
personality	
profession or professional goals	
sports / hobbies	

Formation

Positive	Negative	Question	Wh- Question
Subject + Verb + Complement	**Subject + Verb + Negative + Complement**	**Verb + Subject + Complement**	**Question Word + Verb + Subject (+ complement)**
I **am** Jeanne's sister.	I **am not** Jeanne's sister.	**Are** you Jeanne's sister?	**Who** are you?
You **are** 25 years old.	You **are not** 25 years old.	**Are** you 25 years old?	**How old** are you?
He **is** sad.	He **is not** sad.	**Is** he sad?	**Why** is he sad?
She **is** Polish.	She **is not** Polish.	**Is** she Polish?	**What nationality** is she?
It **is** 10 dollars.	It **is not** 10 dollars.	**Is** it 10 dollars?	**How much** is it?
We **are** from Ottawa.	We **are not** from Ottawa.	**Are** we from Ottawa?	**Where** are we from?
They **are** on vacation.	They **are not** on vacation.	**Are** they on vacation?	**Where** are they?

Remember, the verb *be* does not need an auxiliary verb in negatives or questions.

Incorrect	We do not be from Ottawa.	Do we be from Ottawa?
Correct	We **are not** from Ottawa.	**Are** we from Ottawa?

Adverb placement: Frequency adverbs are placed after the verb *be*.

He is **never** late for work.

Exercise 5

Fill in the blanks with the correct form of the verb *be* in the simple present tense.

We ___are___ from Manitoba.

1. She _____ a doctor.
2. _____ it cold today?
3. They _____ not afraid of the dark.
4. His name _____ Steve.
5. _____ you at home?
6. Kadisha and Kristen _____ my friends.

Exercise 6

Answer each question with a complete sentence.

Is it beautiful?   Yes, it is beautiful.   No, it is not beautiful.

1. Are you an English student? Yes, _____.
2. Is she a teacher? Yes, _____.
3. Is he from Spain? No, _____.
4. Are you and your classmates at school? Yes, _____.
5. Is this room blue? No, _____.

Exercise 7

Change each of the following sentences into a Yes/No question.

I am happy. → Are you happy?

1. Tom and Chris are friends.

   _____?

2. We are at work.

   _____?

3. This book is interesting.

   _____?

4. She is absent.

   _____?

5. You are very smart.

   _____?

Speaking Activity 2
Mini Oral Presentation

Using the information from the Warm-Up activity in Simple Present—The Verb *Be* (on page 47), prepare a short oral presentation about your partner. You can ask him or her additional questions. Then present your presentation to the whole class. Your classmates can ask you or your partner more questions.

Simple Present—The Verb *Have*

The verb *have* has two forms in the simple present, but one form is irregular.

Warm-Up

Find Someone Who . . .

On a separate piece of paper, prepare some Yes/No questions for your classmates. Use the five ideas below to get you started.
Find someone who . . .

- has many hobbies
- has dreams every night
- has a part-time job
- has a doctor's appointment today
- has a good memory

Then ask some of your classmates your questions. If somebody answers "yes" to your question, record his or her name and write the answers in complete sentences. Look at the example to help you.

Questions	Names + Answers
Do you have a laptop?	Sandra has a laptop.

Formation

Positive	Negative	Question	Wh- Question
Subject + Verb (+ object)	**Subject + Auxiliary + Negative + Verb (+ object)**	**Auxiliary + Subject + Verb (+ object)**	**Question Word + Auxiliary + Subject + Verb (+ object)**
I **have** two brothers.	I **do not have** two brothers.	**Do** you **have** two brothers?	**How many** brothers do you have?
You **have** a cold.	You **do not have** a cold.	**Do** you **have** a cold?	**Why** do you have a cold?
She **has** a parrot.	She **does not have** a parrot.	**Does** she **have** a parrot?	**What kind of** pet does she have?
He **has** brown eyes.	He **does not have** brown eyes.	**Does** he **have** brown eyes?	**What** eye colour does he have?
It **has** a sunroof.	It **does not have** a sunroof.	**Does** it **have** a sunroof?	**What** does it have?
We **have** some plans.	We **do not have** any plans.	**Do** we **have** any plans?	**What** plans do we have?
They **have** a cottage in Madawaska.	They **do not have** a cottage in Madawaska.	**Do** they **have** a cottage in Madawaska?	**Where** do they have a cottage?

Exercise 8

Fill in the blanks with the correct form of the verb *have* in the simple present tense.

You _____ **(have)** a dog. → You **have** a dog.

She _____ **(have, negative)** a cat. → She **does not have** a cat.

1. Carolina _____ **(have)** many talents.

2. He _____ **(have, negative)** any allergies.

3. **(have, question)** _____ they _____ any problems?

4. My daughter and I _____ **(have)** curly hair.

5. This hotel _____ **(have)** an indoor pool.

Bringing It All Together

Speaking Activity 3
Partner Interview

Work with a partner. On a separate sheet of paper, make an interview chart like this one. Write some Yes/No questions to ask your partner. Ask about his or her daily habits or weekly routine and record his or her answers in the chart. Look at the example to help you.

You	Your Partner
What time do you usually leave home every day?	I usually leave home at 8:00 AM.

Speaking Activity 4
Find Someone Who . . .

Prepare Yes/No questions for your classmates. Use the information below. Then ask some of your classmates these questions. If somebody answers "yes" to your question, record his or her name, and write the answer in a complete sentence. Look at the example to help you.

Find someone who . . . lives in Ottawa.

Question Do you live in Ottawa?   **Answer** Anne lives in Ottawa.

Find someone who . . .

1. plays a musical instrument

   Question: _____?

   Answer: _____.

2. has a brother or a sister

   Question: _____?

   Answer: _____.

3. usually wakes up early in the morning

   Question: _____?

   Answer: _____.

4. likes chocolate

   Question: _____?

   Answer: _____.

5. drives to school every day

   Question: _____?

   Answer: _____.

Speaking Activity 5
Surveys

Work in small groups. Your teacher will give your group a worksheet with one survey on an assigned topic. Each group member conducts a survey with at least one student from a different group. When you finish the surveys, meet with your group again to tally the responses and to prepare a short presentation of the results to the whole class.

Speaking Activity 6
Game—What's the Profession?

Work in pairs or small groups. Think of a profession, but don't tell your partner or group what it is. Prepare three to four sentences about what a person working in this profession usually does. Your partner or group will try to guess what the profession is. Look at the example to help you.

> This person usually inspects vehicles. He or she often changes oil and replaces car brakes. In general, this person fixes cars. (Answer: a car mechanic)

Reading

Read the passage and answer the questions that follow.

As you read, pay attention to these vocabulary words in the passage: **involved**, **task**, **contribute**, **ensure**, **participation**, **process**, **traditions**, and **interact**.

Weekend Breakfast with Family

The weekend is usually filled with sports, play dates, and errands, but it is also a great opportunity for the entire family to spend time together. A great way to do this is to start with a balanced family breakfast. A balanced breakfast at the beginning of the day is important. It often prepares you and your family for whatever your weekend has in store. Here are some helpful tips for a weekend family breakfast:

Participation

One of the best ways to make breakfast a family affair is to get everyone **involved**. All family members have a **task** to do and **contribute** to making breakfast. To **ensure** everyone's **participation**, a fun recipe is to make banana rollups. In this **process**, one family member spreads Nutella on a slice of whole grain pita, another person tops it off with sliced bananas, and the third rolls it up.

Family Traditions

A weekly family breakfast gives everyone something to look forward to and turns breakfast into a social activity instead of just a meal. It is a nice way to make it one of your family **traditions**, to **interact**, and to spend valuable quality time together.

Extend the Invitation

The weekend is the perfect occasion to spend time with other family members whom you do not usually see during the week. You can welcome everyone—grandparents, cousins, aunts, and uncles. This creates a strong family tradition and leads to closer relationships.

Adapted from "Make Breakfast a Family Affair." *Ottawa Family Living Magazine*, www.ottawafamilyliving.com/make_ breakfast_a_ family_affair.

Comprehension

Answer the questions. Write complete sentences.

1. What activities usually fill up the weekend?

   _____

   _____

2. Why is a balanced breakfast at the beginning of the day important?

   _____

   _____

3. How can each family member be involved in a weekend breakfast?

   _____

   _____

4. In what way is the family weekend breakfast a social activity?

   _____

   _____

5. Whom can you invite to such a breakfast?

   _____

   _____

Analyzing the Reading Passage

Read the passage again and underline all the present tense verbs with a <u>single line</u> and all the frequency adverbs with a <u>double line</u>.

Discussion

1. Agree or disagree with this statement: "A weekend breakfast with family is a good idea." Explain your answer.
2. In your family, do you usually have breakfast together? What other activities do you do with your family members to spend time together?

Listening

Audio 07

Early Classes = Sleepy Teens!

Listen to the audio, which is a podcast about teenagers and sleep. Then answer the questions.

Comprehension

Answer the following True/False questions. Circle the correct response.

T / F   1.   Half of American teenagers get enough sleep on school nights.
T / F   2.   Teenagers sleep 16 to 19 minutes less than they need.
T / F   3.   Many schools start classes as early as 6:00 AM.
T / F   4.   Teens usually go to bed early.
T / F   5.   They are tired in morning classes.
T / F   6.   Michael Breus is a high school teacher.
T / F   7.   Michael Breus has sleep problems.
T / F   8.   Teenagers need 8 to 10 hours of sleep per night.
T / F   9.   If teenagers don't sleep enough, they can get depressed.
T / F 10. When classes start later in the morning, students' marks are better.
T / F 11. The classes at St. George's School started 30 minutes later.
T / F 12. The teachers at that school noticed negative changes in their students' behaviour.

Writing

Choose one of the following topics. Write a short composition (maximum 150 words) about the topic.
- What do you usually do during school breaks or winter or summer vacations?
- How do you usually celebrate your birthday or other family events?

Vocabulary

1.   The words in the chart are in **bold** in the Reading passage on pages 52–53. Look at how the words are used in the passage. Fill in the chart with your definition and a synonym for the word. Use a dictionary or the glossary to help you.

Word or Term	Definition	Synonym
contribute (v.)		
ensure (v.)		
interact (v.)		

involved (v.)		
participation (n.)		
process (n.)		
task (n.)		
traditions (n.)		

2. Replace the <u>underlined</u> words in the following sentences with one of the words from the chart.

   a) Paloma's son studies in Toronto. She calls him every weekend to <u>make sure</u> he is all right.

   b) Mia is a shy girl who doesn't <u>socialize</u> with others much. She prefers to be by herself.

   c) If you want to immigrate to another country, prepare yourself for a long and complicated <u>procedure</u>.

   d) Ramzi is an excellent student. He completes every school <u>activity</u> diligently and gets good grades. His class <u>involvement</u> is also very good.

   e) There are many <u>customs</u> in my family. One of them is to give thanks before eating.

   f) If you want to <u>help</u> and make a difference in your community, get <u>interested</u> in it as much as you can.

3. Fill in the blanks with the vocabulary words listed in the chart in question 1.

   a) Veilia is on the student council because she wants to be more _____ at her school. After school, she volunteers as a tutor to help other students learn to study better.

   b) _____ often bring family or friends together as they celebrate and reinforce values and beliefs from their cultures.

   c) Our to-do list for today is quite long, so before we go out, let's complete at least one _____ from the list.

   d) If you have technical issues with your computer, you need to call an expert who can help you in the _____ of fixing the problem.

   e) There are many effective ways to encourage students to participate and _____ with one another during class. What learning strategies does your teacher use to _____ student _____ in the classroom?

   f) Many musicians _____ to charity organizations several times a year.

Chapter Review

Summary

- We use the simple present for facts, generalizations, and actions that take place on a regular basis.
- With the simple present tense, we use certain keywords or phrases, such as *every day*, *every summer*, or *twice a month*, as well as frequency adverbs, such as *always*, *often*, *sometimes*, and *never*.
- With all verbs except *be*, there are two forms in the simple present. For the pronouns *I*, *you*, *we*, and *they*, use the base form of the verb. For *he*, *she*, and *it*, add -*s* or -*es*.
- The verb *be* is irregular in the simple present and is different for every subject. It has three forms: *am* (*I am*), *are* (*you are*, *we are*, *they are*), and *is* (*he is*, *she is*, *it is*).
- The verb *have* is also irregular, and it has two forms: *have* (*I have*, *you have*, *we have*, *they have*) and *has* (*he has*, *she has*, *it has*).

Exercise 9

Change each of the following positive sentences into the negative. Review the formation charts in this chapter on pages 43, 48, and 50 if you need to. Look at the examples to help you.

Positive You like jazz music.   **Negative** You **do not** like jazz music.

Positive She is a college student.   **Negative** She **is not** a college student.

1. He has breakfast at 8:00 AM.

   _____

2. We usually go out on Fridays.

   _____

3. They are at the shopping mall.

   _____

4. My son calls me every weekend.

   _____

5. I am a mother.

   _____

Exercise 10

Change each of the following sentences into a Yes/No question. Review the formation charts in this chapter on pages 43, 48, and 50 if you need to. Look at the examples to help you.

Statement Anna lives by herself.   **Question** Does Anna live by herself?

Statement My friends are from Montreal.   **Question** Are my friends from Montreal?

1. We get together with our entire family every summer.

   _____?

2. My neighbours are very nice.

   _____?

3. She helps her grandmother every weekend.

_____?

4. I have a toothache.

_____?

5. He is always on time.

_____?

Exercise 11

Change each of the following statements into a Wh- question. The information you want to ask about is in **bold**. Review the Wh- question words on pages 43–44 and the formation charts in this chapter on pages 43, 48, and 50 if you need to. Look at the example to help you.

Statement Canadians celebrate **Thanksgiving** on the second Monday in October.

Question **What** do Canadians celebrate on the second Monday in October?

1. People use computers **all over the world.**

_____?

2. Social people like **to spend time with others.**

_____?

3. Irene and I usually leave for work **at 9:00 AM**.

_____?

4. Camille and Felix take **skating lessons** on Saturday.

_____?

5. Robert has **nine** grandchildren.

_____?

Exercise 12

There are five simple present verb tense errors in the following passage. Find and correct them.

Every Sunday, my parents invites my family for dinner at their house. We usually go there at three o'clock. My daughter and I often helps my mom with the dinner preparation. My husband like to talk with my father. We eat dinner at five o'clock. After, we sit in the living room and we all have coffee while our daughter haves some ice cream. My parents and my family is always happy to spend time with one another.

Exercise 13

Circle the correct choice to complete each sentence.

1. They don't _____ meat. **(eat / eats)**

2. _____ Henry and you know each other? **(Does / Do)**

3. She _____ late for school. **(is sometimes / sometimes is)**

4. Hannah and Jade _____ on a vacation in July. **(go often / often go)**

5. Ottawa _____ the capital of Canada. **(are / is)**

Present Progressive

Overview

We use the present progressive verb tense to express actions that are happening right now, temporary actions, actions in progress, and future arrangements.

Use	Form	Keywords	Example Sentences
right now		now	I **am reading** a book now.
		right now	You **are jogging** right now.
		at the moment	They **are eating** at the moment.
temporary actions		currently	I **am** currently **living** there.
		temporarily	It **is** temporarily **not functioning**.
	am / is / are + base form of a verb + -ing (present participle)	for a week	She **is staying** with me for one week.
longer actions in progress		this week	You **are working** this week.
		this month	They **are travelling** this month.
		this year	We **are renovating** our house this year.
		this semester	He **is taking** math this semester.
future arrangements		tonight	We **are returning** from Florida tonight.
		soon	They **are leaving** soon.

Present Progressive—Regular Verbs

For all verbs, we form the present progressive by combining the present tense of *be* with the present participle (or *-ing* form) of the verb.

Warm-Up

Work in pairs. Read the following conversations out loud.

Conversation 1

> **Partner A:** Hi, John! What are you doing?
> **Partner B:** Hi, Sam. I am studying.
> **Partner A:** Are you studying for our math exam this Friday?
> **Partner B:** No, I'm not. I am studying for my English class.

Conversation 2

> **Partner A:** Excuse me?
> **Partner B:** Yes, how can I help you?
> **Partner A:** I am looking for the Atlantic salmon that is on sale. Do you have any?
> **Partner B:** Sorry. We don't have any in stock right now, but we are getting more this after-noon. Come back after five o'clock or so.
> **Partner A:** Thank you.

Read the warm-up conversations again. Try to guess what the following verbs have in common: *doing, studying, looking, getting.*

Formation

Positive	Negative	Yes/No Question	Wh- Question
Subject + *be* + Verb + *-ing* (+ object / complement)	**Subject + *be* + Negative + Verb + *-ing* (+ object / complement)**	***Be* + Subject + Verb + *-ing*** (+ object / complement)	**Question Word + *be* + Subject + Verb + *-ing* (+ object / complement)**
I **am** talk**ing** now.	I **am not** talk**ing** now.	**Are** you talk**ing** now?	**What** are you doing now?
You **are** study**ing** English this semester.	You **are not** study**ing** English this semester.	**Are** you study**ing** English this semester?	**Why** are you studying English this semester?
He **is** fix**ing** his car right now.	He **is not** fix**ing** his car right now.	**Is** he fix**ing** his car right now?	**What** is he fixing right now?
She **is** paint**ing** her room.	She **is not** paint**ing** her room.	**Is** she paint**ing** her room?	**Whose** room is she painting?
It **is** rain**ing**.	It **is not** rain**ing**.	**Is** it rain**ing**?	**Where** is it raining?
We **are** watch**ing** TV.	We **are not** watch**ing** TV.	**Are** we watch**ing** TV?	**What** are we watching?
They **are** sleep**ing**.	They **are not** sleep**ing**.	**Are** they sleep**ing**?	**Where** are they sleeping?

For a detailed explanation of how to form and use questions and negatives, see Chapter 11.

Spelling Rules for Verbs with *-ing* Ending

Condition	Rule	Examples	
For most verbs	add **-ing** to the base form of the verb	work → working drink → drinking	snow → snowing do → doing
If a verb ends in a silent **-e**	drop the final **-e** and add **-ing**	write → writing arrive → arriving	smile → smiling skate → skating
If a verb ends in **-ie**	change **-ie** to **-y** and add **-ing**	tie → tying	lie → lying
In a one-syllable word that ends in **consonant-vowel-consonant (CVC)** combination	double the last consonant and add **-ing**	clap → clapping jog → jogging fix → fixing	sit → sitting row → rowing play → playing
In a one-syllable word that ends in **w**, **x**, or **y**	do not double the last consonant, just add **-ing**		
In words of two or more syllables that end in a **consonant-vowel-consonant (CVC)** combination			
• if the last syllable is stressed	double the last consonant and add **-ing**	be**gin** → begi**nn**ing	re**fer** → refe**rr**ing
• if the last syllable is not stressed	add **-ing**	**of**fer → **of**fering **fol**low → **fol**lowing	**ha**ppen → **ha**ppening

Exercise 1

Unscramble the following words and make them into sentences or questions.

playing / We / are / soccer → **We are playing soccer.**

1. looking at / Rose / is / her photos

   _____.

2. not / Christie and Jim / flying to Vancouver / are / now

   _____.

3. a shower / taking / Is / David

   _____?

4. is / the floor / Anne-Marie / cleaning

   _____.

5. you / Are / your baby / feeding

   _____?

Exercise 2

Write the correct spelling of the following verbs with an -*ing* ending.

chew → **chewing**

1. talk	_____	9. bike	_____
2. whistle	_____	10. teach	_____
3. discuss	_____	11. laugh	_____
4. cook	_____	12. die	_____
5. go	_____	13. sneeze	_____
6. run	_____	14. sweep	_____
7. pay	_____	15. hop	_____
8. whisper	_____	16. draw	_____

Speaking Activity 1
Spelling Bee

Work in teams. Taking turns, one team chooses a verb from the Base Form column of the chart in Appendix A: Common Irregular Verbs. One member of another team spells the verb with an -*ing* ending. This can be done either orally or in writing on the board, or both. If the spelling is correct, that student's team scores a point. If not, then another team gets a chance to spell it correctly and steal the point instead.

Present Progressive versus Simple Present

Remember, use the simple present for facts, habits, and actions that happen on a regular basis. Use the present progressive for the actions that are happening now. However, we cannot use certain verbs in the present progressive tense, even if the action is right now. Instead, we use the simple present tense for them.

Warm-Up

Read the passage and answer the question that follows.

In this illustration, you **see** a mother and her three children. They **are** at a grocery store. They **are buying** groceries for the entire week, so their shopping cart **is** full of groceries. Right now, the mother **is looking** at the label of a product, and she **is checking** its ingredients. The little boy **is sitting** in the shopping cart, and he **is**

holding a juice carton. The older boy **is looking** at his mom. The girl **is looking** at the groceries, and she **is laughing**. It **seems** they **are having** fun at the store. I **think** they **like** to go shopping with their mom.

Look at the verbs in **bold**. What two verb tenses can you recognize?

Non-Progressive Verbs

Non-progressive verbs describe states or opinions, not activities. A non-progressive verb is a verb that cannot be used in the progressive verb tense.

Category	Non-Progressive Verbs		Verbs That Can Be Either Regular or Non-Progressive		Example Sentences
Senses			hear*	smell*	I **hear** someone at the door.
			see*	feel*	This perfume **smells** nice.
			taste*		He **sees** the difference now.
Possession	belong	possess	have*		That book **belongs** to the teacher.
	own				They do not **possess** a car.
					I **have** a daughter.
Emotions	dislike	love	care*		I **dislike** mushrooms.
	hate	need	want*		I **love** this shirt.
	like	prefer			They **care** about us.
Thoughts	believe	know	feel*	mean*	I **believe** you.
	realize	desire	forget*	remember*	I **know** it's true.
	recognize	understand	imagine*	think*	I **think** it's important.
Being	seem	resemble	appear*	include*	The test **seems** difficult.
	sound	exist	be*	look*	She **resembles** her father.
			cost*	weigh*	She **weighs** 70 kilograms.

The verbs with an asterisk (*) have more than one meaning. They can be used as activities or as states, depending on the context. When used in the progressive tense, their essential meanings change.

		Example Sentences	
Category	Verbs	Non-Progressive Verb Use	Progressive Verb Use
Senses	hear* smell*	I **hear** someone at the door. (the physical sense)	I don't hear anyone. You **are hearing** things. (not hearing, but imagining)
	see* feel*		
	taste*		
Possession	have*	I **have** a daughter. (possession)	I **am having** dinner now. (action of eating)
Emotions	care* want*	They **care** about us. (emotion)	She **is caring** for her mother. (action of providing care)
Thoughts	feel* mean*	I **think** it's important. (thought or belief)	I **am thinking** about what to cook for dinner. (using thought to make a decision)
	forget* remember*		
	imagine* think*		
Being	appear* include*	She **weighs** 70 kilograms. (state or fact)	The nurse **is weighing** the newborn now. (action of finding out the weight)
	be* look*		
	cost* weigh*		

Exercise 3

Fill in the blanks with the correct form of the verbs in the present progressive or simple present.

You _____ **(wash)** dishes now. → You **are washing** dishes now.

She _____ **(like)** flowers. → She **likes** flowers.

1. Right now, my boss _____ **(give)** me instructions.

2. Samuel _____ **(want)** to be a firefighter.

3. We _____ **(think,** negative**)** it's a good idea.

4. I _____ **(know)** the answer to this question.

5. Scott _____ **(clean)** his motorcycle at the moment.

Exercise 4

Change each of the following sentences into a Yes/No question.

I am cooking now. → **Are you cooking now?**

We cook every day. → **Do you cook every day?**

1. Annette is talking on the phone with her friend.

   _____?

2. They work every day.

   _____?

3. My mom calls me every weekend.

   _____?

4. I am preparing lunch for my husband.

   _____?

5. You take good photos.

   _____?

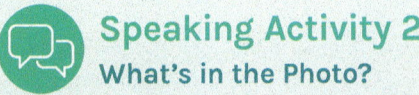 **Speaking Activity 2**
What's in the Photo?

Work with a partner. Your teacher will give you each a photo from a magazine. Don't show your photo to your partner. Describe the photo to your partner by using the present progressive and the simple present. Your partner will draw what he or she thinks your photo looks like. Then your partner will describe his or her photo. Sketch it on a separate sheet of paper. You can ask each other additional questions. At the end of the activity, show your photos to each other.

Bringing It All Together

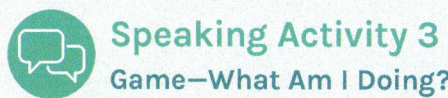

Speaking Activity 3
Game—What Am I Doing?

Work in two teams. Taking turns, a student from one team stands at the front of the classroom, where he or she receives a piece of paper with an action verb on it. The student mimes the action, and his or her group has to guess what the student is doing. If they guess correctly, the team then makes up a sentence that uses the verb in the present progressive. If they provide a correct sentence, they get a point. If the group can't give a correct response in 30 seconds, the other team gets a chance to make up a sentence and score a point.

Speaking Activity 4
Audio 08 🔊
What's That Noise?

Work in pairs. Listen to the audio, in which people and animals are making noises. For each noise, use the following verbs to write a sentence in the present progressive. If you do not know the meaning of some verbs, ask your partner or together look up the words in a dictionary.

| knock | snore | laugh | bark | hum | cough |

1. Tom _____

2. Yuki and Makato _____

3. The dog _____

4. You _____

5. I _____

6. Richard _____

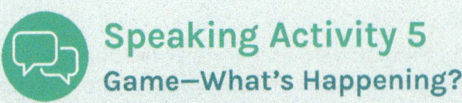

Speaking Activity 5
Game—What's Happening?

Work in pairs. Compete with your partner to write down as many things as possible that are going on in the classroom, outside the window, or in a photo. Give yourselves two to three minutes. The person with the most sentences wins.

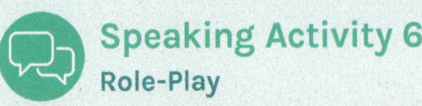

Speaking Activity 6
Role-Play

Work in pairs. Prepare a role-play for the following situation. Then perform it in front of the class.

Situation: Your friend is calling you to invite you for a coffee, but you already have plans. Reject the offer by saying why you are busy. Give a reason using the present progressive.

Reading

Read the passage and answer the questions that follow.

As you read, pay attention to these vocabulary words in the passage: *physical*, *sufficient*, *surveys*, *percent*, *benefits*, *seek*, *role*, and *significant*.

What's Keeping Kids from Being More Active?

Are Kids Doing Enough Physical Activity These Days?

Everybody knows it is important to be physically active. Exercising or any other form of **physical** activity is an essential part of our lives. It <u>enhances</u> our health and helps us develop physical abilities. It's even more <u>crucial</u> in the proper physical and mental development of a child. An active child is healthy and weighs the right amount, and also has high <u>self-esteem</u>. In contrast, an inactive child often <u>suffers</u> from <u>obesity</u> and has an increased risk of developing diseases as an adult.

Many kids do not spend a **sufficient** number of hours on physical activity. According to the Canadian Physical Activity <u>Guidelines</u>, children need to do some physical activities for at least 60 minutes per day. Instead, some **surveys** show that 46 **percent** of kids get three hours or less of active play per week, including weekends.

In school, students usually have physical education classes, but these are often not long enough or are not offered on a daily basis. If those kids do not have any other physical activity after school, then they are not meeting Canadian guidelines for their daily physical activity.

An additional problem is that kids are spending too much <u>sedentary</u> time at home. What are they doing? They are watching TV or playing computer or video games. That keeps them from playing outside and therefore from being more active.

Some parents are trying to make sure their kids are getting enough exercise and the **benefits** that come with it. They are asking their kids to play outside or signing them up for different sports activities. That way, the kids are moving and not sitting in front of the TV or a computer screen.

However, there are also some parents who are not letting their kids play outside because of the fear of something bad happening to them. If these parents care about their kids' activity level, they **seek** organized sport activities for their kids or do some physical activities together as a family. For example, they take their kids for a walk, a swim, or a bike ride.

Parents' **role** in their kids' activity level is really **significant**. Parents <u>determine</u> if their kids are active enough. It's easy to let children stay home safely and spend time in front of a TV or a computer. A better option is for parents to organize physical activities for children, be active as a family, or lead by example and be physically active themselves.

Comprehension

Answer the questions below. Write complete sentences.

1. Why is it important to be physically active?

   _____

2. What is the difference between an active and inactive child?

   _____

3. According to the Canadian Physical Activity Guidelines, how long do kids need to engage in physical activity?

   _____

4. Why aren't kids spending enough time being active? Give two reasons.

   _____

5. What are some parents doing to help their kids be more active?

   _____

6. Why aren't some parents letting their kids play outside?

   _____

7. What do some families do together to get physically active?

   _____

Analyzing the Reading Passage

Read the passage again and underline all the simple present tense verbs with a <u>single line</u> and all the present progressive tense verbs with a <u>double line</u>.

Discussion

What is your opinion on this subject? Do you agree that kids are not active enough? Give some examples to support your opinion.

Listening 1

Listen to the song. Fill in the blanks with the words you hear.

"Tom's Diner" by Suzanne Vega

I _____
In the morning
At the diner
On the corner

I _____
At the counter
For the man
To pour the coffee

And he fills it
Only halfway
And before
I even argue

He _____
Out the window
At somebody
Coming in

"It is always
Nice to see you"
_____ the man
Behind the counter

To the woman
Who has come in
She _____
Her umbrella

And I look
The other way
As they _____
Their hellos and

I' _____
Not to see them
And instead
I pour the milk

I open
Up the paper
_____ a story
Of an actor

Who had died
While he was drinking
It was no one
I had heard of

And I' _____
To the horoscope
And looking
For the funnies

When I' _____
Someone watching me
And so
I raise my head

There's a woman
On the outside
_____ inside
Does she see me?

No she does not
Really see me
'Cause she sees
Her own reflection

And I' _____
Not to notice
That she's hitching
Up her skirt

And while she's
Straightening her stockings
Her hair
Has gotten wet

Oh, this rain
It will continue
Through the morning
As I' _____

To the bells
Of the cathedral . . .
I _____
Of your voice . . .

And of the
Midnight picnic
Once upon a time
Before the rain began

And I finish
Up my coffee
And it's time
To catch the train

Comprehension

Listen to the song again and answer the following questions. Write complete sentences. Use the present progressive tense.

1. Where is this person sitting right now?

   _____

2. What is she doing there?

   _____

3. Why is the man looking out the window?

   _____

4. What is the woman on the outside of the diner doing?

   _____

5. What is the weather like?

   _____

Listening 2
Audio 10 🔊

Busy or Not?

Listen to the audio. You will hear three phone conversations. In each of them, one person is calling and asking to speak to someone. Fill in the following chart. Write complete sentences.

Questions	Conversation 1	Conversation 2	Conversation 3
Is the person busy or not?			
What is the person doing?			
Is the person coming to the phone?			

Writing

Choose a photo of your own or use the one from Speaking Activity 2 on pages 64–65. On a separate sheet of paper, write a short composition (maximum 150 words) about the photo. Make sure you use the present progressive and the simple present verb tenses. Here are some questions to guide your writing:

- What do you see in the photo? Are there any people in the photo? Who are they?
- What are they doing?
- Why do you like/dislike the photo?
- Does the photo remind you of anything?

Vocabulary

1. Read the following sentences. The words in **bold** are from the Reading activity. Use the context to help you understand what the bold words mean.

   a) Their health insurance plan provides many **benefits**, including medical and dental care.
   b) This year, tuition fees are up by 2 **percent**. That is a **significant** increase.
   c) It's important to go for your **physical** checkup once a year.
   d) His **role** in the family is to look after and take care of his younger siblings.
   e) Tom has financial problems. He needs to **seek** advice from his financial advisor.
   f) The main objectives of these two **surveys** are to focus on social media use and screen addiction.
   g) Mona has a **sufficient** income, so her husband can be a stay-at-home dad.

2. Choose the words from the box that match the following definitions. Use a dictionary or the glossary to help you.

benefits	role	sufficient
percent	seek	surveys
physical	significant	

   _____ : one part in 100

   _____ : to attempt to find or get something; search for

   _____ : the position, function, or purpose that someone or something has

   _____ : advantages or profits gained from something

   _____ : something that is enough, adequate

   _____ : something that is important, special, or worthy of attention

   _____ : relating to the body

   _____ : research studies, examinations of something; methods to collect data to gain information on a certain topic

3. Fill in the blanks with the vocabulary words from question 2.

   Human beings, whether they know it or not, continually **1** _____ happiness. Some of them look for it in their careers, money, or status, and others try to find it in family, relationships, or love. Still, many **2** _____ reveal that people who have money, fame, love, and **3** _____ health are not necessarily happy. Therefore, it's not **4** _____ to be successful, rich, or loved. The best way to find happiness is to find your **5** _____ or purpose in life, so you know why you are **6** _____. The **7** _____ are great: you do something that truly matters to you, and you live a meaningful life. That's a 100 **8** _____ guarantee to be happy!

   "The two most important days in your life are the day you are born and the day you find out why."

   —Mark Twain

Summary

- The present progressive shows actions happening at the time of speaking, in progress, or in the near future.
- Keywords we use with the present progressive are *now*, *right now*, *at the moment*, *presently*, *currently*, and *this week*.
- To form the present progressive, use the verb *be* and add the verb with an *-ing* ending.
- There is a difference between the simple present and the present progressive.
- There are non-progressive verbs that we cannot use in the present progressive. Instead, we use the simple present with those verbs.

Exercise 5

Write questions in the present progressive. Use the words provided. Review the formation chart in this chapter on page 60 if you need to.

Where / he / go? → Where is he going?

1. What / you / do / now? _____?

2. Why / she / cry? _____?

3. What kind of tea / he / drink? _____?

4. How many kids / they / bring? _____?

5. What / we / watch? _____?

Exercise 6

There are five verb tense errors in the following passage. Find and correct them.

I really am liking fall. Right now, I am walk in a park and looking at the trees. They change colours now. I am seeing orange, red, and yellow leaves. Oh! And I am hearing how they crunch under my feet. I think fall is my favourite season.

Exercise 7

Change each of the following positive sentences into the negative. Review the formation chart in this chapter on page 60 if you need to.

Elizabeth is teaching now. → Elizabeth is not teaching now.

1. He is swimming now.

_____

2. We are skating at the Rideau Canal now.

_____

3. You are buying a gift for your friend.

_____

4. The printer is printing a document.

_____

5. I am sitting at the park.

_____

Exercise 8

Change each of the following sentences into a Yes/No question. Review the formation chart in this chapter on page 60 if you need to.

My dog is barking now. → Is my dog barking now?

1. Margaret is picking up her daughter from daycare now.

_____?

2. Jose's dad is visiting his relatives in Europe this month.

_____?

3. The doctor and the nurse are making rounds on the fourth floor now.

_____?

4. My guests are coming in now.

_____?

5. We are waiting in a lineup.

_____?

Exercise 9

Change each of the following statements into a Wh- question. The information you want to ask about is in **bold**. Review the formation chart in this chapter on page 60 if you need to. For the list of question words, refer to Chapter 3, pages 43–44.

The student is doing his homework now. → What is the student doing now?

1. Teresa is bothering **her brother**.

_____?

2. Kim and Scott are getting married **this summer**.

_____?

3. My siblings are preparing a party **for me**.

_____?

4. You are paying **bills** at the bank now.

_____?

5. The computer is making a noise **because it is broken**.

_____?

REVIEW
Self-Study

Overview

The self-assessments in this unit give you a chance to review and reinforce the grammar points from Part 1 (chapters 1–4).

Check your knowledge, and if you find areas that need more attention, go back to the appropriate chapter and review the material.

Exercise 1

Unscramble the following words and make them into sentences or questions.

is / Her/ Jane / name → Her name is Jane.

1. languages / Some / difficult / are

   _____.

2. does / How much / cost / it

   _____?

3. two / has / He / dogs

   _____.

4. First / the / to / pre-heat / 260 degrees Celsius / oven

   _____.

5. Is / Mirek / on / sitting / the patio

   _____?

6. at / start / their / They / class / three o'clock / always

   _____.

7. do / need / an / you / When / umbrella

   _____?

8. car / is / That / mine

   _____.

9. yourself / it / Do / by

   _____.

10. Jonathan / her / gives / every / flowers / month

   _____.

Exercise 2

Change each of the following positive sentences into the negative.

I like it. → I do not like it.

1. Sit here. _____

2. These people are nice. _____

3. The average person laughs 15 times per day. _____

4. Henry has many friends. _____

5. My parents help me a lot. _____

Exercise 3

Change each of the following sentences into a Yes/No question.

I am washing my hands now. → Are you washing your hands now?

1. My brother knows a lot about computers.

   _____?

2. My computer is working well today.

   _____?

3. Jake and Murako own a photo shop.

   _____?

4. Those women are coming back from church.

   _____?

5. We have many apple trees in our backyard.

   _____?

Exercise 4

Change each of the following statements into a Wh- question. The information you want to ask about is in **bold**.

She chats with her brother on Sundays. → When does she chat with her brother?

1. Octopuses have **three** brains.

   _____?

2. Our actions are affecting **the future of our planet**.

   _____?

3. **Water** covers 70 percent of the earth's surface.

   _____?

4. It is impossible to sneeze with their eyes open **because sneezing is an involuntary nervous response**.

_____?

5. Your heart **beats** more than 100 000 times a day.

_____?

Exercise 5

Fill in the blanks with the correct form of the verbs in the present progressive or simple present.

Rita ____needs____ **(need)** new shoes. She is at the store now, and she ____is looking____ **(look)** at some shoes.

Nick and Clara **1** _____ **(be)** a young couple. They both **2** _____

(work) full-time. Nick **3** _____ **(be)** a financial adviser, and Clara

4 _____ **(cook)** for a restaurant. This weekend, Nick and Clara

5 _____ **(discuss)** the future plans for their family. At the moment, they

6 _____ **(have, negative)** any children, but they **7** _____

(want) to have some soon. Now they **8** _____ **(look)** at their photo albums

from their childhood, and they **9** _____ **(have)** fun. This is what they usually

10 _____ **(do)** before making serious decisions.

Exercise 6

Correct the errors in the following sentences. The errors are underlined.

1. The dress is fourty dollars.

2. He is celebrating his nineteen birthday today.

3. I am a night person, but I never go to bed past noon.

4. Cats are animals intelligent.

5. This pencils belong to Sarah.

6. I like mine teacher.

7. How many childs do you have?

8. There is 20 students in Annie's class.

9. We have many homeworks to do for next week.

10. He has two watchs.

11. This house is their.

12. My husband works by hisself.

13. He lives in an house.

14. The money is important to some people.

15. My friends goes to Florida every winter.

16. She haves three sheep.

17. I are a plumber.

18. Suzanna is writeing a letter now.

19. Do Mark usually eat breakfast?

20. Not talk so loud!

5 Simple Past

Overview

The simple past expresses an action that is finished or completed in the past.

Use	Form	Keywords and Sample Phrases	Example Sentences
completed action	regular verbs: add -*ed*	yesterday	I work**ed** yesterday.
		last night	We watch**ed** TV last night.
		last summer	They travell**ed** last summer.
specific time in past	irregular verbs: memorize	two years **ago**	She **went** to Cuba two years ago.
		in 1995	He **was born** in 1995.
		when I was a child	I **broke** my arm when I was a child.

Warm-Up

Work in pairs. Read the first paragraph. <u>Underline</u> all the verbs. They are all in the simple present tense. List the verbs in the following chart.

> Sasha and Norman are best friends. They walk to school together in the morning. They play together every day. They go to the park after school. They like the same sports. They always have fun.

Read the second version of the paragraph. <u>Underline</u> all the verbs. List the simple past tense verbs in the middle row in the following chart. What do you notice about their forms? Can you see any patterns?

> Sasha and Norman were best friends. They walked to school together in the morning. They played together every day. They went to the park after school. They liked the same sports. They always had fun.

Simple Present Verbs						
Simple Past Verbs						
Observations						

Simple Past—Regular Verbs

We form the simple past of most verbs by adding *-ed* to the base form of the verb.

Warm-Up

Work in pairs. Read the following conversations out loud.

Conversation 1

> **Partner A:** What did you do last summer?
> **Partner B:** I visited my family in Montreal.
> **Partner A:** How long did you visit them for?
> **Partner B:** I stayed there for a week.

Conversation 2

Partner A: Did he watch TV yesterday?
Partner B: No, he didn't. He worked all day long.

Conversation 3

Partner A: Did they study for their exam last weekend?
Partner B: Yes, they did. They studied for it last Sunday.

Read the warm-up conversations again. Notice that we know the exact timing of the actions in the past. What words or phrases show you that the action is in the past?

Formation

Positive	Negative	Yes/No Question	Wh- Question
Subject + Verb (+ object / complement)	Subject + Auxiliary + Negative + Verb (+ object / complement)	Auxiliary + Subject + Verb (+ object / complement)	Question Word + Auxiliary + Subject + Verb (+ object / complement)
I **visited** my friend last summer.	I **did not visit** my friend last summer.	**Did** you **visit** your friend last summer?	**When** did you visit your friend?
You **stayed** there for a week.	You **did not stay** there for a week.	**Did** you **stay** there for a week?	**How long** did you stay there?
He **watched** them play.	He **did not watch** them play.	**Did** he **watch** them play?	**Who** did he watch play?
She **worked** last Friday.	She **did not work** last Friday.	**Did** she **work** last Friday?	**What** did she do last Friday?
It **started** at five o'clock.	It **did not start** at five o'clock.	**Did** it **start** at five o'clock?	**What time** did it start?
We **decided** a week ago.	We **did not decide** a week ago.	**Did** we **decide** a week ago?	**When** did we decide?
They **studied** last night.	They **did not study** last night.	**Did** they **study** last night?	**What** did they do last night?

There is only **one** form of the verb for all subjects (*I, you, he, she, it, we, they*). The exception is the verb *be* (see pages 83–84).

Follow the same spelling rules for adding the *-ed* ending as for the *-s* ending in the simple present in Chapter 3 on page 45.

For more information about Wh- questions, see Chapter 3, pages 43–44. For a detailed explanation of how to form and use questions and negatives, refer to Chapter 11.

Spelling Rules for Adding the *-ed* Ending

Condition	Rule	Example
For most verbs	add **-ed**	work → worked
If the verb ends in a silent **e**	add **-d**	arrive → arrived
If the verb ends in a **consonant + y**	change **y** to **i** and add **-ed**	study → studied
If the verb ends in a **consonant + vowel + consonant**	double final consonant and add **-ed**	ban → banned

For the pronunciation of the *-ed* endings, see the chart on page 80.

Exercise 1

Answer these questions with complete sentences.

> Did you talk with your teacher? → **Yes**, I talked with my teacher.
>
> Did she wash the dishes? → **No**, she did not wash the dishes.

1. Did you visit any new places during your holiday?

   Yes, _____.

2. Did John study the guitar at music camp last summer?

   No, _____.

3. Did they travel outside Canada two years ago?

   Yes, _____.

4. Did you work during the winter break last year?

   No, _____.

5. Did Marie play volleyball last weekend?

   Yes, _____.

Pronouncing the -ed Ending

There are three ways to pronounce the -ed ending of past tense verbs to make pronunciation easier. Whether we use the /d/, /t/, or /id/ sound depends on the final sound of the verb's base form. Remember it is the **sound** that matters, not the written letter.

Use the Sound	When the Final Sound of the Verb's Base Form Is	Examples
/d/	• a **vowel** sound	stay → stayed (stay/d/)
		follow → followed (follow/d/)
		try → tried (try/d/)
	• one of these voiced consonant sounds: **b, g, j, l, m, n, ng, r, v, z, th, zh**	bob → bobbed (bob/d/)
		fill → filled (fill/d/)
		buzz → buzzed (buzz/d/)
/t/	• one of these voiceless consonant sounds: **f, k, p, s, x, ch, sh, th**	look → looked (look/t/)
		hope → hoped (hope/t/)
		watch → watched (watch/t/)
/id/	• a **d** or **t** sound	end → ended (end/id/)
		want → wanted (want/id/)

Exercise 2

Review your answers in Exercise 1. Place each verb from those answers in the correct column to show the pronunciation of the -ed ending. For the verbs *study* and *work*, use *studied* and *worked*—the positive simple past forms.

/ d /	/ t /	/ id /

💬 Speaking Activity 1
Find the Order

Work in pairs or small groups. Put the following sentences in sequence to make a story. Write a number (1–10) next to each sentence to show the order.

_____ Michelle called her friends on Wednesday to invite them over.

_____ After dinner, they all enjoyed the cookies.

_____ On Saturday morning, Michelle cleaned her house, cooked a wonderful meal, and baked some cookies.

_____ Michelle welcomed her friends and offered them some drinks.

_____ At ten o'clock, they thanked Michelle for a great evening and returned home.

_____ At six o'clock, Michelle served dinner.

_____ They really liked the movie.

_____ Last week, Michelle decided to invite her friends Sylvie and Emma for dinner on Saturday.

_____ Sylvie and Emma arrived at Michelle's house at 5:30.

_____ Next, Michelle popped some popcorn, and they watched a movie.

Simple Past—Irregular Verbs

Some verbs have irregular forms in the simple past. There is no rule for irregular verbs; you have to memorize them. However, there are some patterns.

Warm-Up

Read the following passage. All the verbs are in the simple past tense. <u>Underline</u> them. (Circle) the verbs that do not end in -ed.

Last summer, my family planned to take a camping trip together, but it didn't happen that way. My parents bought a new tent and other camping equipment. They also rented two canoes. My mother organized the food, and I helped my father pack the van. We left early on the Friday morning. We got to the provincial park by 11:00 in the morning. Then we drove to the campsite. We all worked together; we set up the tent and the cooking area. Then my brother and I swam in the lake. When we came back to the campsite, we ate lunch. After lunch, we all went for a hike around the lakeshore. My father slipped on some loose rocks. He fell and broke his ankle. We went back to the van, and my mother took Dad to the hospital. When they came back, we packed up our stuff and went home.

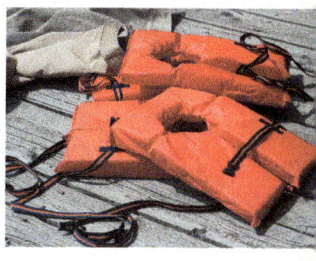

Formation

Positive	Negative	Yes/No Question	Wh- Question
Subject + Verb (+ object / complement)	**Subject + Auxiliary + Negative + Verb (+ object / complement)**	**Auxiliary + Subject + Verb (+ object / complement)**	**Question Word + Auxiliary + Subject + Verb (+ object / complement)**
I **had** lunch.	I **did not have** lunch.	**Did** you **have** lunch?	**What** did you have?
You **wrote** a letter yesterday.	You **did not write** a letter yesterday.	**Did** you **write** a letter yesterday?	**When** did you write a letter?
He **spoke** to Ann.	He **did not speak** to Ann.	**Did** he **speak** to Ann?	**Who** did he speak to?
She **won**.	She **did not win**.	**Did** she **win**?	**What** did she do?
It **took** my shoe.	It **did not take** my shoe.	**Did** it **take** my shoe?	**What** did it take?
We **went** home.	We **did not go** home.	**Did** we **go** home?	**Where** did we go?
They **drove** to get to work.	They **did not drive** to get to work.	**Did** they **drive** to get to work?	**Why** did they drive?

Study the list of the common irregular past tense verbs in Appendix A. When you are ready, test yourself (or a partner) on the formation and spelling of the irregular verbs.

Exercise 3

Change these sentences into the simple past tense.

> He goes to college. → He went to college.

1. You buy magazines. _____

2. I do my homework. _____

3. We read a lot. _____

4. He writes books. _____

5. They speak English very well. _____

Exercise 4

Change each of the following sentences into a Yes/No question.

> We took a trip to Calgary last summer. → Did you take a trip to Calgary last summer?

1. They went to Thailand two years ago.

   _____?

2. Meisha saw the Rocky Mountains on her trip out west.

   _____?

3. Paco and I flew to London to start our holiday.

_____?

4. I bought a lot of souvenirs in Paris.

_____?

5. Bupinder had a great time camping with his friends for a week.

_____?

Simple Past—The Verb *Be*

The verb *be* is irregular. In the simple past there are two forms: *was* and *were*.

Warm-Up

Prepare Yes/No questions for your classmates. Use the five ideas below.
Find someone who . . .

- was absent yesterday
- was born in another country
- was tired this morning
- was able to swim when he or she was a child
- was happy last weekend

On a separate sheet of paper, set up a chart like the following one and prepare some Yes/No questions. Then ask some of your classmates the questions. If somebody answers "yes" to your question, record his or her name and write the answer in a complete sentence.

Questions	Names + Answers
Were you absent yesterday?	Kimiko was absent yesterday.

Formation

The verb *be* has two forms in the simple past tense: *was* and *were*. Notice that the third-person singular has an -*s* ending.
    The verb *be* does not need an auxiliary verb to make negatives or questions.

I	was
he / she / it	was
we	were
you	were
they	were

Positive	Negative	Yes/No Question	Wh- Question
Subject + Verb + Complement	**Subject + Verb + Negative + Complement**	**Verb + Subject + Complement**	**Question Word + Verb + Subject (+ complement)**
I **was** a teacher in the past.	I **was not** a teacher in the past.	**Were** you a teacher in the past?	**What** were you in the past?
You **were** sick yesterday.	You **were not** sick yesterday.	**Were** you sick yesterday?	**When** were you sick?
He **was** at home.	He **was not** at home.	**Was** he at home?	**Where** was he?
She **was** 10.	She **was not** 10.	**Was** she 10?	**How old** was she?
It **was** cold.	It **was not** cold.	**Was** it cold?	**How** was it?
We **were** there.	We **were not** there.	**Were** we there?	**Where** were we?
They **were** famous twins.	They **were not** famous twins.	**Were** they famous twins?	**Who** were they?

Exercise 5

Fill in the blanks with the correct form of the verb *be* in the simple past tense.

You _____ **(be)** very nice. → You **were** very nice.

1. Anna _____ **(be)** away this weekend.

2. My brother and I _____ **(be)** happy to go with our parents on a family vacation.

3. **(be,** question) _____ they in the same class?

4. You _____ **(be,** negative) at home when I called you.

5. Daniel and Samuel _____ **(be)** very good students.

💬 Speaking Activity 2
Exchange Information

Work in pairs. Read the following paragraph about Debbie's childhood. Then tell your partner about yourself when you were a child, using the verb *be*. Record some facts about your partner's childhood and yours in a chart on a separate sheet of paper. Ask each other questions to get more information.

Debbie **was** born in Canada, but her parents **were** Polish. They always spoke Polish at home. When Debbie **was** six years old, she started grade 1. She **was** a tall girl, so everybody thought she **was** seven or eight years old. She **was** also very smart. She **was** able to write well, read fluently in English, and say some words in French. Her teachers **were** happy to have Debbie in their classes. Also, all her friends really liked her. When she got an excellent report card at the end of the year, her parents **were** very proud of her.

You	Your Partner

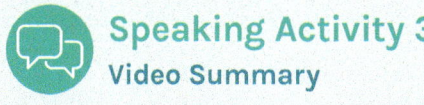

Speaking Activity 3
Video Summary

In small groups, watch a 10- to 15-minute video or movie segment of your choice (from the Internet, TV, or library). Write a short summary of what happened, step by step, in the simple past. Words that indicate time and sequence are listed below to help you write your summary. When you finish, one group member reads the summary out loud while a different group member lists the verb forms used. Together, make a list of the simple past and the base form of each verb.

first	in the beginning	to start
then	next	afterward
finally	at the end	the conclusion

Speaking Activity 4
Telling Stories about the Weekend

Work as a class. One student leaves the classroom while the teacher tells what he or she did last weekend. The remaining students take notes, writing down the main points, using verbs in the simple past. When the teacher finishes the story, the student who left returns to the classroom. Each person who heard the story says one sentence about it or describes an action from it. The returning student tries to tell the whole story to the class. If he or she makes any mistakes, the others should make corrections. Then all the students write out the whole story using the past tense. (This activity can also be done with students telling about their weekends.)

_____

_____

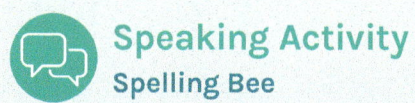

Speaking Activity 5
Spelling Bee

Work in small teams. The teacher will give each team a list of verbs. Taking turns, a team chooses a verb from their list, and one member of another team has to spell the past tense of the verb. This can be done orally or by writing on the board, or both. If the spelling is correct, that student's team scores a point. If not, then another team gets a chance to spell it correctly and steal the point.

Reading

Read the passage and answer the questions that follow.

Our Canada Day

As you read, pay attention to these vocabulary words in the passage: *initially, range, purchase, items, varied, areas, positive,* and *evident*.

July 1, Canada Day, two years ago was the first time we celebrated this holiday in Ottawa. My husband, Larry, my two children, Karl and Alan, and I stayed in Ottawa to be part of Canada's birthday celebration.

We got up early in the morning and walked to the ByWard Market. **Initially**, the market was quiet, but then it got loud and busy as the vendors arrived and needed to set up their stalls. We wanted to have breakfast. We found a little café with a patio where we ate a delicious breakfast of fresh fruit, croissants, and hot chocolate.

After breakfast, we walked around and looked at the market stalls. The vendors had a wide **range** of things for sale. You could **purchase** fresh fruit and vegetables, jewellery, clothing, and souvenirs. The **items varied** in price, but they were all of great quality.

The morning passed very quickly. For lunch, we decided to buy food and have a picnic in one of the many outdoor sitting **areas**. We ate our food and watched other families enjoying the national holiday.

In the afternoon, we decided to take a boat cruise on the Rideau Canal because Karl and Alan were tired from walking. During the tour, we saw many large houses and beautiful gardens.

For dinner, Karl and Alan wanted to buy sausages from a street vendor. We ate dinner sitting on a park bench. What fun!

After dinner, we walked to Parliament Hill. It was very crowded. The music and entertainment were excellent. The fireworks provided the grand finale for the day. Karl, Alan, Larry, and I walked home, tired but happy after spending our first Canada Day in Ottawa. It was such a **positive** experience for our family, and it was **evident** to us why so many people come to Ottawa every year to celebrate this day in the capital of Canada.

Comprehension

Answer the questions. Write complete sentences.

1. What is the date of Canada's birthday?

   _____

2. How many children does the writer have?

   _____

3. Where did the family celebrate Canada Day?

   _____

4. Where did the family have breakfast?

   _____

5. What did the family have for breakfast?

   _____

6. What did the vendors have for sale in their stalls?

_____

7. What did the family do in the afternoon? Why?

_____

8. Where did the family eat dinner?

_____

9. What did the family have for dinner?

_____

10. Where did the family go after dinner?

_____

11. What did the family do in the evening?

_____

12. Did the family have an enjoyable day?

_____

Analyzing the Reading Passage

Read the passage again. Underline all the regular past tense verbs with a <u>single line</u> and all the irregular verbs with a <u>double line</u>.

Discussion

Did you celebrate Canada Day with your family or friends last year? What did you do?

Listening

Audio 11 🔊

Canada Day in Ottawa

Listen to the audio, which is a conversation between two brothers. Then answer the questions.

Comprehension

Write complete sentences. Use the simple past tense.

1. Did Karl and Alan have a good day?

_____

2. Who enjoyed the croissants?

_____

3. Did the two boys swim?

_____

4. Did Alan buy a rope bracelet?

_____

5. What did they have for lunch?

_____

6. Where did they buy lunch?

_____

7. Where did they eat lunch?

_____

8. What did they buy from a street vendor?

_____

9. What did they see on Parliament Hill?

_____

10. Were there a lot of people on Parliament Hill?

_____

Writing

Choose one of the topics below. Write a short composition (maximum 150 words) about the topic.

- What was your favourite holiday when you were a child?
- What is your favourite childhood memory?

Vocabulary

Read the following sentences. The words in **bold** are from the Reading activity. Use the context to help you understand what the words in bold mean. Then match each word with its correct definition, synonym, or antonym. Finally, write your own sentence using the word.

1. Canada's three largest metropolitan **areas** are Toronto, Montreal, and Vancouver.
   Synonym: a) arenas   b) fields   c) regions

   Your sentence: _____

2. It's **evident** that a lot of people want to immigrate to Canada. The country offers great cultural freedom, peaceful living, and good health care.
   Synonym: a) clear   b) vague   c) certain

   Your sentence: _____

3. **Initially**, Kingston was the first capital of the United Province of Canada.
   Definition: a) shows the action happened last   b) shows the action happened at the beginning   c) shows the action happened in the middle

   Your sentence: _____

4. These are some of the **items** that Canada is famous for: West Coast salmon, maple syrup, and First Nations art. Many tourists buy these products as souvenirs.
   Synonym: a) food   b) gifts   c) objects

   Your sentence: _____

5. There are many **positive** sides to living in Canada. In fact, Canada is ranked as the second-best country in the world.
   Antonym: a) additional   b) negative   c) important

   Your sentence: _____

6. For less than $100, Parks Canada lets you **purchase** a one-year Discovery Pass, with access to 80 national parks across Canada. Children get in free.
   Antonym: a) borrow   b) buy   c) sell

   Your sentence: _____

7. Ottawa offers a wide **range** of tourist activities.
   Synonym: a) variety   b) amount   c) degree

   Your sentence: _____

8. Canada's climate **varies** across the country.
   Synonym: a) alternates   b) changes   c) is the same

   Your sentence: _____

Chapter Review

Summary

- The simple past shows a completed action in the past.
- Keywords or phrases such as *last year*, *ago*, or *when I was young* tell you the action was completed in the past.
- All verbs, except *be*, have only one simple past form. For regular verbs, add *-ed* to the base form. Memorize irregular verbs.
- All verbs, except *be*, use *did* and the base form of the verb to create questions and negatives.
- The verb *be* has two forms in the simple past: *was* (*I*, *he*, *she*, *it*) and *were* (*you*, *we*, *they*).
- To create questions with the verb *be*, change the order of the subject and verb.

            s.   v.   v.   s.
  EXAMPLE He was there.   Was he there?

- To create negatives, add *not* after *be*. Do not use *did* with *be*.

  Correct He was not there.   **Incorrect** He ~~did not be~~ there.

Exercise 6

Fill in the blanks with the correct form of the simple past of the verbs in parentheses.

Where _____ (**go, they**) on Saturday? → Where **did they go** on Saturday?

1. Jonathan _____ (**move**) to Sherbrooke two years ago.

2. When Frank _____ (be) young, he _____ (want) to be an astronaut.

3. Amanda _____ (study) Spanish for two years before she _____ (go) to Spain.

4. When _____ (meet, you) Alan?

5. I _____ (know, negative) how to swim until I _____ (be) 20.

Exercise 7

Use the words provided to write Wh- questions. You need to add an auxiliary verb or change the form of the verb. Review the formation charts in this chapter on pages 79, 82, and 84 if you need to. For a detailed explanation of how to form and use Wh- questions, refer to Chapter 11. A chart of question words is in Chapter 3 on pages 43–44.

Why / he / leave / early? → Why did he leave early?

1. How / you / get / here? _____?

2. Where / she / be / born? _____?

3. When / they / write / exams? _____?

4. What movie / she / see / last night? _____?

5. What countries / you / visit / last summer? _____?

Exercise 8

Change each of the following positive sentences into the negative. Review the formation charts in this chapter on pages 79, 82, and 84 if you need to.

I smiled at him. → I did not smile at him.

We ate lunch an hour ago. → We did not eat lunch an hour ago.

They were there last year. → They were not there last year.

1. He called her at five o'clock. _____

2. She was in Europe in 2010. _____

3. Claire visited her parents last month. _____

4. I took my dog for a walk this morning. _____

5. They bought a new house two years ago. _____

Exercise 9

Change each of the following statements into a Wh- question. The information you want to ask about is in **bold**. Review the formation charts in this chapter on pages 79, 82, and 84 and the question word list on pages 43–44 in Chapter 3 if you need to.

Remember: The word order for Wh- questions is usually the same as for Yes/No questions.

He walked to school **this morning**. → **When** did he walk to school?

They went **to Sweden** last summer. → **Where** did they go last summer?

I was absent **because I had an appointment**. → **Why** were you absent?

Julietta enjoyed **the concert**. → **What** did Julietta enjoy?

1. He flew **to Alaska** in 2001.

   _____?

2. Marie drew that picture **when she was six years old**.

   _____?

3. They arrived in Kingston **by train** at eight o'clock.

   _____?

4. They were **16 years old** when they met.

   _____?

5. Sophie packed **her bag** before she left for school.

   _____?

Exercise 10

Fill in the blanks in this letter with the simple past tense of the verbs in parentheses.

Dear Julie,

I **1** _____ (read) about your vacation in Montreal during the summer.

We **2** _____ (go) to Toronto for a weekend.

We **3** _____ (leave) at 8:00 in the morning. The drive on Highway 401

4 _____ (be) good. An accident **5** _____ (happen) around

Belleville, so we **6** _____ (stop) at the new rest stop on the 401 and

7 _____ (have) a coffee.

We **8** _____ **(arrive)** in Toronto at 3:00 in the afternoon. We **9** _____ **(drive)** to our hotel and **10** _____ **(unpack)** our luggage.

We **11** _____ **(eat)** dinner in a restaurant next to the hotel. We **12** _____ **(see)** a play at one of the big theatres. It **13** _____ **(be)** fun.

The next day, we **14** _____ **(take)** the ferry to the Toronto Islands for the afternoon. We **15** _____ **(order)** dinner in a small Greek restaurant.

On Sunday, we **16** _____ **(visit)** Kensington Market and had breakfast. After breakfast, we **17** _____ **(pay)** the bill and we **18** _____ **(go)** to the Ontario Science Centre. Later, we **19** _____ **(return)** to the hotel. We **20** _____ **(check)** out, **21** _____ **(pack)** the car, and **22** _____ **(begin)** our journey back to Ottawa.

We **23** _____ **(have)** a great weekend.

Your friend, Martha

Past Progressive

Overview

- Remember, the simple past expresses an action that ended in the past.
- The past progressive expresses actions that were in progress in the past. It indicates
  - actions that were happening during a limited, specific time in the past
  - temporary actions in progress in the past
  - actions in progress in the past that were interrupted when another action happened
  - actions each in progress at the same time in the past

Use	Form	Keywords	Example Sentences
limited time (in the past)		last month	I **was travelling** last month.
		last week	You **were working** last week.
		last night	He **was studying** last night.
		on Friday	We **were hiking** on Friday.
		on the weekend	I **was visiting** my family on the weekend.
temporary actions (in the past)	*was / were* + base form of a verb + *-ing* (present participle)	at that moment	She **was eating** an apple right then.
		right then	
actions in progress (in the past) when another action happens		while	While we **were walking** in the park, we met Henry.
		as	They saw a fox as they **were driving** through the park.
		when (used with the simple past)	He **was taking** a shower when she called.
actions in progress at the same time (in the past)		while	While you **were sleeping**, I **was studying**.
		as	As Juan **was cooking**, Pedro **was washing** the dishes.

Warm-Up

Work in pairs. Read Paragraph 1. Together, <u>underline</u> all the verbs. List the verbs in order in the first row of the chart that follows.

Paragraph 1 Right now, Sergei and Kumar are sitting on the patio at the café. It is a beautiful day. They are waiting for their friends, Shanda and Meisha. They want to make plans for Saturday night. They are planning a surprise party for Martine's birthday.

Read the second version of the paragraph, Paragraph 2. Together, <u>underline</u> all the verbs. List the verbs in order in the second row of the chart.

Paragraph 2 Yesterday, Sergei and Kumar were sitting on the patio at the café. It was a beautiful day. They were waiting for their friends, Shanda and Meisha. They wanted to make plans for Saturday night. They were planning a surprise party for Martine's birthday.

Verbs				
Paragraph 1				
Paragraph 2				

Compare the verbs in the first row with the verbs in the second row. What do you notice about their forms? Can you see any patterns?

Past Progressive

We form the past progressive of verbs by combining the past tense of *be* with the present participle (or *-ing* form) of the verb.

Warm-Up

Work in pairs. Read the following conversation out loud.

Partner A: Hi, Sandra. I thought I saw you late last night at the college. What were you doing?

Partner B: I was studying in the library, but I fell asleep.

Partner A: It was quite late. How did you get home?

Partner B: I missed the last bus, so I was waiting for my friend to come to get me in his car. He was working when I called him. What were you doing there so late?

Partner A: I was walking by the college on my way home from work.

Read the conversation again. <u>Underline</u> all the verbs. Write them in the correct column in a chart on a separate piece of paper.

Simple Past	Past Progressive
thought	were doing

Read the conversation a third time. Why is the simple past used for some actions and the past progressive used for others?

Formation

Positive	Negative	Yes/No Question	Wh- Question
Subject + *be* + Verb + -*ing* (+ object / complement)	**Subject + *be* + Negative + Verb + -*ing* (+ object / complement)**	***Be* + Subject + Verb + -*ing* (+ object / complement)**	**Question Word + *be* + Subject + Verb + -*ing* (+ object / complement)**
I **was** study**ing** yesterday.	I **was not** studying yesterday.	**Were** you study**ing** yesterday?	**When** were you studying?
You **were** eat**ing** supper.	You **were not** eat**ing** supper.	**Were** you eating supper?	**What** were you eating?
He **was** sleep**ing** on the sofa.	He **was not** sleeping on the sofa.	**Was** he sleep**ing** on the sofa?	**Where** was he sleeping?
She **was** play**ing** a video game.	She **was not** play**ing** a video game.	**Was** she playing a video game?	**What** was she playing?
It **was** snow**ing** at 7 PM.	It **was not** snowing at 7 PM.	**Was** it snowing at 7 PM?	**When** was it snowing?
We **were** sitt**ing** in the front row.	We **were not** sitt**ing** in the front row.	**Were** you sitt**ing** in the front row?	**Where** were you sitting?
They **were** talk**ing** on the phone.	They **were not** talk**ing** on the phone.	**Were** they talk**ing** on the phone?	**How** were they talking?

- Remember that Wh- questions have the same structure as Yes/No questions. The question word replaces specific information in the Yes/No question. Write the question word and add the rest of the question.
- Follow the formation rules for *be* for questions and negatives in the past progressive.
- For a detailed explanation of how to form and use questions and negatives, refer to Chapter 11.
- To review the spelling rules for verbs with the -*ing* ending, see Chapter 4, page 61.

Contractions

We often join the verb *be* and *not,* and the auxiliary verb and *not,* to form contractions or shorter forms. Join the two words together and use an apostrophe (') to replace the letter *o.*

Be + not	Auxiliary + not
is not → isn't	does not → doesn't
are not → aren't	do not → don't
was not → wasn't	did not → didn't
were not → weren't	

I am not is the exception. We make the contraction only with the pronoun *I* because a contraction using *am* and *not* is difficult to pronounce.

I am not → I'm not

Refer to Appendix B for a complete chart of the contractions used with the verb tenses presented in this book.

Exercise 1

Fill in the blanks with the past progressive form of the verbs in parentheses.

While I _____ **(make)** supper, my friend called. →

While I **was making** supper, my friend called.

I _____ **(sleep,** negative). I was eating supper. →

I **was not (wasn't) sleeping.** I was eating supper.

1. Last Sunday, we _____ **(come)** home on the bus.

2. Paul _____ **(talk,** negative) to his friend.

3. They _____ **(begin)** to do their homework.

4. Marie-Josée _____ **(hum)** a song.

5. _____ it _____ **(rain)**?

Exercise 2

Answer these questions in the positive or negative, as indicated. Write complete sentences.

Question Were you listening to the songs on your iPod?

Answer Yes, I was listening to the songs on my iPod.

Question Was she dancing?

Answer No, she was not (wasn't) dancing.

1. Was Maria chatting with her friend on the phone?

Yes, _____.

2. Were you doing your homework?

No, _____.

3. Were John and Isabel sitting together in the cafeteria?

Yes, _____.

4. Were you and your friend walking downtown on Saturday afternoon?

   Yes, _____.

5. Was Malek playing soccer with his friends?

   No, _____.

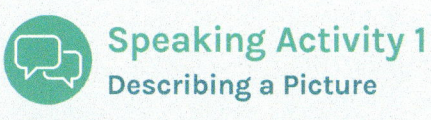 **Speaking Activity 1**
Describing a Picture

Work in pairs. Look at the picture of people in a restaurant. First, write your own sentences to describe what was happening in the restaurant at noon yesterday. Use the past progressive. Share your sentences with your partner. Then share your sentences with other pairs. Below are some verbs to help you get started.

talk	order	sit
wait for	serve	stand
look at	carry	walk

Past Progressive versus Simple Past

Warm-Up

Walk around the class and interview three students. Ask the questions from the following chart and record your answers on a separate sheet of paper. Share your findings with the rest of the class. Your findings might look like this.

> Henrik stayed home last night. At 6:00 PM, he was taking a nap. While he was taking a nap, the phone rang.

Questions	Student 1	Student 2	Student 3
1. What did you do last night?			
2. What were you doing at 6:00 last night? Did anything happen while you were doing that?			
3. What were you doing at 8:30 last night? Did anything happen while you were doing that?			
4. What were you doing at 11:00 last night? Did anything happen while you were doing that?			

Formation

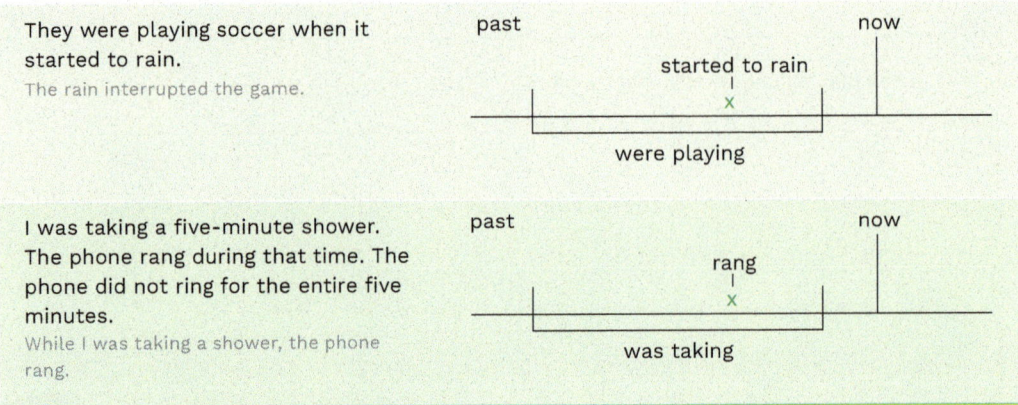

They were playing soccer when it started to rain. *The rain interrupted the game.*	past ... now ... started to rain ... x ... were playing
I was taking a five-minute shower. The phone rang during that time. The phone did not ring for the entire five minutes. *While I was taking a shower, the phone rang.*	past ... now ... rang ... x ... was taking

Both actions in the example sentences are in the past. The past progressive action happened over a limited time in the past. The simple past action interrupted or happened during the other action.

Remember that *while* and *as* are usually keywords or signals to use the past progressive. *When* is usually the keyword for the simple past.

Non-Progressive Verbs

Remember that certain verbs cannot be used in the present progressive tense. The same rule applies to the past progressive tense. These non-progressive verbs include verbs that express the senses, emotions, thoughts, possession, and being. For more information, review the non-progressive verb chart on page 63 in Chapter 4.

Exercise 3

Fill in the blanks with the correct form of the verbs in parentheses. Use the past progressive or the simple past.

While I _____ (wash) the dishes, someone _____ (ring) the doorbell. →
While I **was washing** the dishes, someone **rang** the doorbell.

1. Yan _____ **(meet)** his wife while they _____ **(go)** to university.

2. Susan _____ **(fix)** her bicycle when her friend _____ **(drop)** by.

3. When she _____ **(hear)** the noise, she _____ **(look)** out the window to see what _____ **(happen)**.

4. While we _____ **(fly)** to Vancouver, there _____ **(be)** a terrible thunderstorm.

5. I _____ **(walk)** down the street when I _____ **(find)** a wallet.

Exercise 4

Change the following statements into Wh- questions. The information you want to ask about is in **bold**. Refer to the formation chart on page 95 and the question-word list on pages 43-44 in Chapter 3 if you need to. Note: For a detailed explanation of how to form and use questions, refer to Chapter 11. Look at the examples to help you.

Max was doing **his homework** in the library. → **What** was Max doing in the library?

We cooked the chicken **while she was cleaning the house**. → **When** did you cook chicken?

They were **sleeping** at midnight. → **What** were they doing at midnight?

1. Juan **was playing basketball** when I saw him.

_____?

2. We **were packing for our trip** when Angelica came to visit us.

_____?

3. I was driving **to the store** when I saw the accident.

_____?

4. The students were checking **their emails** before the teacher arrived.

_____?

5. **Seven** students were still writing the exam when the fire alarm rang.

_____?

6. Jonathan was taking notes during class **to use them to study later**.

_____?

Speaking Activity 2
Scrambled Parts

Work in small groups. Your teacher will give each group four piles of cards with words on them. Discuss and arrange the cards from each pile to form complete sentences. The group that finishes first and has the most correct answers wins.

_____

_____

_____

_____

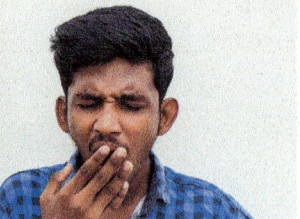

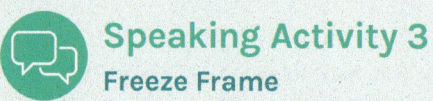

Speaking Activity 3
Freeze Frame

Work in teams. Write down action verbs to act out, such as "scratching your head" or "yawning." Write one or two action verbs for each person in your group. You can act them out alone or as a group. Your teacher will ask a team to act out an action. After 10 seconds, your teacher will say "stop" or "freeze." Hold your positions. The teacher will ask another team to answer the question "What was he or she doing?" or "What were they doing?" If the team doesn't guess correctly, the teacher will ask the student, "What were you doing?" The teams take turns acting out the actions. The team with the most correct answers wins.

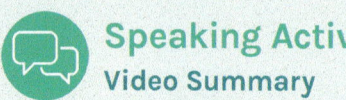

Speaking Activity 4
Video Summary

Work in pairs. Your teacher will show a short video clip. Pay attention to what is happening in the video. When your teacher stops the video, write as many sentences as you can describing the actions in the video. Use the past progressive and the simple past. Compare your sentences with your partner's. Did you miss any actions? Read your sentences out loud to another pair of students.

Reading

Read the passage and answer the questions that follow.

As you read, pay attention to these vocabulary words in the passage: *define*, *derives*, *immigrants*, *environment*, *consequently*, *illustrate*, *similar*, and *link*.

Canadian Folklore: Myths, Legends, and More

We usually **define** folklore tales as an oral or spoken form of storytelling passed on from generation to generation. These tales are often ways of explaining nature, notable events, or spiritual beliefs and often have a teaching point, especially for children. Of course, oral traditions extend beyond folklore and include oral history, and they are a way to pass on knowledge to the next generation.

Folklore in Canada has three main sources as a result of our historical background: Indigenous, English, and French traditions. Indigenous folklore **derives** from First Nations, Métis, and Inuit storytelling and legends. The English Canadian folktales have their origins in English, Scottish, Irish, and Welsh folklore. Of course, the French Canadian folktales originated in France. French- and English-speaking **immigrants** continued to tell their familiar tales in their new country, and because the stories were originally an oral tradition, they evolved to suit the new **environment** of Canada. Many other people from all around the world who immigrated to Canada brought their traditions and stories as well. **Consequently**, folklore in Canada is very rich.

Recently, while I was listening to a CBC Radio broadcast, the hosts were giving some background information on storytelling, myths, legends, and so on. They were explaining the differences: many myths and some legends use characters who are half animal and half human or who are animals that speak to humans, for example, to **illustrate** the point of the story. In folktales of all origins, we hear about shapeshifters, such as the Windigo, werewolves, or vampires.

While the hosts were saying that myths and legends have **similar** traits, they also pointed out that there are differences; however, there is often a fine line between those differences. Myths are a way to explain traditions or mysterious or religious events. For example, the stories about Hercules are myths. In other words, they probably didn't really happen. Those stories were created long ago to explain things.

Legends are very similar because they explain things, but they often have some **link** to actual facts. Either the places were real places, or some of the characters or people did actually exist, such as Robin Hood. The place existed and the king was really a king, but we don't know how much of the rest of the story was real or not. Both myths and legends often provide lessons too.

There are also urban legends, which are <u>contemporary</u> folktales. Some are based on real <u>incidents</u>, but many are <u>embellished</u> beyond what most people believe to be possibly true. Their purpose is to caution, to scare, or to entertain.

Ghost stories have much in common with urban legends. Most ghost stories told around a campfire or in the dark, late at night, don't really relate to actual events, but again, their purpose is to scare or entertain.

One thing that is certain is that folklore is always <u>adapting</u> and evolving. It's also always entertaining and often a good learning experience.

Comprehension

Answer the questions. Write complete sentences.

1. What are the three main sources of Canadian folklore?
   _____
   _____

2. Why were the stories of French and English immigrants easy to change to suit their new lives and the environment in Canada?
   _____

3. Why is Canada's folklore so rich?
   _____

4. Give a few examples of the types of characters that are often used in myths and legends.
   _____
   _____

5. What is one difference between myths and legends?
   _____

6. What is one difference between urban legends and ghost stories?
   _____

Analyzing the Reading Passage

Read the passage again. Underline all the simple past tense verbs with a <u>single line</u>. Then underline all the past progressive tense verbs with a <u>double line</u>.

Discussion

Stories, such as myths and legends, are passed on from one generation to another in all cultures. Can you think of any stories you heard as a child? Do you think these kinds of stories still provide us with useful lessons or explanations today?

Listening

Audio 12

Urban Legends

Listen to the audio, which is a segment of a radio show on urban legends. Then answer the questions.

The renovated Ottawa jail

Comprehension

(Circle) the letter of the correct answer.

1. Marlena Rankin is a professor of folklore at Laurentian University.

    a) True

    b) False

2. Folklore includes stories, legends, and myths that

    a) are orally passed on from one generation to another

    b) often vary from one area to another

    c) both a) and b)

3. Urban legends are often cautionary tales. Cautionary means

    a) entertaining

    b) warning

    c) true

4. In the legend "The Hook," what frightened both the boy and the girl?

    a) the radio announcement about the escaped killer

    b) the scratching sound on the car door

    c) both a) and b)

5. What did the Ottawa jail become after it closed?

    a) a restaurant

    b) a hostel

    c) a hotel

6. According to the guests at the former Ottawa jail, what was the ghost doing when they woke up in the middle of the night?

    a) He was screaming.

    b) He was eating food.

    c) He was standing at the foot of the bed.

7. Urban legends are only for entertainment; they are not part of our folklore and culture.

    a) True

    b) False

Writing

Write your own version of a legend or myth you know, either traditional or more contemporary. You can also create your own brand-new legend.

Vocabulary

1. The words in the box are in **bold** in the Reading passage on pages 100-101. Look at how the words are used in the passage. Use that context and what you know about word forms to help you match the words from the box with their correct definitions. Then use a dictionary to find another form of the word (such as an adjective, a noun, a verb, or an adverb) and add it to the chart. An example is provided.

define (v.)	derives (v.)	immigrants (n.)	environment (n.)
consequently (adv.)	illustrate (v.)	similar (adj.)	link (n.)

Word or Term	Definition	Adjective / Noun / Verb / Adverb
1.	a) to create a picture or a physical or mental image of something in order to explain it more clearly	
2.	b) a connection between things or something in common with others	
3. consequently	c) as a result; as a consequence of something; therefore	consequent (adj.) consequence (n.)
4.	d) has its origins in; comes from	
5.	e) people who move, usually permanently, from one area or country to another	
6.	f) to provide a clear explanation of the meaning of something	
7.	g) having a lot of characteristics in common but not completely the same	
8.	h) the situation or conditions around you; surroundings	

2. Replace each <u>underlined</u> word in the following sentences with one of the words from the chart and the box in question 1.

    a) The <u>newcomers</u> needed to adjust to their new <u>situation</u> in their new country.

Chapter Review

Summary

- The past progressive expresses actions that were in progress in the past and shows
    - actions that were happening during a limited, specific time in the past
    - temporary actions in progress in the past
    - actions in progress in the past that were interrupted when another action happened
    - actions in progress at the same time in the past
- The simple past expresses an action that is finished or completed in the past.
- *While* and *as* are usually keywords or signals to use the past progressive.
- *When* is usually the keyword for the simple past.
- Non-progressive verbs cannot be used in the past progressive tense. The non-progressive verbs include verbs that express the senses, emotions, thoughts, possession, and being. Review the non-progressive verb chart on page 63 in Chapter 4.

Exercise 5

In the following paragraph, change the verbs that are in the simple present to the simple past, and change the verbs that are in the present progressive to the past progressive.

When I arrive home from work, my roommate is preparing supper. While I am changing my clothes, he says we need to study for an exam. While we are eating our meal, we start to ask each other questions about the exam. We are studying while we are having our supper. We continue to ask questions while we are doing the dishes. By the time we finish the dishes, we know what we need to review. I like to study that way.

Exercise 6

There are five errors in the use of the past progressive or the simple past in the following paragraph. Find and correct them.

I was hearing a story on the radio about why some Indigenous peoples began to make dreamcatchers. One day, an old woman was watch a spider. The spider was spinning its web. The woman's grandson wanted to kill the spider, but she was stopping him. The spider was so grateful that he showed the woman how to make a web. While it showed her how to do it, the spider explained that only good dreams passed through the web. The web was trapping all the bad dreams.

Exercise 7

Use the words provided to write sentences or questions in the past progressive. You need to change the verb into the past progressive. Review the formation chart in this chapter on page 95 if you need to.

Where / he / go? → Where was he going?

1. The singer / sing / my favourite song

   _____.

2. Frank and his friends / play / soccer

   _____?

3. Samantha / take / the bus to work

   _____.

4. the children / feed / some animals at the zoo

   _____?

5. my friend / cut / my hair

   _____.

Exercise 8

Change the following sentences into Yes/No questions. Review the formation chart in this chapter on page 95 if you need to.

My dog was barking at that moment. → Was my dog barking at that moment?

1. It was raining at 10:00 last night.

   _____?

2. We were trying to find the answer to the question.

_____?

3. I was sewing a button onto my shirt.

_____?

4. The players were waiting for the game to begin.

_____?

5. Guillermo was taking a nap.

_____?

Exercise 9

Circle the letter of the correct word or phrase to complete the sentences.

1. George was talking on the phone _____ I got home.
   a) when   b) while

2. It _____ when I left work.
   a) rained   b) was raining

3. The man _____ to catch the bus when I saw him.
   a) ran   b) was running

4. While you were sleeping, I _____ to the store.
   a) went   b) was going

5. When the teacher explained the lesson, I _____ it.
   a) understood   b) was understanding

Exercise 10

Change each of the following positive sentences into the negative. Review the formation chart in this chapter on page 95 if you need to. Look at the example to help you.

Elizabeth was teaching yesterday. → **Elizabeth was not (wasn't) teaching yesterday.**

1. I was speaking to my boss about the problem at work.

_____

2. Yesterday, we were studying for the test.

_____

3. She was walking the dog at that time.

_____

4. They were watching a movie on TV.

_____

5. We were celebrating our anniversary at the restaurant.

_____

7 Adjectives and Adverbs

Overview

- Adjectives describe nouns or pronouns.
- Use comparative adjectives to compare two things.
- Use superlative adjectives to describe three or more things and indicate that one of them is of the highest (or lowest) degree.
- Adverbs describe verbs and modify adjectives or other adverbs.
- Use comparative adverbs to compare two actions.
- Use superlative adverbs to compare three or more actions and show that one of these actions is of the highest (or lowest) degree.
- Use equative adjectives and adverbs to indicate that two things or actions are—or are not—the same.

Warm-Up

Read the following proverbs and their explanations. Underline any adjectives with a <u>single line</u> and any adverbs with a <u>double line</u>.

1. Good conscience is a soft pillow. = You sleep peacefully if you are not guilty of anything.
2. A bad tree does not yield good apples. = If you are a bad parent, most likely your kids are bad too.
3. Good management is better than a good income. = You can lose your money fast if you do not manage it well.
4. Be swift to hear, slow to speak. = Listen carefully before you speak.
5. A good example is the best sermon. = It's better to show by doing than by giving advice.
6. Great oaks grow from small acorns. = Some things start really small before they become big and well known.
7. Love is blind. = A person in love often can't see the negative sides of the person he or she loves.
8. Nobody is perfect. = Everyone makes mistakes.
9. The first step is the hardest. = It's hard to start something.

> Proverbs are well-known sayings that express basic truths or advice.

Adjectives

Warm-Up

Think of three nouns. In the following chart, write those nouns in the first column. Then, in the second column, write a word that describes each of those nouns.

Noun	A Word That Describes the Noun
house	new
classmates	funny

Formation

Formation	Example Sentences
Adjectives modify or qualify nouns or pronouns.	A **bad** tree does not yield **good** apples. It's **hard** to start something.
Place adjectives before a noun or after the verbs *be* or *become*.	**Good** conscience is a **soft** pillow. Love is **blind**. They become **big** and **well known**.
Adjectives are always singular even if the noun or pronoun is plural.	**Great** oaks grow from **small** acorns.

Exercise 1

Describe each of the following people or things. Use at least three adjectives. Write complete sentences.

   oranges: Oranges are orange, round, and sweet.

1. athletes

   _____

2. babies

   _____

3. cats

   _____

4. school

   _____

5. this book

   _____

Speaking Activity 1
A Good Friend Is . . .

Work in pairs. Look at the examples of some qualities that make a good friend. By yourself, order the qualities from 1 (very important) to 10 (not very important). Share your list with your partner and explain the reasons for choosing this order. Then add other qualities that are not on the list but are important to you both.

_____ honest	_____ energetic	_____ attentive
_____ funny	_____ intelligent	_____ generous
_____ reliable	_____ well behaved	_____ punctual
_____ unselfish	_____ forgiving	_____ rich

Other qualities

_____   _____   _____

_____   _____   _____

Adverbs

Warm-Up

Think of three verbs. Write those verbs in the first column on the right. Then, in the second column, write a word that describes each of those verbs. Look at the examples (on the left) to help you.

Verb	A Word That Describes the Verb	Verb	A Word That Describes the Verb
laugh	loudly		
run	fast		
speak	clearly		

Formation

Formation	Example Sentences
Adverbs modify or qualify verbs, adjectives, or other adverbs.	Listen **carefully** before you speak. Some things start **really** small before they become big and **well** known. She drives **extremely carefully.**
Use adjectives to form adverbs. General rule: add **-ly** to the end of an adjective.	Louis is a **slow** eater. Louis eats **slowly**. That was a **quick** answer. He answered it **quickly**. It was an **informal** conversation. We spoke **informally**.
For adjectives ending with **e**, add **-ly**.	She has **nice** clothes. She dresses **nicely**.
For adjectives ending with a consonant + **y**, change **y** to **i** and add **-ly**.	They have a **happy** life. They live **happily**.
For adjectives ending with **-le**, delete **e** and add **-y**.	My new sofa is **comfortable**. I am sitting **comfortably** on my new sofa.
For adjectives ending with **-ic**, add **-ally**.	Cecile is a **sympathetic** listener. She always listens **sympathetically**.
There are also irregular adverbs.	Eerie is a **good** singer. Eerie sings **well**. Those players are **fast**. They play **fast**. Brian is a **hard** worker. He works **hard.**

Exercise 2

Change each of the following adjectives into an adverb.

1. quiet _____
2. easy _____
3. terrible _____
4. perfect _____
5. safe _____

6. tragic _____
7. hard _____
8. good _____
9. soft _____
10. basic _____

Speaking Activity 2

What's the Adverb?

Work in pairs. Look back at Speaking Activity 1 on page 109. There are 11 adjectives that you can change to adverbs. Write a sentence with each of those adverbs. Compare your sentences with another pair's sentences.

honest → honestly   **Sentence** My friend always speaks honestly.

Comparative Adjectives

We use comparative adjectives to compare **two** things, places, people, or groups of people. Comparative adjectives show us how those **two** things are different.

Warm-Up

Work in pairs. Compare the people and the objects you see in the photos. Use adjectives.

Can you guess how we form comparative adjectives?

Formation

Adjective Types	Examples	Rule	Example Sentences
one-syllable adjectives	tall	add **-er** to adjective, and add **than**	Xiang is **taller than** Micha.
one-syllable adjectives ending with an **e**	nice	add **-r** to adjective, and add **than**	Today is **nicer than** yesterday.
one-syllable adjectives ending with a consonant-vowel-consonant	big	double the last consonant, add **-er**, and add **than**	Their house is **bigger than** ours.
two-syllable adjectives ending with a **y**	busy	change **y** to **i**, add **-er**, and add **than**	York Street is **busier than** Park Avenue.
adjectives with two or more syllables	creative	insert **more** or **less** before the adjective, and add **than**	Carl is **more creative than** Sam. Sam is **less creative than** Carl.
irregular adjectives	good bad far (distance)	No rules; memorize those adjectives.	Water is **better than** juice. This car is **worse than** that one. My school is **farther* than** yours.

*Note: *farther* relates to distance and *further* relates to degree.

Which city is **farther** from you—Halifax or Vancouver?   Do you need **further** explanation?

Exercise 3

Fill in the blanks with the comparative form of the adjectives in parentheses. Note that the example below has two possible answers.

You are _____ (athletic) than he is. → You are **more athletic** than he is. *or*

→ You are **less athletic** than he is.

1. Juan's desk seems to be _____ **(neat)** than Meagan's.

2. Trent is _____ **(young)** than his brother Travis.

3. Children are often _____ **(happy)** than adults because they don't have many things to worry about.

4. My cousin likes sports, but I like art. When we paint, my cousin is _____ **(artistic)** than I am.

5. Are dogs _____ **(smart)** than cats?

Superlative Adjectives

Superlative adjectives show that one noun (a person, place, or thing) out of a group of three or more has the highest or lowest degree of that quality. We do **not** use superlatives to compare two things but to show that **out of three (or more)** things, **one** is of the highest or lowest degree of quality.

Warm-Up

Work in pairs. Read the following conversations out loud.

Conversation 1

Partner A: This was the best workshop ever!

Partner B: Yep! And the longest.

Partner A: You mean you didn't like it?

Partner B: Oh no! I loved it! Out of all the workshops, it was the most interesting one.

Conversation 2

Partner A: Stella, tell me about your kids. How are they?

Partner B: They're growing up, and the three of them are surely keeping me busy.

Partner A: Are they still shy like the last time I saw them?

Partner B: Well, yes, a bit. But the youngest one, Chloe, is now the most social one.

Partner A: What about the oldest one? Is she the quietest one?

Partner B: Yes. She is the quietest and the least problematic of the three of them.

In the above conversations, what are the speakers doing?

a) They are comparing something or the person they are talking about with something or someone else.

b) They are stating that out of many things or people, this one shows the most extreme degree of a quality.

In the above conversations, <u>underline</u> all the superlative adjectives. Can you guess how we form superlative adjectives?

Formation

There are two superlative forms: *the* followed by **adjective + -est** or *the most* + **adjective**.

Adjective Types	Examples	Rule	Example Sentences
one-syllable adjectives	tall	insert **the** before the adjective, and add **-est**	Xiang is **the tallest** student in our class.
one-syllable adjectives ending with an **e**	nice	insert **the** before the adjective, and add **-st**	Today is **the nicest** day of my life.
one-syllable adjectives ending with a consonant-vowel-consonant	big	insert **the** before the adjective, double the last consonant, and add **-est**	Their house is **the biggest** on the street.
two-syllable adjectives ending with a consonant + **y**	busy	insert **the** before the adjective, change **y** to **i** and add **-est**	York Street is **the busiest** street in this city.
two- (or more) syllable adjectives	creative	insert **the most** or **the least** before the adjective	Carl is **the most creative** artist that I know.
	punctual		Sam is **the least punctual** worker in our company.
irregular adjectives	good	insert **the** before the adjective; memorize the irregular adjectives	Water is **the best** drink to quench your thirst.
	bad		This car is **the worst** car in history.
	far (distance)		My school is **the farthest*** place I walk to every day.

*Note: *farthest* relates to distance and *furthest* relates to degree.

Icarus is **the farthest** star from Earth.

Dan's statements were **the furthest** from the truth.

Exercise 4

Fill in the blanks with the superlative form of the adjectives in parentheses.

> Carmela competes in many sports. She is _____ (athletic) person I know. →
> Carmela competes in many sports. She is **the most athletic** person I know.

1. The Lamborghini Veneno is _____ **(expensive)** car in the world.

2. The Trans-Canada Highway is 7821 kilometres long. It's _____ **(long)** national highway in the world.

3. Burj Khalifa is the world's _____ **(tall)** building. It's 828 metres tall.

4. My wedding was _____ **(happy)** day of my life. It was a wonderful day.

5. Miya was married three times. Her first two husbands were very good, but her third husband was _____ **(good)**.

Comparative and Superlative Adverbs

Comparative adverbs tell us about the difference between how **two** people, animals, or objects do something.
Superlative adverbs show us that among three or more people, animals, or objects, one performance is of the highest or lowest degree.

Warm-Up

Circle the letter of the correct word or phrase to complete the sentences.

1. If you want fresh food every day, buy your groceries _____
   a) once a week.
   b) more frequently than once a week.

2. You got good marks last semester, but if you want better marks next semester, study _____
   a) harder than last semester.
   b) the same.

3. Of all the contestants, Sally sang _____
   a) beautifully.
   b) the most beautifully.

4. Kenyan had many car accidents last year. In his family, he drives _____

    a) the worst.

    b) the worse.

Sentences 1 and 2 use comparative adverbs. Can you see how we form such adverbs?

_____

Sentences 3 and 4 use superlative adverbs. Can you see how we form such adverbs?

_____

Formation

Adverb Type	Examples	Rule	Example Sentences
one-syllable adverbs	fast hard	**Comparative**: add **-er** and add **than** adverb + -er + than	Kiefer runs **faster than** Yoko.
		Superlative: insert **the** before the adverb, and add **-est** the + adverb + -est	Of all the kids, Kiefer runs **the fastest**.
adverbs of two or more syllables	slowly carefully	**Comparative**: insert **more** or **less** before the adverb, and add **than** more / less + adverb + than	Kim writes **more / less slowly than** Jane. Ken drives **more / less carefully than** Ben.
		Superlative: insert **the most** or **the least** before the adverb the most / the least + adverb	Who writes **the most / the least slowly**? Who drives **the most / the least carefully?**
exception: *early*	early	**Comparative**: change **y** to **i**, add **-er**, and add **than**	Shannon finished the test **earlier than** Matt.
		Superlative: insert **the** before the adverb, change **y** to **i**, and add **-est**	Who finished the test **the earliest**?
irregular adverbs	well badly	No rules; memorize these adverbs. **Comparative**: **better / worse + than**	Katia reads **better** in French **than** in English. I feel **worse** today **than** I did yesterday.
		Superlative: **the best / the worst**	Melodie did **the best** on the math test. Sandrine did **the worst** in the science class.

Just like with the adjectives, add *than* after a comparative adverb and *the* before a superlative adverb.

Exercise 5

Fill in the blanks with the correct comparative or superlative adverb of the words in parentheses.

1. **Patrick:** Hey, Tom! I guess I'm late. Sorry.

   Tom: Oh no, you're not late at all. I came a bit _____ **(early)** than we agreed on.

   Patrick: Really? That's good. And look, David is not here yet at all.

   Tom: He actually was here already, an hour ago. He arrived _____ **(early)**, but he didn't feel well. He called me and told me that he went home.

   Patrick: Too bad! I hope he feels _____ **(well)** soon.

2. **Lynne:** Bon appétit, Betty!

Betty: Thank you! Are you having lunch too?

Lynne: I already finished my lunch a couple minutes ago. I ate it _____ **(fast)** than usual because I still have a lot of homework to do for my science class.

Betty: I see. By the way, how are you doing in that class? I find the class very difficult.

Lynne: I did badly last year, but this year I think I'm doing fine. Last year's teacher didn't

explain the things clearly, but this year's teacher seems to teach _____ **(skillfully)**. If you find the class difficult, I can help you out.

Betty: That's nice of you. Thanks.

3. **Damian:** Shawn! I was watching carefully as you were playing. Wow, man! Out of all the

drummers I know, you play drums _____ **(well)**.

Shawn: Well, thanks, but I think my friend Austin plays drums _____ **(well)** than I do.

Damian: Are you serious?

Shawn: Yeah. He learned how to play drums when he was very young. He is way

faster and plays _____ **(precisely)** than I do.

Speaking Activity 3
Conversation

Work in pairs. First, read the conversations from Exercise 5 out loud. Then create similar conversations by using comparative and superlative adverbs. Act them out in front of your other classmates.

Equatives

We use equatives to make a comparison between two things or actions that are equal (the same). We use both adjectives and adverbs with this structure.

Warm-Up

Here are some idioms that compare equality. Match the numbered idioms with their lettered definitions.

> Idioms are phrases that have hidden meanings. They do not mean exactly what they state.

Idiom	Definition
1. as easy as pie _____	a) very calm, in control of your emotions
2. as clean as a whistle _____	b) not able to see well
3. as blind as a bat _____	c) very old
4. as stubborn as a mule _____	d) able to do what you desire; no worries or responsibilities
5. as good as gold _____	e) something that you can do without difficulty
6. as cool as a cucumber _____	f) not dirty at all; spotless
7. as free as a bird _____	g) well behaved
8. as old as the hills _____	h) don't want to do what others tell you to do

Formation

To form the comparison of equality, use the following structure:

Positive   as . . . as = the same
Negative   not as . . . as = less so

The test was **as <u>easy</u> as** the assignment.
                              adj.

The test was **not as <u>easy</u> as** the assignment.
                                  adj.

Angie walks **as <u>quickly</u> as** her mother.
                              adv.

Angie does not walk **as <u>quickly</u> as** her mother.
                                      adv.

Exercise 6

Use an equative with each set of words to make a sentence. Look at the example to help you.

Biking / dangerous / mountain climbing → Biking is not **as dangerous as** mountain climbing.

1. Our trip to Spain last year / exciting / our trip to France in 2011

   _____

2. Girls / learn / fast / boys

   _____

3. Celeste / presents / interestingly / Marie-France

_____

4. Fruit / sweet / ice cream

_____

5. Bees / hardworking / ants

_____

Bringing It All Together

Speaking Activity 4
Role-Plays

Work in pairs. Prepare a role-play for each of the following situations. Then perform them in front of the class.

Situation A: You are 19 years old, and you want to get married to your partner. Your dad or mom thinks you are too young for marriage. Try to persuade your parent by telling him or her how good your boyfriend or girlfriend is. Use adjectives and adverbs.

Situation B: You are at a job interview. First, the interviewer asks you to tell him or her a few of your strong points. Then the interviewer asks you about your weak points. Answer the interviewer. Use adjectives and adverbs when possible.

Speaking Activity 5
Game—Guess the Action

Work in two teams. Your teacher will have two boxes: one containing cards with verbs and the other one containing cards with adverbs. A member of one team goes to the front of the class and draws one verb and one adverb out of the boxes. The student acts out the words. If his or her team correctly guesses both words, they get a point. If the team can't give a correct response in 30 seconds, the other team gets a chance to make a guess and score a point.

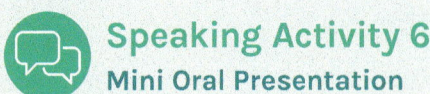

Speaking Activity 6
Mini Oral Presentation

Work in pairs. Choose a topic from the following list or use your own idea. Prepare a short presentation on the topic. Use as many comparative and superlative adjectives and adverbs as possible. Give your mini presentation to the rest of the class.

- Compare living in the city with living in the country.
- Compare living with parents with living on your own.
- Compare being married with being single.
- Compare PCs with Mac computers.

Reading

Read the passage and answer the questions that follow.

Multiple Intelligences and Learning Styles

Did you know that your type of intelligence determines your learning style? A learning style is the way you learn best. People learn in different ways. For example, they learn by seeing, hearing, or doing. It's important to know what your learning style is, as it can **impact** your grades and help you learn more efficiently. To **identify** what your best way of learning is, you need to know your type of intelligence. There are eight types of intelligence, called "multiple intelligences."

Among many **theories** on this topic, Dr. Howard Gardner's Theory of Multiple Intelligences is the most famous one. He developed it in 1983. According to the theory, people have eight different intelligences. The type of intelligence people have can determine the way they process new information and learn. The following are descriptions of the eight types of intelligence and their connections to a person's learning style.

As you read, pay attention to these vocabulary words in the passage: *impact, identify, theories, design, issues,* and *complex.*

Spatial

People with spatial intelligence have an ability to visualize well with their minds. They can imagine, draw, and **design** well. They learn quickly with visual aids.

Linguistic

People who have linguistic intelligence are good with words and languages. They learn more easily by reading, writing, listening, or discussing **issues**.

Logical-Mathematical

People who display this type of intelligence are logical and rational. They like to know how things work, and they show high mathematical abilities, as well as capabilities for **complex** reasoning and scientific thinking. They learn best by asking questions, doing experiments, and solving problems.

Bodily-Kinesthetic

People who have bodily-kinesthetic intelligence are skillful in physical activities, sports, and dance. They learn efficiently by incorporating movement into their learning experience.

Musical

Those with musical intelligence have a great ability to create and appreciate music, so they often sing or play a musical instrument. They learn typically by listening to lectures, music, or other audio material.

Interpersonal

People who have a high interpersonal intelligence are social, and they interact well with other people. They understand others easily. They learn <u>predominantly</u> by working with others in a group, as they enjoy collaborative activities.

Intrapersonal

Individuals with intrapersonal intelligence know themselves very well. They have an ability to reflect on their own behaviour. They are often independent, so they learn best by studying alone.

Naturalistic

People who display naturalistic intelligence connect well with nature. They enjoy being outdoors and caring for animals and plants. They learn best in a natural environment where they can observe and relate the studied material to the world around them.

So, which intelligences do you have? According to Gardner, we are born with all of the intelligences, but each of us develops our own set of different types of intelligence. Therefore, you might have a few of them or even show some characteristics of each of them. Remember, you learn most efficiently if you know what your learning style is, and your learning style depends on what type or types of intelligence you have.

Adapted from Douglass Fliess, Sue. "Multiple Intelligences: Understanding Your Child's Learning Style." Education.com, 2009; Gardner, Howard. *Frames of Mind*. Basic Books, 1983.

Comprehension

Answer the questions. Write complete sentences.

1. What is a learning style?

   _____

   _____

2. Why is it important to know your learning style?

   _____

   _____

3. What did Dr. Gardner develop? When did he develop it?

   _____

   _____

4. Add the missing information in the chart below.

Type of Intelligence	The Best Way to Learn
spatial	_____
linguistic	_____, _____, _____, _____
_____	by asking questions, _____, _____
bodily-kinesthetic	_____
musical	_____
_____	by working with others in a group
intrapersonal	_____
naturalistic	_____

Analyzing the Reading Passage

List ten adjectives from the reading passage.

_____   _____

_____   _____

_____   _____

_____   _____

_____   _____

List five adverbs from the reading passage.

_____

_____

_____

_____

_____

Discussion

What types of intelligences do you possess? What is your best learning style? Does it correspond to the type or types of intelligence you have?

As you listen, pay attention to the vocabulary words *relevant* and *negative* and the context in which they are used.

My Future Spouse

Listen to the audio. You will hear three young people describe what qualities they would like their future spouse to have.

Comprehension

1. Fill in the chart below based on what you heard.

Questions	Wendy	Simon	Eveline
What does this person want his or her spouse to be like?			
What is the most important quality of a spouse?			
What are the least important qualities of a spouse?			
What is an absolute no-no?			

2. Now, based on your notes from the chart in question 1, answer the following True/False questions. Circle the correct response.

Wendy

T / F   1.   She wants her future husband to be cheerful, affectionate, and romantic.

T / F   2.   The most important quality of a future husband is that he's adventurous.

T / F   3.   She wants her husband to work a lot because then they will have money to spend time together.

T / F   4.   Wendy's future husband needs to be a generous person.

Simon

T / F   1.   He only cares about his future wife's physical appearance.

T / F   2.   Simon needs his future wife to be an optimistic person because he's optimistic too.

T / F   3.   Simon enjoys cooking, so he doesn't care if his future wife is able to cook or not.

T / F   4.   His last relationship ended because his girlfriend broke up with him.

T / F   5.   Simon hopes that his future wife is a jealous person.

Eveline

T / F   1.   Her future husband doesn't need to be devoted to his family.

T / F   2.   What matters most to Eveline is that her future husband is a loving husband and a great father.

T / F   3.   Eveline wants a rich, handsome husband.

T / F   4.   She wouldn't be able to be with someone who is unfaithful.

Writing

Write a short composition (maximum 150 words) about your personality. In the first paragraph, describe yourself. Use as many adjectives and adverbs as possible. In the second paragraph, use the same or different adjectives to compare yourself with someone else (for example, your sibling or a friend). In the last paragraph, write about what characteristics you want to develop in the future. Below are some example sentences and a list of descriptive adjectives and their opposites to help with your writing.

I am an **enthusiastic** teacher, and my students tell me that I teach **well**.

Compared with my friend, I am **calmer** than she is.

In the future, I want to be **less selfish** and to help others **more frequently**.

caring / indifferent	generous / stingy	open-minded / closed-minded
considerate / inconsiderate	humble / arrogant	patient / impatient
disciplined / undisciplined	kind / unkind	punctual / unpunctual
flexible / stubborn	mature / immature	respectful / disrespectful
friendly / unfriendly	optimistic / pessimistic	self-confident / insecure

Vocabulary

1. Read the following sentences. The words in **bold** are from the Reading and Listening activities. Use the context to help you understand what the **bold** words mean.

   a) The most **complex** organ in the human body is the brain. Billions of neurons make up this organ.

   b) The connectivity of a bilingual person's brain is **designed** differently. Bilingual people are usually better and more creative at solving a novel problem.

   c) Functional Magnetic Resonance Imaging (fMRI) is used to observe brain structures and to **identify** which areas of the brain are more active during various cognitive tasks.

   d) A brain injury can lead to problems with how the brain processes information. This, in turn, can **impact** a person's mood, thinking, behaviour, memory, and learning.

   e) Among some other **issues** in the latest research in neuroscience is the link between the brain and the gut. Scientists believe that the gut could contribute to anxiety and depression.

   f) Some of the most commonly felt **negative** emotions are fear, anger, sadness, and loneliness.

   g) Brain research is highly **relevant** to education. Understanding how the brain works can help teachers create successful lessons that will meet the needs of a diverse student population.

   h) Despite the many existing **theories** developed to comprehend the human brain, there is still so much to learn about it.

2. Fill in the chart with your definition and a synonym for each word. Use a dictionary or the glossary to help you.

Word or Term	Definition	Synonym
complex (adj.)		
design (v.)		

identify (v.)			
impact (v.)			
issues (n.)			
negative (adj.)			
relevant (adj.)			
theories (n.)			

3. Circle the best choice of word for the following sentences. Think about the meaning and how it is used in the sentence.

   a) What is the most **complex / negative** organ in the body?
   b) There is a free app to **design / identify** plants. Take a photo and the app gives you information about the plant.
   c) Students learn better if the material is **complex / relevant** to them.
   d) Do you want to make a world a better place? It takes very little to positively **identify / impact** other people's lives.
   e) There are a number of **issues / theories** about how the universe was formed.

Chapter Review

Summary

- Adjectives modify nouns and pronouns.
- Adverbs modify verbs, adjectives, and other adverbs.
- Comparative adjectives compare two people or things. Form them by adding *-er* or *more than / less than*.
- Comparative adverbs compare two actions. Form them the same way as comparative adjectives.
- Superlative adjectives express that one thing, place, or person (out of many) is of the highest (or lowest) degree of quality. Form them by adding *-est* or *the most / the least*.
- Superlative adverbs compare three or more actions and show that one of these actions is of the highest (or lowest) degree. Form them the same way as superlative adjectives.
- The equative structure "as . . . as" is used with adjectives and adverbs. Equatives indicate that two things or actions are—or are not—the same.

Exercise 7

Fill in the blanks with either an adjective or an adverb. Use the words in parentheses.

Paper burns _____ (quick). → Paper burns **quickly**.

1. The weather was _____ (terrible) yesterday.

2. Could you please spell your name _____ **(slow)**?

3. This soup is _____ **(delicious)**.

4. They lost the game because they played _____ **(bad)**.

5. Grant speaks _____ **(fast)**.

Exercise 8

Fill in the blanks with the comparative, superlative, or equative form of the adjectives or adverbs in parentheses.

1. The state of Florida is _____ **(big)** than England.

2. Fadel won the gold in the 100 metres at the last track-and-field meet. He ran

   _____ **(fast)**.

3. The _____ **(long)** word in the English language, according to the *Oxford*

   Dictionary of English, is *pneumonoultramicroscopicsilicovolcanoconiosis.*

4. Mont Blanc, in Europe, is not _____ **(tall)** as Kilimanjaro, in Africa.

5. Victoria came to Canada one year ago. She speaks Russian _____ **(fluently)**

than she speaks English.

Exercise 9

There are seven adjective or adverb errors in the following passage. Find and correct them.

> In 2008, Jose left his native country, Portugal, and immigrated to Canada to live with his more old cousin. He found a lot of differences between the two countries and the people. First, Canada was much cold than Portugal. He had to buy warmest clothes. Second, he found that people in Canada were always walking fastly. But the biggest surprise to him was that in the morning, on the way to work, he would see people on the bus carrying their coffee travel mugs instead of stopping by a café and having a nicer cup of coffee there. A year passed, and one day as Jose was going to work, he smiled as he saw his reflection in a store window: he was in a puffy winter coat, walking quick, and holding on to his warm travel mug!

Exercise 10

Circle the letter of the correct word or phrase to complete the sentences.

1. This snowmobile is _____ that one.
    a) better   b) as good as   c) the best

2. The giant squid has _____ eyes in the world.
    a) the large   b) the largest   c) larger

3. Who is _____ student today?
    a) most tired   b) the most tiredest   c) the most tired

4. This lamp is _____ that one.
    a) the brightest   b) as bright   c) brighter than

5. Turtles are known to move very _____.
    a) slowly   b) more slowly   c) slow

Exercise 11

Unscramble the following words and make them into sentences or questions.

This / that / easier / exercise / than / one / is → This exercise is easier than that one.

1. than / My / neighbours / friendlier / are / yours

    _____.

2. Milos / well / cook / very / Does

    _____?

3. longest / is / river / What / in the world / the

    _____?

4. yesterday / as / Today / as / was / hot

    _____.

5. speaks / than / Hector / his son / faster

    _____.

Word Choice, Word Pairs

Overview

- Homonyms are words that sound the same but have different spellings and meanings.

- Commonly confused words sometimes sound or look similar or are sometimes mispronounced, but they have different meanings and uses.

- Certain word pairs, such as *really* and *very*, *some* and *any*, and certain prepositions often cause difficulty. Sometimes, we can use either one of the pair to mean the same thing, but in other situations, we cannot use the words in the same way.

- The verbs *listen*, *hear*, *look*, *see*, and *watch* sometimes cause confusion. The meanings of the verbs change when there is a preposition after them.

Warm-Up

Work in pairs. Read the following sentences. Focus on the words in **bold**.

> **You're here to hear** the **two** bands play, aren't you? Are **your** friends **here too**?

> We **live** near the arts centre, and we **really** enjoy going to concerts there to **listen to live** music. We also like to **watch** films in the IMAX theatre **very** much.

Now listen to your teacher read the four sentences. What do you think is the same and what is different about those words? First, focus on the first two sentences. What are the pairs or groups of words that sound the same? What do you think the difference is between them? Next, identify the pairs of words in the next two sentences. What do you think the difference is between them?

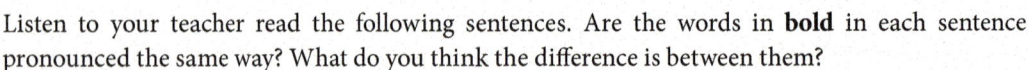

Homonyms and Commonly Confused Words

Homonyms are pairs or groups of words that sound the same, but their spelling and their meanings are different.

Commonly confused words look or sound a little similar, or they are sometimes pronounced incorrectly, but their meanings and uses are different.

Warm-Up

Listen to your teacher read the following sentences. Are the words in **bold** in each sentence pronounced the same way? What do you think the difference is between them?

1. The **two** boys want **to** go **to** the party **too**.
2. **His** sister **is** in **their** house, but **he's** over **there**.
3. **You're** not angry with **your** brother. **You're** angry with **your** sister.
4. The dog is chasing **its** tail. **It's** funny.

Homonyms

Formation

Form	Meaning and Use	Example Sentences
it's	*It's* is the contracted or short form for *it is*.	**It's** a beautiful day today.
its	*Its* is the possessive adjective and pronoun for the third-person singular (for things and animals, never people).	Look at this flower and **its** colour!
you're	*You're* is the contracted or short form for *you are*.	**You're** visiting a friend.
your	*Your* is the possessive adjective for the second-person singular and plural (for people only).	Does **your** sister have a car?

they're	*They're* is the contracted or short form for *they are*.	**They're** walking to the park.
their	*Their* is the possessive adjective for the third-person plural (for people, things, and animals).	My friends moved into **their** new apartment today.
there	We use *there* + *be* to introduce the existence of something or someone. *There* is also an adverb of place (away from this place).	**There** are a lot of students in the class. Where is your car? It's over **there**.
hear	*Hear* is a verb. It's the action you do with your ears. (Tip: *ear* is in the word *hear*.) We use *here* + *be* to present something or someone.	I **hear** a dog barking. **Here** is your book.
here	*Here* is also an adverb of place (in this place).	I'll put it **here** on the desk.
to	*To* is a preposition. We use it • with the infinitive of a verb • with an indirect object • to show direction	Jean needs **to** work. Please give it **to** me. Let's go **to** the park. I want **to** go **to** the store **to** buy a gift **to** give **to** Julia.
too	*Too* is an adverb. It emphasizes or intensifies the word it is modifying. Sometimes, *too* means *also*. It usually comes at the end of a sentence.	We have **too** many things to do today. They want to go swimming **too**.
two	*Two* is the number 2. *Two* can come before a plural noun or appear on its own.	I have **two** assignments to do too.
one	*One* is the number 1. *One* can come before a singular noun or appear on its own.	I have two cookies. Would you like **one**?
won	*Won* is the simple past tense of the verb to *win*.	My friend **won** the writing competition.

Tips for Using Homonyms

they're, you're, **and** *it's*
If the word has an apostrophe, rewrite the word as two words. Is it still correct?

> **They're** at home. → **They are** at home.

their, your, **and** *its*
If the word seems to be a possessive form, is there a noun after the word? Replace it with a different possessive adjective. Is it still correct?

> **Their** book is there. → **Your** book is there.

there **and** *here*
If the word refers to a place, replace it with another adverb or phrase that refers to a place. Is it still correct?

> Their book is **there**. → Their book is **here**. (on the table)

Always check the words that follow. Do you need to add a <u>verb</u> or is it already there?

> **There** <u>is</u> a book over **there**.
> **Here** <u>are</u> your keys over **here** on the table.

to, too, and ***two***

Check the words after *to*. *To* can come before a verb, a noun, or a pronoun.

> I want **to** go **to** the movies.

If you see the words *much* or *many*, use *too*, not *to* or *two*, before them.

> I can't go to the movies because I have **too** <u>much</u> homework to do.

Replace *too* with *also*. Is it still correct?

> I enjoy going to the movies **too**. → I enjoy going to the movies **also**.

Replace *two* with another number. Is it still correct?

> I have **two** brothers. → I have **three** brothers.

one and ***won***

Replace *one* with another number. Is it still correct?

> I have **one** dollar. → I have **two** dollars.

Replace *won* with *lost*, the past tense of *lose*. Is it still correct?

> I **won** 10 dollars. → I **lost** 10 dollars.

Exercise 1

Circle the correct word in the parentheses to complete each sentence.

1. Are **(they're / their / there)** many books in the library? Yes. **(It's / Its)** great to have a lot of variety when **(you're / your)** doing research for school projects. I sometimes go **(to / too / two)** the library **(to / too / two)** borrow audio books. **(They're / Their / There)** is a pretty good selection of those **(to / too / two)**.

2. Did you **(hear / here)** that loud noise coming from the next room? What do you think they were doing in **(they're / their / there)**? I don't know, but it was certainly loud in **(hear / here)**.

3. Sylvain and I each **(one / won)** a prize at the party. I chose a DVD. Sylvain got a different **(one / won)**.

Exercise 2

Fill in the blanks to correctly complete the sentences. Use words from the box. Not all the words are used.

it's / its	your / you're	they're / their / there	hear / here	to / too / two

1. Please put the keys on the counter over _____.

2. Please turn up the volume. It's _____ quiet. I want to _____ the

   broadcast of the New Year's Eve show _____.

3. Is that Marco's new car? Wow, _____ great!

4. The teacher asked the students to bring _____ books to class.

5. Please come _____. I want to look at _____ ring more closely.

Exercise 3

There are five word choice errors in the following paragraph. Find and correct them.

My friend Vladimir has a big family. Their are five boys and two girls. They live in a house on you're street. Do you want to go by his house to see if he wants to go too play street hockey with us? Its not far from hear.

Speaking Activity 1
Creative Sentences

Work in pairs. Together, on a separate piece of paper, write one sentence for each of the homonyms in the Formation chart on pages 128-129. Then try to write one sentence that includes all homonyms in each group. Compare your sentences with another pair's sentences.

Here is my book.

I **hear** the phone ringing.

Do you **hear** the neighbours talking from in **here**?

Commonly Confused Words
Formation

Form	Meaning and Use	Example Sentences
as	*As* introduces equality. *As* can come before • an adjective • an adverb • a subject and verb There is no / h / sound at the beginning.	It's **as** cold **as** ice. He moves **as** slowly **as** a snail. You take the same bus **as** I take.
has	*Has* is a simple present form of the verb *have*. *Has* comes after a singular noun or a subject pronoun (*he*, *she*, *it*). It has an / h / sound at the beginning.	He **has** the same class schedule as I do.
is	*Is* is a simple present form of the verb *be*. *Is* comes after a singular noun, a subject pronoun (*he*, *she*, *it*), or a question word. There is no / h / sound at the beginning.	Franz **is** my friend. It **is** late. What **is** her address?
his	*His* is the possessive adjective and pronoun for the third-person singular. It has an / h / sound at the beginning.	He trims **his** beard every morning.
he's	*He's* has an apostrophe, so it is the contracted or short form of *he is*. It has an / h / sound at the beginning.	**He's** from Guatemala.

Form	Meaning and Use	Example Sentences
live	*Live* is the verb that means to have life. *Live* has the short / i / sound and comes after a noun or a subject pronoun. *Live* (with a long / i / sound, as in *life*) describes an activity as it is happening.	We **live** in Ottawa. Franklin **lives** with his family. The program is streaming **live** online. It's a **live** broadcast.
life	*Life* is a noun that means the time from birth to death or existence. (*Lives* is the plural form.)	The **life** of a student is often difficult and fun at the same time.
leave	*Leave* is the verb that means to go away from a place. *Leave* comes after a noun or a subject pronoun.	The train **leaves** at 9:15.
where	*Where* is a pronoun that refers to a place.	**Where** do you live?
were	*Were* is a simple past tense form of the verb *be*.	You **were** sad yesterday. We **were** at the college on the weekend. They **were** in the pool all day.
than	We use *than* to compare people and things (see Chapter 7).	I like strawberries more **than** I like apples.
then	*Then* refers to a time in the past, or it introduces the next thing or action in a series.	He was at home **then**. (at that time) I need to finish my work first. **Then** I want to go to the movies.

Tips for Using Commonly Confused Words

as and *has*

Change the person and replace *has* with *have* or another verb. Is it still correct?

He has a twin brother. → **I have** a twin brother.

As compares equals. Is there an adjective or adverb in the middle?

That car is **as old as** the hills.

He moves **as slowly as** a snail.

is, *his*, and *he's*

Change the person and replace *is* with *am* or *are*. Is it still correct?

The dog is in the kitchen. → **The dogs are** in the kitchen.

Replace *his* with a different possessive adjective. Is it still correct?

His car is in the garage. → **My** car is in the garage.

Rewrite the word *he's* as two words. Is it still correct?

He's busy. → **He is** busy.

live, *life*, and *leave*

Change the person to *he, she,* or *it,* and replace *live* with *lives.* Is it still correct?

I live in Ontario. → **He lives** in Ontario.

If *live* doesn't act like a verb, replace it with another adjective. Is it still correct?

We enjoy **live** performances. → We enjoy **beautiful** performances.

Check the words before and after *life*. Is there an article or adjective before *life* or a verb or a phrase after it?

> The **life** of a politician must be very stressful.

> I enjoy my **life**.

Change the person to *he, she,* or *it* and replace *leave* with *leaves*. Is it still correct? Be careful: *leaves* is also the plural of the noun *leaf*.

> I often **leave** for school at 7:00 am. **He** often **leaves** for school at 7:00 AM.

where and *were*
Always check the words that follow. Is the word a pronoun or a verb? Do you need to add a verb or is it already there?

> I don't know **where** it is.

> **Where were** you last night? We **were** at the movies.

than and *then*
Replace the word *than* or *then* with *at that time* or *next*. Is it still correct?

> I have more fun at school **than** at work.
> It's a comparison, so using *at that time* doesn't make sense.

> I knew him **then**. → I knew him **at that time**.

> I work for five hours; **then** I go home. → I work for five hours; **next** I go home.

Exercise 4

Fill in the blanks to correctly complete the sentences. Use words from the box. Not all the words are used.

as / has	is / his / he's	lives / life / leave	where / were	than / then

1. _____ was Jim when the storm started? _____ not answering

   _____ cellphone. I'm beginning to worry about him.

2. My brother _____ three years younger _____ I am. He still

   _____ at home with our parents. He _____ one more year of high

   school to finish; _____ he's going to _____ our town to go to

   university in another city.

Word Pairs

Certain word pairs cause difficulty because we can use them similarly in some cases but not in others.

Warm-Up

Work in pairs. Read the following sentences out loud and focus on the words in **bold**.

1. You were **going home** while I was **going to** work. Now you're **at** home and I'm **at** work.
2. When the teacher walked **into** the room, Jorge was already **in** there.
3. She made the cake **from** scratch. The cake pan is made **of** aluminum.

How are the words in each pair of words different? Is there a difference in their meaning?

Formation

Form	Meaning and Use	Example Sentences
really very	*Really* and *very* are both adverbs that have the same meaning. They both intensify the meaning of the adjective or adverb they come before. However, only *really* can modify a verb and only *very* can modify *much*.	Your friend is **really** nice. Your friend is **very** nice. I **really** like to play basketball. He likes to watch soccer **very** much.
some any	*Some* and *any* introduce non-countable nouns and nouns with indefinite quantities. (We don't know how much or how many things there are.) Use *some* in positive sentences. Use *any* in questions and in negatives.	I have **some** money. He has **some** visitors this weekend. I have **some** money in my wallet. Do you have **any** money? He does**n't** have **any** visitors today.
no not any	*No* and *not any* show the absence or lack of something. In English, there can only be **one negative signal**. For example, you can say "no" or "not any," but you cannot say "not no."	Correct I have **no** energy today. Correct I **don't** have **any** energy today. Incorrect I **don't** have **no** energy today. (There are two negatives in the sentence.)
to	*To* indicates a direction, some movement, and an end location.	Tristan drives **to** Montreal every Friday. (This sentence has movement and a destination.)
at	*At* presents a specific location. With the verb *go*, *to* usually comes before the destination, except with *home*.	Frank is sitting **at** his desk. We are **at** home, and he is **at** school. (This sentence has no movement, but a specific location) I **go to** work on Monday morning. I **go home** after work.
from	*From* gives the origin of someone or something or tells how something was made.	Yuliya is **from** Russia. This sweater is made **from** wool.
of	*Of* gives us information about the original material of a thing.	This purse is made **of** leather. The desk is made **of** wood.
for	*For* indicates a quantity of time.	He lived in Germany **for** three years.
during	*During* indicates the period of time.	**During** that time, he worked at the university in Hamburg.
in	*In* refers to something that is static (not changing place). It means that someone or something is inside a space.	The students are **in** the classroom.
into	*Into* gives the idea of movement or going inside some space.	The doctor came **into** the patient's room. (This sentence has movement.)
on	*On* is also static, and it means that someone or something is on the surface of something else.	The suitcases are **on** the station platform.
onto	*Onto* gives the idea of movement to the top of that surface.	They stepped off the train and **onto** the platform. (This sentence has movement.)

Exercise 5

Fill in the blanks to correctly complete the sentences. Use the words from the box. Use each word only once.

any	during	really	to	very	in	at	from	on	for

1. I studied Spanish _____ two months.

2. Sanda enjoys dancing _____ much.

3. Please put it _____ the kitchen counter.

4. Hank is _____ Winnipeg.

5. I think your glasses are _____ the drawer.

6. I don't have _____ money.

7. We are going _____ the gallery.

8. They didn't know each other _____ that time.

9. I was _____ school today.

10. Maria _____ enjoyed her trip to Australia.

Speaking Activity 2
Concentration Game

Work in small groups. Your teacher will give each group two sets of cards. One set has sentences with a missing word. The other set has the missing words. Shuffle both sets. Arrange the cards of one set face down on the left side of the desk. Place the other cards face down on the right side. Take turns revealing one card from the left group and one card from the right. The object is to match the sentence with its missing word. If there is no match, turn the cards face down again, and try to remember what words were on the cards. If there is a match, set the pair aside. The player in each group with the most matched pairs wins, and the team to finish first also wins.

Listen, Hear, Look, See, Watch

The meanings of the verbs *listen*, *hear*, *look*, *see*, and *watch* can be confusing. In addition, the meanings of the verbs change when there is a preposition after them.

Warm-Up

Work in pairs. Read the following sentences out loud and focus on the words in **bold**.

> When I **listen to** music on the radio, I often **hear** information about the musicians.
>
> When you **look at** a painting, what do you **see**?
>
> When you **are watching** people in the park, what do you **see**?

What do you think the difference in meaning is between the pairs of verbs?

Formation

Form	Meaning and Use	Example Sentences
hear	To *hear* is the ability to perceive sound with your ears. *Hear* is often followed by *about*.	I **hear** children laughing in the park. (physical ability) I **heard** about your promotion. Congratulations! (message received and understood)
listen to	To *listen* is to actively or purposely pay attention to what you hear. *Listen* is always followed by *to* when a noun follows it.	I always **listen to** the radio on my way to work. (actively paying attention) I like to **listen to** music. **Listen!** Do you hear that noise?
see	To *see* is the ability to see with your eyes.	I **see** birds in the trees. (physical ability)
look at	To *look at* is to purposely observe something.	She is **looking at** her watch. (a fixed look)
watch	To *watch* involves purposely seeing and observing action or movement.	We **watched** TV last night. (observing the action)
look for	To *look for* means to search for something that is missing or cannot be seen.	I'm **looking for** my keys. I can't find them.
watch for	We use *watch for* when someone expects something is going to happen.	He is **watching** the clouds **for** signs of a storm.
look out	To *look out* means you are inside looking at a scene outside.	I was **looking out** the window when I saw him.
watch out	Both *watch out* and *look out* mean a warning to be careful.	**Watch out!** (Look out!) There's a car coming.

Exercise 6

(Circle) the correct words in the parentheses to complete each sentence.

1. My family enjoys **(listening to / looking at / watching)** movies in the evening.

2. What are you **(looking / seeing / watching)** at?

3. Did you **(hear / listen to)** someone at the door?

4. John **(was looking for / was looking at / was watching for)** his glasses; they were on his head.

5. Look **(at / for / out)**! The sign says "wet paint."

Bringing It All Together

Speaking Activity 3
Spelling Bee

Work in two teams. Your teacher will read a short sentence and repeat the word you need to spell. A member of Team 1 writes the correct spelling of the word on the board. If the answer is correct, that team scores a point. If not, Team 2 gets a chance to spell it correctly and steal a point. Your teacher will then read another sentence and word for Team 2. The team with the most points wins.

Speaking Activity 4
Scrambled Sentences

Work in teams of three or four. Your teacher will give your group five sets of cards. Each set has all the parts of a sentence. The objective is to put the sentences together in the correct order. The team that finishes first wins.

Reading

Read the passage and answer the questions that follow.

The English Language

Languages **constantly** evolve and change, especially with the <u>influences</u> of other languages. The English language is no exception. Old English had a large vocabulary, but many of the more common words were short one-syllable words like *hard*, *go*, or *get*. However, there were many **considerable** influences on the language as it continued to develop. For example, the names of the days of the week have Norse and Anglo-Saxon beginnings. *Thursday* comes from the name of the Norse god Thor. The Romans and the French had a big influence on the vocabulary and the **structure** of the English language too. Their **major** influence happened during the **periods** in history when England was under their **domination** or under their control. Later, English had its turn to be an influence. In fact, the spread of the English language has its <u>roots</u> in the <u>colonization</u> of the countries <u>conquered</u> by the British Empire.

English continues to <u>expand</u> its influence today. Mandarin Chinese, Spanish, and English are the three most commonly spoken languages in the world. Although English is third, it is becoming a *lingua franca* (a universal or shared language). In fact, today, more people speak English as a second language than as their first language.

The English language also continues to expand. We are constantly creating new words and <u>adopting</u> others from foreign languages. As a result of that inclusive **approach** to vocabulary expansion, there is no <u>accurate</u> count of the number of words currently used in English, but many <u>experts</u> think it's more than one million. With so many words, and in particular so many influences from other languages, it's no wonder that there are some confusing **aspects** of the language structure and uses of words in English.

As you read, pay attention to these vocabulary words in the passage: ***constantly, considerable, structure, major, periods, domination, approach,*** and ***aspects.***

Comprehension

Circle the best answer to the questions.

1. What are three examples of Old English words?

   a) hard, go, major

   b) go, get, hard

   c) turn, go, get

2. Which language does the word *Thursday* come from?

   a) French

   b) Anglo-Saxon

   c) Norse

3. How did the English language spread?

   a) colonization

   b) domination by the Romans

   c) the Internet

4. What is a *lingua franca*?

   a) a second language

   b) a universal language

   c) the most commonly spoken language

5. People continue to create new words, and we take new words from other languages to use as part of the English language.

   a) True

   b) False

6. There are approximately two million words in the English language.

   a) True

   b) False

Analyzing the Reading Passage

Read the passage again. Underline the homonyms and commonly confused words studied in this chapter. Seventeen of them are used at least once.

Discussion

Other languages influenced English vocabulary, and English influenced other languages' vocabularies. Do you think that is the same for other languages? Does your first language contain words from other languages? Is it a good thing that languages adopt new words from other languages?

Listening

Audio 14

Listen to the song. In the song lyrics below, fill in the blanks with the words you hear.

"What a Wonderful World"
by George David Weiss and Robert Thiele

I see trees of green, red roses _____

I _____ them bloom for me and you

And I think to myself what a wonderful world.

I _____ skies of blue and clouds of white

The bright blessed day, the dark sacred night

And I _____ to myself what a wonderful world.

The colors of the rainbow so pretty in the sky

Are _____ on the faces of people going by

I _____ friends shaking hands saying how do you do

They're _____ saying I love you.

I _____ babies crying, I _____ them grow

They'll learn much more _____ I'll never know

And I think to myself what a wonderful world

Yes I think to myself what a wonderful world.

Comprehension

Listen to the song again. Answer the questions.

1. Why do trees, flowers, blue skies, and white clouds make this a wonderful world?

   _____

2. What does it mean that the colours of the rainbow are on the faces of the people?

   _____

3. Why does "friends shaking hands" mean the same thing as "saying I love you"?

   _____

4. Why does watching babies grow make this a wonderful world?

   _____

Discussion

Listen to the song again. What do you think it's about? How does it make you feel?

Writing

Work in small groups. Your teacher will give each group a starting sentence. Each person in the group adds two sentences to create a complete story. Use as many of the homonyms and commonly confused words (in the charts) from this chapter as possible. Share your short stories with the other groups.

Vocabulary

1. The words in the chart are from the Reading activity. Look at how they are used in the passage. Then match each word with its correct definition.

Word	Definition
1. approach (n.) ___	a) quite large; significant
2. aspects (n.) ___	b) the organization or patterns of the many parts of something
3. considerable (adj.) ___	c) important; significant
4. constantly (adv.) ___	d) a considered or thought-out way of doing something or thinking about something
5. domination (n.) ___	e) without stopping or change; continuously
6. major (adj.) ___	f) extended or specific lengths of time
7. periods (n.) ___	g) having control over someone or something; supremacy
8. structure (n.) ___	h) specific parts, characteristics, or features of something

2. The following list of words are in **bold** in the Reading. Beside them are three possible synonyms. Circle the two words or phrases that are the closest in meaning to the vocabulary word. Look at the example to help you.

   approach: way / condition / path

   a) aspects: patterns / characteristics / parts
   b) considerable: extensive / minor / significant
   c) constantly: consistently / continually / steadily
   d) domination: supremacy / control / submission
   e) major: extensive / insignificant / primary
   f) periods: eras / unknown timeframes / durations
   g) structure: pattern / organization / aspect

3. The following vocabulary words have three possible antonyms (opposites) beside them. Circle the two words or phrases that are the most opposite in meaning to the vocabulary word. Look at the example to help you.

   approach: lack of direction / access / departure

   a) aspects: whole / complete / parts
   b) considerable: small / sufficient / insignificant
   c) constantly: steadily / irregularly / variably
   d) domination: strength / inferiority / weakness
   e) major: minor / main / insignificant
   f) periods: unknown durations / months / open timeframes
   g) structure: fixed / disorganization / lack of form

> Look at your answers to question 2 (identifying synonyms) to help you identify antonyms for these words.

Chapter Review

Summary

- People sometimes confuse homonyms because the words sound the same, but we spell and use them differently.
- Commonly confused words, such as *where* and *were*, are words that look or sound similar or are sometimes mispronounced but have different spellings and meanings.
- Certain word pairs, such as *really* and *very,* and *to* and *at*, can be confusing because we can use them in a similar way in some situations but not in others.
- Some verbs, such as *listen, hear, look, see,* and *watch,* have close but different meanings. In addition, the meanings of the verbs change with different prepositions.

Exercise 7

Circle the correct word in parentheses to complete the sentences.

1. I like **(you're / your)** new apartment **(really / very)** much.

2. When I **(look / see / watch)** the first flower bloom **(in / into)** the spring, I feel really happy.

3. First, they went to visit **(they're / their / there)** friends. **(Than / Then)** they went shopping.

4. Carlos's team **(one / won)** the championship game. **(It's / Its)** their first time ever.

5. Didn't you **(hear / listen)** what the teacher said? You weren't **(hearing / listening)** to the teacher, as usual.

Exercise 8

There are five word choice errors in the following paragraph. Find and correct them.

I don't have some idea what to get Suzanne and Zara for there new apartment. I know they very enjoy plants. Do you think buying a nice flowering won for them is a good idea? Their also fond of music. What do you think?

Exercise 9

Circle the letter of the correct word or phrase to complete the sentences.

1. When does your flight _____?
   a) live   b) life   c) leave

2. Mohammad is from Iran. _____ in my English class.
   a) Is   b) He's   c) His

3. Do you know _____ Marie lives?
   a) were   b) we're   c) where

4. We have classes _____ four hours in a row.
   a) during   b) for   c) from

5. Gina _____ a new car.
   a) as   b) has   c) his

Exercise 10

Fill in the blanks to correctly complete the sentences. Use the words from the box. Use each word only once.

looking	of	really	too	watch	in	at	to	hear	here

1. _____ out! That chair is broken.

2. That costs _____ much.

3. The glasses are _____ the kitchen.

4. This dress is made _____ cotton.

5. That blouse is _____ pretty.

6. I like _____ at photos.

7. Put it _____ (in this place).

8. Did you _____ that noise?

9. I went _____ school today.

10. He's _____ home.

REVIEW
Self-Study

Overview

The self-assessments in this unit give you a chance to review and reinforce the grammar points from Part 2 (chapters 5–8).

Check your knowledge and if you find areas that need more attention, go back to the appropriate chapter and review the material.

Exercise 1

Unscramble the following words and make them into sentences or questions.

it / When / happen / did → When did it happen?

1. more / This flower / than / beautiful / that flower / is

   _____.

2. were / Where / this morning / they

   _____?

3. really / I / comedies / love

   _____.

4. the test / well / The students / on / did

   _____.

5. new / you / any / have / Do / ideas

   _____?

6. to / you're / your / Now / going / class

   _____.

7. she / study / for / too / Did / hours / two

   _____?

8. was / Ursula / when / her husband / cooking / came back

   _____.

9. likes / music / Joshua / to / rock / listen to

   _____.

10. class / the / person / Sarah / interesting / in / most / our / is

    _____.

Exercise 2

Change each of the following positive sentences into the negative.

We went to Greece last summer. → We did not (didn't) go to Greece last summer.

1. It rained heavily last night.

   _____

2. I was checking my emails yesterday between seven and eight o'clock.

   _____

3. Our biology project is as good as yours.

   _____

4. Carol won the competition.

   _____

5. The musicians were great.

   _____

Exercise 3

Change the following sentences into Yes/No questions.

I was yawning when she was talking. → Were you yawning when she was talking?

1. They were clapping while others were singing a song.

   _____?

2. Samantha moved to Miami two years ago.

   _____?

3. Mona and Ted had a wedding anniversary party last weekend.

   _____?

4. He was eating an apple when his tooth fell out.

   _____?

5. My parents-in-law were happy to come for a visit last summer.

   _____?

Exercise 4

Change these statements into Wh- questions. The information you want to ask about is in **bold**.

You submitted **the essay** late. → **What** did you submit late?

1. The game tug-of-war became an official event **at the second modern Olympic Games** in 1900.

   _____?

2. In 1945, the first Slinky toys were **one dollar each**.

   _____?

3. In 1969, Neil Armstrong was famous **because he was the first person to set foot on the moon**.

   _____?

4. The first Ford cars had **Dodge** engines.

   _____?

5. George Stanley and John Matheson designed **the flag of Canada** in 1965.

   _____?

Exercise 5

Fill in the blanks with the correct form of the verbs in parentheses. Use the past progressive or simple past. Look at the example to help you.

Sergio: Do you remember that I ____*lost*____ **(lose)** my car keys yesterday morning? I finally

____*found*____ **(find)** them later on that day!

Manuel: Where ____*were*____ **(be)** they?

Sergio: While I ____*was getting*____ **(get)** my jeans ready to wash, they ___*fell*___ **(fall)** out of the pocket.

Amy: What **1** _____ **(happen)** to you yesterday? **2** _____ you

_____ **(forget)** about our project meeting at five o'clock?

Brianna: What? Oh, no! I totally **3** _____ **(forget)**. Sorry.

Amy: But I **4** _____ **(call)** you three times between 5:15 and 6:00. What

5 _____ you _____ **(do)**?

Brianna: I **6** _____ **(be)** tired, so I **7** _____ **(sleep)**. I

8 _____ **(hear,** negative**)** the phone. **9** _____ you **(start)** the

project without me?

Amy: No way! I **10** _____ **(want,** negative**)** to start it all by myself. It's a

team project.

Brianna: You're right. Let's meet tomorrow.

Exercise 6

Circle the letter of the correct word or phrase to complete the sentence.

1. Harvey is always so calm. He's _____ as a cucumber.
   a) cooler   b) as cool   c) the coolest

2. Martina sings _____.
   a) very good   b) very best   c) very well

3. Do you like pizza _____ poutine?
   a) more than   b) the most   c) as more than

4. She is _____ when she is listening to music.
   a) the happiest   b) the most happy   c) the happier

5. Francisco can run _____ Alfredo.
   a) the faster than   b) faster than   c) fast than

Exercise 7

Correct the errors in the following sentences. The errors are <u>underlined</u>.

1. She <u>studyed</u> for the test all weekend long.

2. We were sleeping <u>while</u> the phone rang.

3. He always took time to <u>watch</u> my paintings and to give me feedback.

4. <u>Reds</u> apples are sweeter than green apples.

5. I was <u>waiting Abdul</u> when you called me on my cellphone.

6. Yesterday, I bought <u>too</u> sweaters, not one.

7. Both drivers <u>was</u> speeding.

8. He was dancing with <u>he's</u> girlfriend when he tripped and fell.

9. I don't have <u>no</u> money.

10. When did he <u>live</u> the hotel?

11. The store closed earlier <u>then</u> usual.

12. <u>Were</u> are the kids?

13. I didn't <u>worked</u> at the university in 2019.

14. The weather was <u>badder</u> yesterday than it is today.

15. They <u>bringed</u> many souvenirs from their trip to Nova Scotia.

16. Hiroko is <u>least competitive</u> child in our family.

17. The tongue is <u>the most strong</u> muscle in the human body.

18. <u>Its</u> a very pretty necklace.

19. <u>Their</u> are 20 students in my chemistry class.

20. Vanilla ice cream is as <u>yummier</u> as chocolate ice cream.

Simple Future—
Will and
Be Going To

Overview

In English, there are two main verb formations to express future plans and actions: *will* and *be going to*.

Use	Form	Keywords	Example Sentences
• for spontaneous, voluntary, or probable actions • for predictions	*will* + verb	later on today in the morning / afternoon tomorrow **next** weekend / week / year	I **will study** later. It **will rain** in the morning. We **will invite** them in the afternoon. He **will come** tomorrow. They **will help** us next week.
• for planned future actions • for predictions	*be going to* + verb	**next** summer / vacation / holiday in the future in five years **this** week / year / Sunday soon on May 5 (specific date) in 2022 (specific year) **when** I get home . . . **after** he finishes school . . .	I **am going to work** next summer. You **are going to graduate** in two years. She **is going to study** in Canada this year. It **is going to rain** soon. We **are going to graduate** on June 10. They **are going to call** us when they get there.

Warm-Up

On a separate piece of paper, create a survey chart like the following one. Walk around the classroom. Ask three of your classmates the questions from the chart and record their answers.

Name	Tonight	Next Weekend	After You Graduate
	What are your plans for tonight?	What are your plans for next weekend?	What are your plans after you graduate?

Will

One of the ways to express a future action is with *will*. We use this form for spontaneous, voluntary, or probable actions and predictions.

Warm-Up

At the end of high school, students get a yearbook with photos of students, teachers, and activities that took place during the year. Graduating students often submit a few words of wisdom to go along with their senior portraits. Some students also include their future plans, especially about who they want to be in the future.

Work in pairs. Look at the yearbook photos of the graduating high school students and the descriptions next to each photo. Use the information to form complete sentences about these students' futures.

1	Name: Yoshi Kuma Plans: go to university, move to another country Future profession: a businessperson	
2	Name: Emilia Smith Plans: have lots of kids Future profession: a stay-at-home mom or a kindergarten teacher	
3	Name: Mat Sanders Plans: open an auto-body shop, fix cars Future profession: a car mechanic or a car designer	
4	Name: Hoda Miseri Plans: travel a lot, learn about different cultures Future profession: a journalist	

Formation

Positive	Negative	Yes/No Question	Wh- Question
Subject + Auxiliary + Verb (+ object / complement)	Subject + Auxiliary + Negative + Verb (+ object / complement)	Auxiliary + Subject + Verb (+ object / complement)	Question Word + Auxiliary + Subject + Verb (+ object / complement)
I **will** do it now.	I **will not** do it now.	**Will** you do it now?	**Why** will you do it now?
You **will** get this job.	You **will not** get this job.	**Will** you get this job?	**How** will you get this job?
He **will** get better soon.	He **will not** get better soon.	**Will** he get better soon?	**When** will he get better?
She **will** have the best marks.	She **will not** have the best marks.	**Will** she have the best marks?	**What** marks will she have?
It **will** be sunny tomorrow.	It **will not** be sunny tomorrow.	**Will** it be sunny tomorrow?	**When** will it be sunny?
We **will** keep in touch.	We **will not** keep in touch.	**Will** we keep in touch?	**How** will we keep in touch?
They **will** travel this summer.	They **will not** travel this summer.	**Will** they travel this summer?	**Where** will they travel this summer?

- *Will* is an auxiliary.
- The contracted forms of the subject + *will* are *I'll, you'll, she'll, he'll, we'll,* and *they'll*.
- The negative contracted form of *will + not* is *won't*.

> For a detailed explanation of how to form and use questions and negatives, refer to Chapter 11.

Exercise 1

Fill in the blanks with *will* and the correct form of the verbs in parentheses.

He decided that he _____ **(become)** a computer programmer. →
He decided that he **will become** a computer programmer.

1. Marianna is tired tonight, so she _____ **(do)** homework tomorrow.

2. _____ it _____ **(be)** windy this weekend?

3. They _____ **(stay,** negative**)** for long.

4. We _____ **(miss)** you.

5. _____ you _____ **(call)** me later?

Exercise 2

Change each of the following sentences into a Yes/No question.

They will take the train. → Will they take the train?

1. The plane will depart at noon.

   _____?

2. Theodora will pay her phone bill next week.

   _____?

3. We'll see you tomorrow.

   _____?

4. I will go to bed late.

   _____?

5. Joan's brother will answer that question.

   _____?

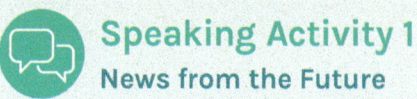

Speaking Activity 1
News from the Future

Work in small groups. Read the following magazine articles from the future. Talk with your classmates about each article, and then below each article, rewrite it together. Change the sentences that have any other verb tenses to sentences that express the future with *will*. Make all other necessary changes. To help you, the possible changes are underlined. The first article is done for you.

First Hotel on the Moon Finally Opens

August 23, 2025—<u>Today</u>, a new chapter in space tourism <u>begins</u>. Rod Markham and his wife-to-be, Susan Millster, <u>arrived</u> safely on the moon to spend five days as the first guests at the Starbright Hotel, which the owners <u>set up</u> for this purpose <u>two years ago</u>. They <u>are not</u> only the first hotel guests on the moon, but they <u>also set</u> a new record for most-expensive accommodation since the price <u>was</u> US$3.7 million per night, per person. However, the price <u>included</u> the exclusive transfer from Earth to the hotel.

Example On August 23, 2025, a new chapter in space tourism **will begin**. Rod Markham and his wife-to-be, Susan Millster, **will arrive** safely on the moon to spend five days as the first guests at the Starbright Hotel, which the owners **will set up** for this purpose **in 2023**. They **will not only be** the first hotel guests on the moon, but they **will also set** a new record for most-expensive accommodation since the price **will be** US$3.7 million per night, per person. However, the price **will include** the exclusive transfer from Earth to the hotel.

1. Icelandic Hydrogen Finally Pushed Gasoline off the Road

    November 19, 2040—<u>Today</u> <u>was</u> a historic day for Iceland when its president at a symbolic ceremony officially <u>shut</u> down the last gasoline pump in the country. Iceland <u>is</u> a model country when it comes to the fuel transition from gasoline to hydrogen, and it <u>became</u> <u>today</u> the first country in the world to complete it.

    _____

    _____

    _____

    _____

    _____

    _____

    _____

2. Do the Anti-Aging Drugs Work?

    March 20, 2035—There <u>was</u> a lot of buzz around the life-extension drugs that <u>hit</u> the market <u>a decade ago</u>. They <u>didn't promise</u> you a life forever, but they <u>gave</u> you a chance to maybe extend your life with an extra 5 to 10 years. But <u>do</u> they <u>work</u>?

    _____

    _____

    _____

    _____

    _____

    _____

    _____

    _____

Adapted from News of the Future, www.newsoffuture.com.

Be Going To

We use the form *be going to* to express a future action that is already planned. We also use this form to make predictions.

Warm-Up

Work in pairs. Look at the following pictures. Use the verbs in the box to finish the sentence beside each picture.

| jump out | rain | fall | snow | be warm |

1. Tonight, it _____
_____
_____

2. Tomorrow _____
_____
_____

3. It was cold this week, but this weekend _____
_____
_____

4. Look out! That glass _____
_____
_____

5. Henry is ready. He _____
_____
_____

Formation

Positive	Negative	Yes/No Question	Wh- Question
Subject + *be* + *going to* + Verb (+ object / complement)	Subject + *be* + Negative + *going to* + Verb (+ object / complement)	*Be* + Subject + *going to* + Verb (+ object / complement)	Question Word + *be* + Subject + *going to* + Verb (+ object / complement)
I **am going to** speak with her.	I **am not going to** speak with her.	**Are** you **going to** speak with her?	**Who** are you going to speak with?
You **are going to** pass this course.	You **are not going to** pass this course.	**Are** you **going to** pass this course?	**How** are you going to pass this course?
He **is going to** be 18 years old next week.	He **is not going** to be 18 years old next week.	**Is** he **going to** be 18 years old next week?	**How old** is he going to be next week?
She **is going to** travel to Asia this summer.	She **is not going to** travel to Asia this summer.	**Is** she **going to** travel to Asia this summer?	**Where** is she going to travel this summer?
It **is going to** snow tomorrow.	It **is not going to** snow tomorrow.	**Is** it **going to** snow tomorrow?	**When** is it going to snow?
We **are going to** buy a new house in two years.	We **are not going to** buy a new house in two years.	**Are** we **going to** buy a new house in two years?	**What** are we going to buy in two years?
They **are going to** leave soon.	They **are not going to** leave soon.	**Are** they **going to** leave soon?	**When** are they going to leave?

Remember: The verb *be* does not need an auxiliary verb in negatives or questions.

Exercise 3

Read each sentence and determine if it expresses a plan or a prediction.

After class, I am going to go home. _plan_____

My husband is going to be well-known one day. _prediction_____

1. I'm hungry. I'm going to make myself a sandwich. _____

2. Stan is very sick today. He is going to stay home tomorrow. _____

3. The sky is grey. It's going to rain. _____

4. Next year, my daughter is going to join the gymnastics team. _____

5. Luke and Carmen are in love. I think they are going to get married. _____

Exercise 4

Fill in the blanks with *be going to* and the correct form of the verbs in parentheses.

Shaun _____ **(watch)** TV tonight. → Shaun **is going to watch** TV tonight.

1. You _____ **(have)** a quiz tomorrow morning.

2. _____we_____ **(do)** a group project this semester?

3. Abdul _____ **(move,** negative) to Canada.

4. _____the course notes_____ **(be)** available online?

5. Tomorrow, I _____ **(write)** a letter to my uncle in Morocco.

💬 Speaking Activity 2
Bingo—Find Someone Who...

Walk around the classroom and ask questions to find someone who is going to do each of the actions in the boxes. Write that person's name in the box. If you get a horizontal, diagonal, or vertical line of four boxes, you get a Bingo and you win.

_____ is going to cook dinner tonight.	_____ is going to do laundry tomorrow.	_____ is going to sleep in on Saturday.	_____ is going to get an A in this class.
_____ is going to go to the park this afternoon.	_____ is going to clean his or her house this weekend.	_____ is going to graduate in a year.	_____ is going to dine at a restaurant tonight.
_____ is going to buy groceries next week.	_____ is going to see a doctor soon.	_____ is going to text his or her friend later.	_____ is going to have coffee after class.
_____ is going to study on Friday night.	_____ is going to travel to another city this month.	_____ is going to go to the movies this week.	_____ is going to have three kids in the future.

Time Markers

After some specific words called **time markers**, we don't use *will* or *be going to* to express the future. Instead, we use the simple present tense to talk about the future.

Warm-Up

Work in pairs. Ask your partner what he or she will do

- after he or she leaves this class
- when he or she gets home
- before he or she goes to sleep tonight

Then tell the whole class about what your partner will do.

Formation

These are some examples of time markers:

when	before	after	as soon as	as long as	unless

After the time markers, use the simple present tense.

Correct	I will pay off my student loan **when** I **graduate**.
Incorrect	I will pay off my student loan **when** I **will graduate**.
Correct	**After** I **find** a job, I will buy a house.
Incorrect	**After** I **will find** a job, I will buy a house.
Correct	**As soon as** I **buy** a house, I will get married.
Incorrect	**As soon as** I **will buy** a house, I will get married.
Correct	I will travel a lot **before** I **have** kids.
Incorrect	I will travel a lot **before** I **will have** kids.
Correct	I will work **as long as** I **enjoy it**.
Incorrect	I will work **as long as** I **will enjoy it**.
Correct	I will retire **unless** I **don't have** enough money.
Incorrect	I will retire **unless** I **won't have** enough money.

Exercise 5

Fill in the blanks with the correct form of the verbs in parentheses.

> I will tell you a secret as long as you _____ (tell, negative) anyone. →
> I will tell you a secret as long as you **don't tell** anyone.

1. Ryan will have driving lessons before he _____ (take) the driving test.

2. We _____ (go, negative) to the park unless it stops raining.

3. I'll lend her some money as long as she _____ (give) it back next week.

4. They will have some coffee after they _____ (eat) dinner.

5. When Liam gets back home, he _____ (call) his friend.

6. We will email you as soon as we _____ (arrive).

7. After Rihna finishes her degree, she _____ (go) on a trip to Pakistan.

8. You won't pass this course unless you _____ (study) hard.

9. She _____ (be) happy when her friends come over tonight.

10. _____ you _____ (help) me when I need you?

Speaking Activity 3
Phone Messages

Audio 15

Comprehension
Listen to the audio, in which three different people leave phone messages for someone. Answer the questions. Work with a partner and check your answers.

Phone message 1
1. Why is Pablo calling Ivan?

   _____

2. When will Pablo call Ivan back?

   _____

Phone message 2

3. When is Mr. Adams's appointment?

_____

4. What will Dr. Yu do when Mr. Adams comes to see her?

_____

Phone message 3

5. Why is Kendra late for her meeting with Sonia?

_____

6. When will Kendra leave work?

_____

Bringing It All Together

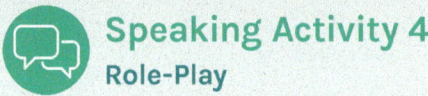

Speaking Activity 4
Role-Play

Work in pairs. Prepare a role-play for each situation. Then perform them in front of the class.

Situation A: You are stuck in traffic. Call your partner to tell him or her that you will be late for dinner.

Situation B: Your friend is moving to a new house this weekend. He or she calls you to ask for help with the move. Make plans.

Situation C: You have a doctor's appointment and can't go to class tomorrow. Call your teacher and explain your situation. Ask for homework and about the possibility to meet with the teacher the following day.

Speaking Activity 5
Dictation

Work in pairs. Your teacher will give each pair some sentences that express the future. Dictate them to your partner. Your partner will write the sentences on a separate sheet of paper. When you and your partner finish, check for mistakes and correct them.

Speaking Activity 6
Agendas and Plans

Work in pairs. Look at the following agendas. On a separate sheet of paper, write sentences to describe what Angela, Erik, and Stephan's plans are. Use *will* and *be going to*.

1. Angela's To-Do List

September 14

10:00	go to doctor's appointment
1:00	attend English class
4:00	meet with Kate for coffee
7:00	after supper, call parents

2. Erik's To-Do List

December 23

8:00	finish packing
10:00	buy last Christmas gifts
2:00	take train to Toronto
6:00	call Pat before train arrives
9:00	go out with Pat and Moe

3. Stephan's To-Do List

June 15

8:00	have breakfast with Mary
11:00	pay bills
2:00–4:00	study for the final math exam
8:00	celebrate the end of the school year

Reading

Read the passage and answer the questions that follow.

As you read, pay attention to these vocabulary words in the passage: *evaluate, financial, investments, establish, proceed,* and *achieve.*

New Year's Resolutions

Often, New Year's Eve makes us reflect on the past year, evaluate our present, and think about the future. As a result, it might also inspire us to do something to change our looks, habits, or future in general. On this day or around this time, a lot of people make New Year's resolutions. Resolutions are like goals. Among some popular ones are to exercise more, to eat healthy food, to be organized, to make better financial investments, to quit bad habits, or for many students, to do better in school.

If you ever want to make a New Year's resolution, you will see that following that resolution will be difficult. One of two things will happen. You will either persist and succeed or you will not keep your resolution and fail. Here are a few tips that can help you follow through on your resolution.

First, to reach your goal, you will need to have strategies. It's good to establish how you are going to do the things you plan to do. To proceed, you will need to write those strategies down. A written plan is going to help you focus on your goal.

Once you have a plan, you will finally take action and commit to what you want to achieve. There will probably be days when you feel like giving up. Therefore, to succeed, you will need a lot of motivation. Also, when you don't feel like continuing, it will be good if you let a few friends know about your resolution. In hard times, they will support you and encourage you to go on.

It will be a challenge for sure, but in the end, you will be happy and proud of yourself.

Comprehension

Answer the questions. Write complete sentences.

1. On New Year's Eve, why do people often decide to change something about themselves?

   _____

2. Find another word for *resolutions.*

   _____

3. Give some examples of New Year's resolutions.

   _____

4. What will you need to do if you want to reach your goal?

   _____

5. What will you need to do next after you have your plan?

   _____

6. Why is it good to let your friends know that you made a resolution?

_____

7. What are the rewards or benefits of accomplishing your resolution?

_____

Analyzing the Reading Passage

Read the passage again and <u>underline</u> all the uses of *will* and *be going to*.

Discussion

Will you ever make a New Year's resolution? If yes, what will it be? If not, why not?

Listening

Audio 16

As you listen, you will hear the words *legal* and *assistant*. In this context, a *legal assistant* refers to a professional who provides administrative support for a lawyer, law firm, or legal department.

What Are Your Goals?

Listen to the audio. You will hear three people each talk about themselves and their aspirations for the future.

Comprehension

1. Fill in the chart based on what you heard.

Questions	Person 1: Makila	Person 2: Renata	Person 3: Hans
1. What will this person do in the next year?			
2. What are this person's goals for the next five years?			
3. How will he or she achieve these goals?			
4. What does he or she say about the future?			

CHAPTER 9 Simple Future–*Will* and *Be Going To*   161

2. Based on your notes from the chart, answer the following True/False questions. (Circle) the correct response.

Makila

T / F   1.   She wants to buy a house.

T / F   2.   She will go on many vacations.

T / F   3.   She is pessimistic about her future.

Renata

T / F   1.   She came to Canada when she was small.

T / F   2.   She is looking for a job as a lawyer.

T / F   3.   She thinks it is difficult to start a second career in a different country.

Hans

T / F   1.   He wants to start working right away.

T / F   2.   He met his spouse when he was travelling.

T / F   3.   In the future, he wants to have a farm.

Writing

Write a short composition (maximum 150 words) about your future goals.

Vocabulary

1. Read the following sentences. The words in **bold** are from the Reading and Listening activities. Use the context to help you understand what the words in bold mean.

   a) Many people have a goal of living a rich lifestyle or retiring early to enjoy life. To **achieve** that goal, they need to have enough savings or make good **investments**.

   b) Use a monthly budget to **establish** what your income and expenses are. Then you will be able to **evaluate** your budget and see how much money you can spend or need to save.

   c) Help your child learn how to manage money: as your **assistant**, your child can help make decisions about spending household money.

   d) If you have too much debt, you will need to seek the **legal** advice of a **financial** advisor. He or she will help you understand how to **proceed** to fix your finances.

2. Look at the following words from the Reading and Listening activities. For each word, there is a list of words with similar meaning. (Circle) the two words closest in meaning to the **bold** word. The first one is done as an example.

   a) **financial**: monetary, budgetary, economic

   b) **achieve**: accomplish, fulfill, begin

   c) **assistant**: painter, helper, aide

   d) **establish**: create, envision, start

   e) **evaluate**: examine, resolve, assess

   f) **investments**: losses, assets, profits

   g) **legal**: judicial, lawful, invalid

   h) **proceed**: go on, stop, continue

3. Now, on a separate piece of paper, write your own sentences using the vocabulary words. Try to use the simple future.

Chapter Review

Summary

- There are two verb formations that we can use to express a future action: *will* and *be going to*.
- Use *will* for spontaneous, voluntary, or probable actions and for predictions.
- Use *be going to* for planned or intended future actions, as well as for predictions.
- After time markers, use the simple present tense and not *will* or *be going to*.

Exercise 6

Circle the letter of the correct word or phrase to complete the sentences.

1. _____ they go to the fair next week?
   a) Are   b) Will   c) Do

2. The tea is still hot. I _____ a few minutes.
   a) will to wait   b) going to wait   c) am going to wait

3. I'll give you a call _____ I get back from work.
   a) until   b) when   c) while

4. We don't have much money, so we probably _____ any souvenirs.
   a) won't buy   b) don't buy   c) willn't buy

5. _____ Ela and Karim going to visit us this summer?
   a) Is   b) Will   c) Are

Exercise 7

Fill in the blanks with *will* and the correct form of the verbs in parentheses.

There _____ **(be)** a lot of people there. → There **will be** a lot of people there.

1. How old _____ he _____ **(be)** next month?

2. We _____ **(have)** dinner tonight at six o'clock.

3. I _____ **(help)** you.

4. They _____ **(travel,** negative**)** to England this summer.

Exercise 8

Fill in the blanks with *be going to* and the correct form of the verbs in parentheses.

I _____ **(go)** to a park this Saturday. → I **am going to go** to a park this Saturday.

1. They _____ (study) in our class next week.

2. The plane _____ (arrive) a little late.

3. _____ you _____ (do) homework tonight?

4. She _____ (work, negative) tomorrow.

Exercise 9

Unscramble the following words and make them into sentences or questions.

be / Cassandra / here / tomorrow / will → Cassandra will be here tomorrow.

1. are / They / not / together / study / going to

   _____.

2. going to / the / eleven / Is / movie / at / start

   _____?

3. this / will / What / summer / do / you

   _____?

4. arrive / call / We / when / in Moscow / will / our parents / we

   _____.

5. winter / go / I / to / not / Calgary / next / will

   _____.

Exercise 10

There are six future tense errors in the following passage. Find and correct them.

Min is a very good student. He is always organized. Next Monday, he had an exam, so he are going to plan his time well. Tomorrow, for example, he wants to spend a few hours on reviewing his course notes. Then, this weekend, he will study on Saturday evening after he will come back from work. He wont go out with his friends as usual. Finally, on Sunday when he will get up, he will study all day long. He will relax only in the evening. He is going watch a movie and go to bed early.

10 Modals

Overview

- Modals are auxiliary (helping) verbs that add another aspect to the action of the main verb. Some modals indicate tense, but that is not their main function.

- *Can* and *could* are used with the main verb to show ability.

- *Have to* and *must* are used with the main verb to show necessity and prohibition (lack of permission).

- *Should* is used with the main verb to show advice.

- *May*, *would*, *could*, and *can* are used with the main verbs to make polite requests and offers.

Warm-Up

Work in pairs. Read the following conversation out loud. Underline the modals with a <u>single line</u> and the verbs that follow them with a <u>double line</u>.

> **Partner A:** Would you like another piece of cake?
>
> **Partner B:** I really shouldn't have another.
>
> **Partner A:** You don't have to go right now, do you?
>
> **Partner B:** Well, I should go soon. I have to be at work at five.
>
> **Partner A:** You can stay a little longer. I can drive you to work.
>
> **Partner B:** Thanks. Then I would like another piece of cake. It's delicious.

What do you think these modals add to the main verbs?

Modals of Ability

Can and *could* are used with the main verb to show ability. *Can* shows present ability, and *could* shows past ability.

Warm-Up

Work in pairs. Read the following two paragraphs. <u>Underline</u> all the verbs.

> When we were younger, we did many more physical activities. I played basketball, and my friend Juan did gymnastics. Now we aren't able to do those activities as well as we did back then. What did you do when you were younger that you don't do now?

> When we were younger, we could do many more physical activities. I could play basketball, and my friend Juan could do gymnastics. Now we can't do those activities as well as we could back then. What could you do when you were younger that you can't do now?

Read the paragraphs again. What is the difference between them? What do the modals *can* and *could* add to the second paragraph? What do you notice about the structure of the sentences with *can* and *could*?

Formation

Can and Could

Positive	Negative	Yes/No Question	Wh- Question
Subject + Modal + Verb (+ object / complement)	**Subject + Modal + Negative + Verb (+ object / complement)**	**Modal + Subject + Verb (+ object / complement)**	**Question Word + Modal + Subject + Verb (+ object / complement)**
I **can** play the guitar.	I **cannot** (**can't**) play the guitar.	**Can** you play the guitar?	**What** can you play?
You **can** do it now.	You **cannot** (**can't**) do it now.	**Can** you do it now?	**When** can you do it?
He **can** sing well.	He **cannot** (**can't**) sing well.	**Can** he sing well?	**How** can he sing?
We **can** drive.	We **cannot** (**can't**) drive.	**Can** we drive?	**What** can we do?
They **can** win the race.	They **cannot** (**can't**) win the race.	**Can** they win the race?	**What** can they win?

I **could** play the guitar.	I **could not** (**couldn't**) play the guitar.	**Could** you play the guitar?	**What** could you play?
You **could** do it then.	You **could not** (**couldn't**) do it then.	**Could** you do it then?	**When** could you do it?
He **could** sing well.	He **could not** (**couldn't**) sing well.	**Could** he sing well?	**How** could he sing?
We **could** drive.	We **could not** (**couldn't**) drive.	**Could** we drive?	**What** could we do?
They **could** win the race.	They **could not** (**couldn't**) win the race.	**Could** they win the race?	**What** could they win?

- There is no need to conjugate the verbs. The form of *can* or *could* stays the same for each person.
- Note that *can* in the full form of the negative is one word—*cannot*. It's the only modal that adds *not* to create one word.

> For a detailed explanation of how to form and use questions and negatives, refer to Chapter 11. Refer to Appendix B for more information on contractions.

Exercise 1

Circle the correct modals in the parentheses to complete the sentences.

1. I really enjoy music. I **(can't / couldn't)** play a musical instrument, but I **(can / could)** sing pretty well.

2. When Frank was a young man, he **(can / could)** play hockey really well. Now that he's in his sixties, he **(can / could)** still skate, but he **(can't / couldn't)** play a full game of hockey. However, he **(can / could)** still play ball hockey with his grandchildren.

3. Samar had perfect vision until she turned 40. She **(can / could)** see things clearly near and far. Now she wears glasses, and she **(can't / couldn't)** see very much without them.

4. In the 1970s, a person **(can / could)** attend college or university for much less money than they can now. People also earned less money then.

5. I am not very good at cooking. How about you? **(Can / Could)** you cook well?

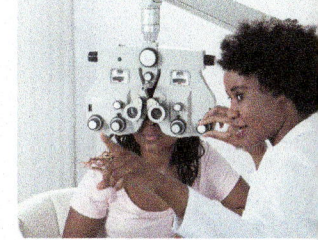

Speaking Activity 1
Q&A

Work in pairs. Ask your partner about his or her present and past abilities or talents. Record the answers on a separate piece of paper. Use *can* or *could*. Look at the following suggestions.

Questions	**Answers**
Can you play a musical instrument?	Dorota can play piano.
Could you do other activities when you were younger?	Dorota could play handball when she was younger.

Modals of Necessity or Prohibition (Lack of Permission)

Have to and *must* are used with the main verbs to show the idea of necessity in positive sentences and lack of necessity or prohibition (lack of permission) to the main verbs in negative sentences.

Warm-Up

Work in pairs. Read the conversation out loud.

Partner A: Didn't you have to go to work today?

Partner B: No, I booked it off because I must finish my sociology project by tomorrow.

Partner A: Do you have to hand it in tomorrow?

Partner B: Yes, first thing in the morning. I mustn't be late or the teacher will take off marks.

Read the conversation again, and <u>underline</u> the modals *have to* and *must*. What do you think they add to the meaning of the sentences? Do you notice anything unique about the structure of *have to*? Review the Modals of Ability section on pages 166–167 for clues.

Formation

Have to

	Positive	Negative	Yes/No Question	Wh- Question
	Subject + *have / has / had to* + Verb (+ object / complement)	Subject + Auxiliary + Negative + *have to* + Verb (+ object / complement)	Auxiliary + Subject + *have to* + Verb (+ object / complement)	Question Word + Auxiliary + Subject + *have to* + Verb (+ object / complement)
Present	I **have to** study tonight.	I **do not (don't) have to** study tonight.	**Do** you **have to** study tonight?	**When** do you have to study?
	You **have to** go there.	You **do not (don't) have to** go there.	**Do** you **have to** go there?	**Where** do you have to go?
	He **has to** practise speaking.	He **does not (doesn't) have to** practise speaking.	**Does** he **have to** practise speaking?	**What** does he have to practice?
	We **have to** work hard.	We **do not (don't) have to** work hard.	**Do** we **have to** work hard?	**How** do we have to work?
	They **have to** win.	They **do not (don't) have to** win.	**Do** they **have to** win?	**What** do they have to do?
Past	You **had to** go home.	You **did not (didn't) have to** go home.	**Did** you **have to** go home?	**Where** did you have to go?

- Adding the word *to* to the verb *have* changes it into a modal of necessity. *Have to* is not a true modal and therefore must follow the structure rules for the verb *have*. There are two forms in the simple present tense: *has* and *have*. You must use *do, does,* and *did* to make negative sentences and questions in the simple present and simple past tenses. It is the only modal that has two forms.
- The modal *have to* can express both present (*has to/have to*) and past necessity (*had to*).

Must

Positive	Negative	Yes/No Question	Wh- Question
Subject + Modal + Verb (+ object / complement)	Subject + Modal + Negative + Verb (+ object / complement)	Modal + Subject + Verb (+ object / complement)	Question Word + Modal + Subject + Verb (+ object / complement)
I **must** drive slowly.	I **must not (mustn't)** drive slowly.	**Must** you drive slowly?	**How** must you drive?
You **must** do it at home.	You **must not (mustn't)** do it at home.	**Must** you do it at home?	**Where** must you do it?
He **must** sing.	He **must not (mustn't)** sing.	**Must** he sing?	**What** must he do?
They **must** talk to the teacher.	They **must not (mustn't)** talk to the teacher.	**Must** they talk to the teacher?	**Who** must they talk to?

- The modal *must* expresses present necessity in positive sentences; *must* is a stronger, more formal way to express *have to*.
- *Must not* expresses prohibition (lack of permission) in negative sentences.
- *Must* does not have a past tense form. Use *had to* for past necessity.

Exercise 2

What ideas do *have to* and *must* add to the following sentences? Write *necessity*, *lack of necessity*, or *prohibition (lack of permission)* in the space provided.

She **has to** have surgery. ___necessity___

I do **not have to** cook today. ___lack of necessity___

Bonnie **must not** drive because she doesn't have a licence. ___prohibition___

1. I have to leave by 6:00. _____

2. You must not take things that don't belong to you. _____

3. I didn't have to take that course last semester. _____

4. You must arrive at the airport an hour before your flight. _____

5. He doesn't have to work tomorrow. _____

Exercise 3

Fill in the blanks with the correct form of *have to* or *must*.

When I lived at home, I _____ **had to** _____ do some chores on Saturdays.

1. Sami _____ (**negative**) leave so early. He has the day off tomorrow.

2. _____ you _____ do as much homework when you took this course last year?

3. You _____ (**negative**) drink alcohol and drive. It's against the law.

4. Philippe _____ finish his assignment by Thursday.

5. We _____ (**negative**) go to school tomorrow. It's a holiday.

Speaking Activity 2
To Do or Not to Do

Work in pairs. Make a list of actions that are necessary, that are not necessary, and that are prohibited. Use *have to*, *must*, *don't have to*, and *must not* in complete sentences. Compare your lists and sentences with those of other pairs. An example of each type of action follows.

Necessary	I have to do a load of laundry. I don't have any clean clothes to wear.
Not necessary	I don't have to withdraw any money. I have enough cash in my wallet.
Prohibited	You mustn't park here. It's a fire route.

Modals of Advice

The modal *should* is used with the main verb to give advice.

Warm-Up

Work in pairs. Read the conversation out loud.

Partner A: Why are you limping?

Partner B: I twisted my ankle playing soccer. It's my own fault. I was wearing sandals. I shouldn't wear sandals to play a sport like soccer, I know.

Partner A: You're right. You should wear running shoes or soccer shoes to play soccer. I think you should go to the doctor's office or the emergency room. It looks like you should get an X-ray.

Read the conversation again and <u>underline</u> *should* and *shouldn't*. What idea do you think *should* and *shouldn't* add to these sentences?

Formation

Should

There is only one form of *should*; it stays the same for each person.

Positive	Negative	Yes/No Question	Wh- Question
Subject + Modal + Verb (+ object / complement)	**Subject + Modal + Negative + Verb (+ object / complement)**	**Modal + Subject + Verb (+ object / complement)**	**Question Word + Modal + Subject + Verb (+ object / complement)**
I **should** leave by 10:00.	I **should not** (**shouldn't**) leave by 10:00.	**Should** you leave by 10:00?	**When** should you leave?
You **should** do it.	You **should not** (**shouldn't**) do it.	**Should** you do it?	**What** should you do?
He **should** lose weight.	He **should not** (**shouldn't**) lose weight.	**Should** he lose weight?	**Why** should he lose weight?
We **should** study for two hours.	We **should not** (**shouldn't**) study for two hours.	**Should** we study for two hours?	**How long** should we study?
They **should** go to the party.	They **should not** (**shouldn't**) go to the party.	**Should** they go to the party?	**Where** should they go?

Exercise 4

Unscramble the following words and make them into sentences or questions.

our friends / visit / on the weekend / should / We → We should visit our friends on the weekend.

1. if / should / home / are / You / stay / you / sick

   _____.

2. on / we / to / Saturday / Should / the / go / library

   _____?

3. stop / doctor / I / smoking / My / said / should

_____.

4. stay / or / I / I / go / Should / should

_____?

5. really / for / They / study / the / should / test

_____.

Speaking Activity 3
Dear Know-It-All

Many newspapers have advice columns. Work in small groups. Look at the example below. First, work by yourself and write a short letter to the Dear Know-It-All column, asking for advice about a problem. It can be funny or serious. Exchange letters with your group members. Write a response to the letter, giving your advice about how to solve the problem. Use *should*.

Dear Know-It-All,

My friend thinks it's okay to talk on his phone at the movies. He doesn't seem to understand when people around him get angry. How should I explain it to him?

Help.

Modals for Polite Requests, Permission, Offers, and Desire

Warm-Up

1. Work in pairs. Read the conversation below out loud.

Partner A: May I help you?

Partner B: Yes. I'm looking for a pair of winter boots, size 8.

Partner A: We have a good selection over here, and these are on sale this week.

Partner B: Could I try on this pair?

Partner A: Certainly.

Partner B: They're perfect. I'll take them. Can I pay by debit?

Partner A: Sure. Would you like your receipt in the bag?

Partner B: Yes. Thanks.

2. <u>Underline</u> the modals in the conversation.

Formation

These modals indicate different levels of formality, especially in polite requests.

may	most polite or formal
would	↑
could	↑
will	↑
can	most informal

There is only one form for each of *may*, *would*, *could*, and *can*. These modals stay the same for each person. However, they are mainly used with *I*, *we*, and *you* for polite requests and permission.

Modal	Use	Polite Requests	Permission
may	asking permission (formal)	May I leave?	Yes, you may leave.
		May I help you?	Yes, you may help me.
would	making polite requests (formal)	Would you help me move the table?	
		Would you pass the salt please?	
could	making polite requests (less formal)	Could you help me?	
		Could you tell me the time?	
can	asking permission (informal)	Can I use that?	Yes, you can use that.
		Can I have another piece?	Yes, you can have another piece.
		Offers	**Desire**
would like	expressing offers or desires	Would you like another cup of coffee?	Yes, I would like another cup of coffee.
		Would you like to go to the movies?	Yes, I would like to go to the movies.

- Never use *may you* in a question.
- Polite requests are made in question form.
- You can ask for permission in a question or express it in a statement form.
- *Would* used alone expresses polite requests.
- *Would* used with *like* + a noun or *like to* + a verb expresses offers or desire.

Exercise 5

Ⓒircle the correct modals in the parentheses to complete the sentences.

1. Good afternoon. **(May / Would)** I help you?

2. **(Could / May / Would)** you like to make an appointment to see the doctor?

3. **(Could / May)** you close the window?

4. I **(could / may / would)** like to buy a ticket to Toronto.

5. **(May / Would)** we leave early? We have an appointment.

Exercise 6

Change each of the following impolite statements or questions into a polite request, an expression of polite desire, or an offer. There is often more than one way to express it.

Do you want some help? → **May I help you?** *or* **Would you like some help?**

1. Give me the salt.

   _____

2. Do you want some juice?

   _____

3. Give me your notebook.

   _____

4. I want to use your washroom.

   _____

5. What do you want?

   _____

Speaking Activity 4
Role-Play

Work in pairs. Prepare short role-plays for the following situations. Use the polite request formations. Take turns asking and answering the questions. Then perform them in front of the class.
- Ask your partner to give you directions to the library.
- Ask your partner to help you with your homework assignment.
- Ask your partner if he or she needs help with the homework.
- Ask your partner to join you for lunch.
- Ask your partner to help you do something outside of the classroom.
- Ask your partner if he or she would help organize a party for the class.

Bringing It All Together

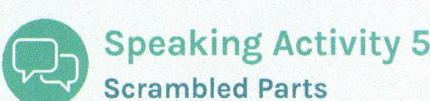

Speaking Activity 5
Scrambled Parts

Work in teams. Your teacher will give each team five sets of cards. Each set has all the parts of a sentence on separate cards. Put the parts of each sentence together in the correct order. The team that finishes first wins.

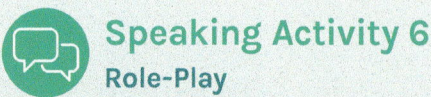

Speaking Activity 6
Role-Play

Work in pairs. Prepare short role-plays for these situations. Then perform them for the class.

Situation A

Partner A: You are a doctor. Your patient has diabetes. Give the patient some advice about diet and exercise and ask him or her to make an appointment with the dietitian.

Partner B: You are a patient. Your doctor just told you that you have diabetes. You love fast food and sweet desserts, and you don't get much exercise.

Situation B

Partner A: You took a trip to Europe (or somewhere else) last summer. Your friend (Partner B) is going there this summer. Give your partner advice about where to go, where to stay while there, and so on.

Partner B: You're planning a trip to Europe (or somewhere else) this summer. Your friend (Partner A) went there last summer. Ask your friend for some information and advice.

Reading

Read the passage and answer the questions that follow.

Working and Studying

As you read, pay attention to these vocabulary words in the passage: *income*, *coordinate*, *restricts*, *individuals*, *sector*, and *acquire*.

Studying at college or university in Canada can be <u>expensive</u>. Most students look for full-time jobs during the summer months and use their <u>savings</u> from that **income** to pay some of the cost of continuing their education. However, more and more students feel they have to work at part-time jobs during the school year so that they can support themselves while they are studying. Four <u>decades</u> ago, only one in four post-secondary students worked part-time from September to May. Now, more than 50 percent of full-time students work part-time during the school year.

According to Statistics Canada, Canadian students work an average of 16 hours a week and earn around $6,000 during the academic year. Also, 96 percent of those students work in the <u>service industry</u>. Their jobs include work in restaurants, retail stores, and grocery stores. Because students have to **coordinate** their school and work schedules, these are the kinds of jobs that can <u>accommodate</u> them. Students are usually only available to work evenings and weekends, and that **restricts** their employment options. The fact that **individuals** don't have to have a lot of experience is another reason for the large number of students working in the service **sector**.

Although many of the part-time jobs that students have seem to be <u>unrelated</u> to their studies, there are some benefits. Students can earn money while they are studying. They can also <u>gain</u> some valuable experience and **acquire** skills that will help them prepare for the careers they would like to begin when they graduate.

Adapted from Audrey, Sam. "Students Working More, Studying Less?"; Marshall, Katherine. "Employment Patterns of Postsecondary Students," https://www150.statcan.gc.ca/n1/pub/75-001-x/2010109/article/11341-eng.htm; Ouellette, Sylvie. "Study: How Students Fund Their Postsecondary Education," https://www150.statcan.gc.ca/n1/en/catalogue/81-595-M2006042.

Comprehension

Answer the questions. Write complete sentences.

1. What do most students use to pay for some of their education?

_____

2. Do many students think they need to work part-time during the school year? Why?

_____

3. How many students worked part-time during the school year 40 years ago?

_____

4. What kinds of part-time jobs do the majority of students have?

_____

5. Give two reasons why so many students work in the service industry.

_____

6. What are two benefits of having a part-time job while you are studying?

_____

Analyzing the Reading Passage

Read the passage again and <u>underline</u> the modals.

Discussion

Do you think students should work part-time while they are studying full-time? Explain your answer.

Listening

Audio 17

Interview with a College Counsellor

Listen to the audio. Then match the following questions and answers.

Comprehension

Match each numbered question with the correct lettered answer.

1. Who is David Williams?	a)	money
2. What do students have to balance?	b)	school results and health
3. What do students worry about?	c)	organize their time
4. What can being too stressed affect?	d)	to relax
5. What is the first thing a student should look for?	e)	studying and working
6. What does a regular work schedule help students to do?	f)	a college counsellor
7. How should students treat their studies?	g)	other ways to pay for school
8. What should students make time for?	h)	like a job

As you listen, pay attention to the vocabulary words **affect** and **shift** and the context in which they are used.

Writing

Write a short composition (maximum 150 words) about your opinion on full-time students working at part-time jobs. Use the modals studied in this chapter.

Vocabulary

1. The words in the following box are from the Reading and Listening activities. Choose the best words from the box to replace the underlined words in the following sentences. If necessary, use a dictionary or the glossary to help you.

    | acquire | affect | coordinate | income | individuals | restricts | sector | shift |

    a) Mehul often has to be available to work at a different period of time during the day for his job in the medical industry. He doesn't like shift work because it can have an impact on his home life. He and his partner have to organize and match their schedules to complete their everyday activities and make time for each other and their children.
    b) People who do volunteer work can obtain new skills and experience.
    c) Having a low salary, as most students do, limits your lifestyle choices in areas such as housing and social activities.

2. Use a dictionary to find other forms of the vocabulary words to complete the chart.

Noun	Verb	Adjective	Adverb
	acquire		
	affect		
	coordinate		
income			
individuals			
	restrict		
sector			
shift			

3. Fill in the blanks with the vocabulary words in the box in question 1.

    1_____ who work in the manufacturing 2_____ often have to be prepared to change their work 3_____ to meet the needs of their employer. Some find it a great way to 4_____ the 5_____ they want so they can afford the things they would like to have, and they find it is easy to 6_____ their activities with family and friends outside of work hours. However, other people find that working evenings or nights can 7_____ their sleep patterns and their mood, and they feel that shift work 8_____ their family and social life.

Summary

- Modals are auxiliary (helping) verbs that add another aspect to the action of the main verb.
- *Can* is used with the main verb to show present ability, and *could* shows past ability.
- *Have to* and *must* are used with main verbs to show necessity or prohibition (lack of permission). *Have to* is the only modal that has more than one form—*has to, have to* (in the present), or *had to* (in the past).
- *Should* is used with the main verb to show advice.
- *May, would, could,* and *can,* used with the main verb, express polite requests and offers. They are used mainly in a question form. You can use *may* for permission in both statement and question forms.
- *Would like* expresses an offer or desire.

Exercise 7

Which concepts do the modals add to the following sentences? Write *ability, advice, polite request, offer, desire, necessity, lack of necessity,* or *lack of permission* in the space provided.

Would you like to come for a visit?   _____ offer _____

1. We have to do our homework.   _____

2. May I help you look for something?   _____

3. You should come to the picnic. We'll have fun.   _____

4. You mustn't eat in the computer lab.   _____

5. Jorge would like to learn to play the guitar.   _____

6. I don't have to do it, but I want to.   _____

7. He couldn't fix his car by himself.   _____

8. You should ask someone to help you.   _____

9. Could you tell me how to do it?   _____

10. Your friend can speak Spanish very well. _____

Exercise 8

Rewrite the following sentences. Use modals to replace the words in **bold.**

It's necessary for you to pay your bills on time. →

You must pay your bills on time. *or* **You have to** pay your bills on time.

1. **It would be a good idea for us to** study together.

    _____

2. Xavier **has the ability to** play the trumpet quite well.

_____

3. **Do you want** some pizza?

_____

4. **It's against the law for you to** drive a car without a licence.

_____

5. **It's not necessary for Guillermo to** work tomorrow.

_____

Exercise 9

Rewrite the following passage. Replace the words in **bold** with *should* or *have to*. Add *you* when necessary.

Before you change a light fixture, you **need to** shut off the power supply. **It's a good idea to** check that you have all of the necessary tools ready. First, you **need to** disconnect the old fixture. **It's really important to** keep all of the wires from touching each other. **The next step is to** connect the wires of the new fixture to the correct wires. **It's important to** make sure the connections are tight. Then you **need to** attach the fixture to the ceiling or wall. Finally, you **need to** turn on the power supply and try out the new light.

_____

_____

_____

_____

_____

_____

_____

Exercise 10

There are five modal errors in the following paragraph. Find and correct them.

When you are applying for a job, you should to do some research about the company and the kinds of positions that are available. You has to revise your resumé and cover letter to reflect the needs of the position you would like to get. In addition, your resumé and cover letter must'nt have any errors. If you get an interview, you must also prepare for that. You should practise answering the kinds of questions the employer will ask. You don't have memorize your answers, but you should feel comfortable with them. You should always to dress appropriately and be confident.

Exercise 11

Fill in the blanks to correctly complete the sentences. Use the modals from the box. Use each modal only once.

can	can't	should	shouldn't	has to	didn't have to	would

A: Hey, Charles! _____ you like to go to the concert tonight?

B: Sure, but what about Amanda? Weren't you planning to go to the concert together?

A: She _____ make it. She caught the flu and _____ stay in bed.

B: That's too bad. _____ you stay home with her?

A: I offered, but she said I _____ stay.

B: How much was the ticket?

A: I'm not sure. Amanda gave them to me for my birthday.

B: Okay, then I _____ go to the bank, so I _____ buy the drinks at the concert.

11 Questions, Negatives, and Short Answers

Overview

- To communicate with others, you need to be able to ask and answer questions of all types: positive and negative, spoken and written.

- This chapter reviews question and negative formation and introduces short answers for all the verb tenses and modals learned in this level.

- In Yes/No and Wh- question formation, the auxiliary verb, the modal, or *be* comes before the subject. If the main verb in the statement form is only one word, you need to use an auxiliary verb, except for the main verb *be*.

- In negative sentence formation, *not* goes after the auxiliary verb, the modal, or *be*. If the main verb in the positive sentence is only one word, you need to use an auxiliary verb. The main verb *be* is the exception; never use the auxiliary *do* with *be*.

- In short answers, use the first word of the verb in the question—the auxiliary, the modal, or *be*—to create the short answer:

Yes + subject + auxiliary / modal / *be*

No + subject + auxiliary / modal / *be* + *not*

Warm-Up

Work in pairs. Read the following conversation out loud.

Partner A: Hi. How was your trip to Mexico?
Partner B: It was great.
Partner A: When did you get back?
Partner B: We didn't get back until late last night. Our flight was delayed for 18 hours.
Partner A: Was it delayed because of the storms?
Partner B: Yes, it was. But Mexico was fantastic!
Partner A: Do you have time to get a coffee and to tell me about it?
Partner B: I don't right now. I have to get to class. Don't you have a class now too?
Partner A: Oh, yes, I do. Would you like to get together later?
Partner B: Yes, I would. Where do you want to meet?
Partner A: At the coffee shop near your place.
Partner B: Great idea! I'll see you there around five.

Write the questions and sentences from the conversation under the correct headings in the chart below. Note: Do not include the following word groups in the chart: "Hi," "At the coffee shop near your place," and "Great idea!".

Yes/No Questions	1. _____
	2. _____
	3. _____
	4. _____
Wh- Questions	1. _____
	2. _____
	3. _____
Positive Sentences	1. _____
	2. _____
	3. _____
	4. _____
	5. _____
Negative Sentences	1. _____
	2. _____
Short Answers	1. _____
	2. _____
	3. _____

Do you recognize any patterns? What do you notice about the short answers?

Questions with Simple Tenses

Warm-Up

Work in pairs. Read this set of questions from one side of a telephone conversation:

a) Did Oleg call you last night?

b) Was he at work at the time?

c) Does he want to buy your TV?

d) Is it still for sale?

e) Will he call you tomorrow?

f) Are you going to need any help?

<u>Underline</u> the first word of the verb and the main verb in each question. What pattern do you notice?

Formation

Questions in the Simple Present and Simple Past—All Verbs except *Be*

Review the formation chart for simple present in Chapter 3 and the chart for simple past in Chapter 5.

	Positive	Yes/No Question	Wh- Question
	Subject + Verb (+ object / complement)	**Auxiliary + Subject + Verb (+ object / complement)**	**Question Word + Auxiliary + Subject + Verb (+ object / complement)**
Simple Present	I **like** music.	**Do** you **like** music?	**What** do you like?
	You **want** to study.	**Do** you **want** to study?	**What** do you want to do?
	Guy **enjoys** reading to relax.	**Does** Guy **enjoy** reading to relax?	**Why** does Guy enjoy reading?
	It **has** two bedrooms.	**Does** it **have** two bedrooms?	**How many** bedrooms does it have?
	We **do** the dishes together.	**Do** you **do** the dishes together?	**How** do you do the dishes?
	They **work** in the evening.	**Do** they **work** in the evening?	**When** do they work?
Simple Past	You **stayed** until 3:00.	**Did** you **stay** until 3:00?	**How long** did you stay?
	He **ate** at 7:00.	**Did** he **eat** at 7:00?	**When** did he eat?
	We **went** to the movies.	**Did** you **go** to the movies?	**Who** went to the movies?
	They **did** their homework.	**Did** they **do** their homework?	**What** did they do?

- There are two forms of the verb *do* in the simple present: *do* and *does*. *Does* is only for the third-person singular—*he, she,* or *it*.
- *Did* is the only form of the verb *do* for all persons in the simple past.
- In questions, use the auxiliary *do* or *does* in the present and *did* in the past and the base form of the main verb.
- In questions, the *-s* for the third-person singular in the present is only on the auxiliary, not on the main verb. There is no *-ed* on the main verb in the past.

Questions in the Simple Present and Simple Past—*Be*

In Yes/No question formation, *be* comes before the subject.

	Positive	Yes/No Question	Wh- Question
	Subject + Verb + Complement	**Verb + Subject + Complement**	**Question Word + Verb + Subject (+ complement)**
Simple Present	I **am** sad.	**Are** you sad?	**Why** are you sad?
	You **are** 20.	**Are** you 20?	**How old** are you?
	It **is** very cold.	**Is** it very cold?	**How** is it?
Simple Past	I **was** sick yesterday.	**Were** you sick yesterday?	**When** were you sick?
	You **were** at home.	**Were** you at home?	**Where** were you?
	He **was** here.	**Was** he here?	**Who** was here?

- *Be* has three forms in the simple present (*am*, *is*, and *are*).
- *Be* has two forms in the simple past (*was* and *were*).
- *Be* always changes its position with the subject to form questions. Never use the auxiliary *do, does,* or *did* with the verb *be*.

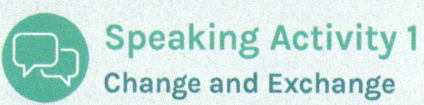

Speaking Activity 1
Change and Exchange

Work in pairs. Your teacher will dictate 10 positive sentences using the simple present and the simple past. Each of you will write them on a separate sheet of paper. Compare your sentences with your partner's. Correct any errors. Next, rewrite the positive sentences as Yes/No questions. Compare and revise the questions. Raise your hand as soon as you finish. The first pair to finish with the correct sentences wins.

Questions with Progressive Tenses

Formation

Questions in the Present Progressive and Past Progressive

Review the formation chart for the present progressive in Chapter 4 (page 60) and the chart for the past progressive in Chapter 6 (page 95).

	Positive	Yes/No Question	Wh- Question
	Subject + *be* + Verb *-ing* (+ object / complement)	***be* + Subject + Verb *-ing* (+ object / complement)**	**Question Word + *be* + Subject + Verb *-ing* (+ object / complement)**
Present Progressive	I **am reading** a book.	**Are** you **reading** a book?	**What** are you reading?
	It **is wagging** its tail.	**Is** it **wagging** its tail?	**What** is it doing?
	We **are going** to work.	**Are** you **going** to work?	**Where** are you going?
Past Progressive	I **was dancing**.	**Were** you **dancing**?	**What** were you doing?
	She **was talking** to her friends.	**Was** she **talking** to her friends?	**Who** was she talking to?
	They **were doing** their homework last night.	**Were** they **doing** their homework last night?	**When** were they doing their homework?

- We form the progressive tenses with the verb *be*, so they have to follow the rules for *be*.
- *Be* always changes its position with the subject to form questions. Never use the auxiliary forms *do, does,* or *did* with the verb *be*.

Speaking Activity 2
What Do You See?

Work in pairs. Look at the picture here. First, write five Yes/No questions about what **is happening** in the picture. Use the present progressive. Second, pretend the actions in the picture happened two weeks ago. Write five Yes/No questions about what **was happening**. Use the past progressive. Try to use different actions. Compare your questions with another pair's questions.

Questions with Future Tenses

Review the formation charts for *will* and *be going to* in Chapter 9 (pages 151 and 154).

Formation

	Positive	Yes/No Question	Wh- Question
	Subject + Auxiliary + Verb (+ object / complement)	Auxiliary + Subject + Verb (+ object / complement)	Question Word + Auxiliary + Subject + Verb (+ object / complement)
will	You **will** need some money.	**Will** you need some money?	**What** will you need?
	He **will** stay.	**Will** he stay?	**What** will he do?
	They **will** be tired.	**Will** they be tired?	**Why** will they be tired?
be going to	I **am going to** go.	**Are** you **going to** go?	**What** are you going to do?
	It **is going to** be okay.	**Is** it **going to** be okay?	**How** is it going to be?
	We **are going to** meet them there.	**Are** we **going to** meet them there?	**Where** are we going to meet them?

- Questions with *will*: There are two words in the verb (*will* + verb base form), so to form questions, the auxiliary *will* changes its position with the subject.
- Questions with *be going to*: To form questions, *be* always changes its position with the subject.
- Never use the auxiliary *do, does,* or *did* with *will* or *be*.

Speaking Activity 3
Fortune Teller

A fortune teller is someone who claims to be able to tell what's going to happen in another person's future.

Work in pairs. Take turns playing the role of a fortune teller. Ask the fortune teller questions about your future. The fortune teller must answer, telling you about your future. Use the future tense with *will* and *be going to*. Then switch roles. Have fun!

Questions Using Modals

Review the formation charts for modals in Chapter 10 (pages 166–167, 168, 170, and 172).

Formation

Positive	Yes/No Question	Wh- Question
Subject + Modal + Verb (+ object / complement)	**Modal + Subject + Verb (+ object / complement)**	**Question Word + Modal + Subject + Verb (+ object / complement)**
I **can** swim.	**Can** you swim?	**What** can you do?
You **could** run faster 10 years ago.	**Could** you run faster 10 years ago?	**How** could you run 10 years ago?
He **should** try to relax.	**Should** he try to relax?	**What** should he try to do?
She **may** leave at 10:00.	**May** she leave at 10:00?	**When** may she leave?
It **would** be nice to join them.	**Would** it be nice to join them?	**What** would it be nice to do?
We **would** like to help.	**Would** you like to help?	**What** would you like to do?
They **must** go to the store.	**Must** they go to the store?	**Where** must they go?
You **have to** make dinner.	**Do** you **have to** make dinner?	**What** do you have to make?
He **has to** fix the car.	**Does** he **have to** fix the car?	**Who** has to fix the car?

- All the modals except *have to* have only one form for all persons.
- Because there are two words in the verb structure (modal + verb base form), the modal changes its position with the subject to form questions; the exception is *have to*.
- Never use the auxiliary *do* with modal verbs except with the modal *have to*.
- *Have to* must follow the structure rules for the verb *have*. There are two forms in the present tense: *has* and *have*.
- Use *do* or *does* to make questions with *have to* in the simple present and *did* in simple past.

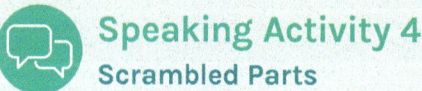

Speaking Activity 4
Scrambled Parts

Work in teams. Your teacher will give each team six sets of cards. Each set has all the parts of a Yes/No question using modals. Put the parts of each question together in the correct order. The team that finishes first wins.

Exercise 1

Change each of the following sentences into a Yes/No question.

We **took** the bus to Toronto. → **Did** you **take** the bus to Toronto?

He **can speak** English well. → **Can** he **speak** English well?

1. Marianna was baking a cake for the party.

   _____?

2. They went to the market first thing in the morning.

_____?

3. We have to study for our test tonight.

_____?

4. Pietra is going to meet us at the movie theatre.

_____?

5. I should tell him about the advertisement I saw in the paper.

_____?

6. Those students are in my biology class.

_____?

7. His friend could play the trombone really well when he was in college.

_____?

8. She drives to school every day.

_____?

9. We will catch the train at 8:00.

_____?

10. Mr. Dubec taught English in Japan.

_____?

Wh- Questions

In Wh- questions, the question word (*where*, *what*, *when*, etc.) asks about a specific part of the sentence. The question formation is the **question word + auxiliary / modal / *be* + subject + verb**, except when the question word replaces the subject.

Warm-Up

Work in pairs. Read the following questions and answers.

Where is the book?	The book is on the table.
What is on the table?	The book is on the table.
When will Jan arrive home?	Jan will arrive home at 7:00.
Who will arrive home at 7:00?	Jan will arrive home at 7:00.
How many books do you have?	I have three books.

Circle the words in the answers that the question words ask for. Read the questions again. Underline the main verbs and any auxiliary verbs in the questions. What pattern do you notice in the order of the subjects and verbs? What is different about the second and fourth question?

Formation

Question words ask about a specific piece of information in a sentence.

Question Word	Use to Ask About	Example Sentences	
		Positive Sentence	**Wh- Question**
what	animals, things, or actions	Ian bought **a puppy**.	**What** did Ian buy?
		I have **a new car**.	**What** do you have?
		Mariko **is studying**.	**What** is Mariko doing?
who	people	He should see **a doctor**.	**Who** should he see?
when	time	The train leaves **at 6:00**.	**When** does the train leave?
where	place	We have to go **to class**.	**Where** do we have to go?
why	reason	She went home **to study**.	**Why** did she go home?
		Carlos is going to stay home **because he is sick**.	**Why** is Carlos going to stay home?
how	manner, state (health)	It was **cold** last night.	**How** was it last night?
how many	quantity with countable nouns	There were **four** books.	**How many** books were there?
how much	quantity with non-countable nouns	You have **enough** money.	**How much** money do you have?
how far	distance	We are **10 kilometres** from home.	**How far** are we from home?
how long	duration of time	The students will have **20 minutes** to finish the test.	**How long** will the students have to finish the test?

Questions about the Verb or Action

What asks about actions.

Positive Sentence	Wh- Question
Amy **is driving**.	What **is** Amy **doing**?
Frank **works** every Saturday.	What **does** Frank **do** every Saturday?
I **visited** my grandparents during the holidays.	What **did** you **do** during the holidays?
Sheena **will graduate** in June.	What **will** Sheena **do** in June?

After the question word, use the usual question word order—**question word + auxiliary / modal / be + subject + verb**—but replace the main verb with the verb *do*.

Do must be in the same tense as the verb it is replacing.

Questions about the Subject

Who or *What* asks about the subject of the sentence.

Positive Sentence	Wh- Question
Raj was washing his car.	**Who** was washing his car?
Anna likes chocolate.	**Who** likes chocolate?
Lightning hit the tree.	**What** hit the tree?
The book is on the table.	**What** is on the table?

When the question words *who* or *what* ask about the subject of the sentence, the question word replaces the subject, and the rest of the sentence (the verb and object/complement) stays in the same order (question word + verb + object/complement).

Questions with *How Many* and *How Much*

Positive Sentence	Wh- Question
There were **four** children.	**How many children** were there?
I have **two** tests tomorrow.	**How many tests** do you have tomorrow?
You have **enough** milk.	**How much milk** do you have?
We do **a lot of** homework after class.	**How much homework** do you do after class?

How many and *how much* replace information about specific nouns or noun phrases in the sentence. Place those nouns or noun phrases that relate to the missing information after the question words.

Correct	How many children were there?
Incorrect	How many were there children?

Exercise 2

Change the following sentences into Wh- questions. The information you want to ask about is in **bold**.

Sofia likes **to go dancing**. → **What** does Sofia like **to do**?

My brother is playing music **at a club**. → **Where** is your brother playing music?

1. His plane arrived **at 9:30**.

   _____?

2. There are **20** students in our class.

   _____?

3. I must remember to call **Julio** this evening.

   _____?

4. Francesca has to **get up** at 6:00.

   _____?

5. The students were studying **to prepare for their exam**.

   _____?

6. **Angelo** works from 5:00 to 10:00 on Friday evenings.

   _____?

7. My parents took a trip **to Brazil** last year.

   _____?

8. I'm feeling **better** today.

_____?

9. We have **a lot of** homework to do tonight.

_____?

10. **Too much fast food** can be bad for your health.

_____?

Negative Sentences

In negative sentence formation, *not* goes after the first word of the verb—the auxiliary, the modal, or *be*. If there is only one word of the main verb, it needs an auxiliary verb. The exception is the main verb *be*.

Warm-Up

Work in pairs. Read each pair of sentences.

Positive	Negative
1. I have to get eight hours of sleep to feel rested.	1. I do not have to get eight hours of sleep to feel rested.
2. Jacques will meet us at nine.	2. Jacques will not meet us at nine.
3. Ali was at home last night.	3. Ali was not at home last night.

Underline the verbs and circle the negative words. What do you notice about the sentence structure?

Formation

Simple Present and Simple Past—All Verbs except *Be*

Review the formation charts for the simple present in Chapter 3 (pages 43, 48, and 50) and the charts for the simple past in Chapter 5 (pages 79, 82, and 84).

	Positive	Negative
	Subject + Verb **(+ object / complement)**	**Subject + Auxiliary + Negative + Verb** **(+ object / complement)**
Simple Present	I **like** to skate.	I **do not** (don't) **like** to skate.
	It **has** many good points.	It **does not** (doesn't) **have** many good points.
	We **travel** together.	We **do not** (don't) **travel** together.
Simple Past	I **watched** TV.	I **did not** (didn't) **watch** TV.
	He **spoke** to his friend.	He **did not** (didn't) **speak** to his friend.

- To create a negative sentence, you must use the auxiliary verb *do* or *does* in the present and *did* in the past.
- *Not* comes after the auxiliary verb.

Simple Present and Simple Past—*Be*

	Positive	Negative
	Subject + Verb + Complement	**Subject + Verb + Negative + Complement**
Simple Present	I **am** tired.	I **am not** (I'm not) tired.
	You **are** a student.	You **are not** (aren't) a student.
	He **is** funny.	He **is not** (isn't) funny.
Simple Past	I **was** at home yesterday.	I **was not** (wasn't) at home yesterday.
	You **were** in Haiti.	You **were not** (weren't) in Haiti.
	She **was** with her classmates.	She **was not** (wasn't) with her classmates.

Be does not need an auxiliary verb, so the negative word *not* comes after *be*.

Present Progressive and Past Progressive

Review the formation chart for the present progressive in Chapter 4 (page 60) and the chart for the past progressive in Chapter 6 (page 95).

	Positive	Negative
	Subject + *be* + Verb-*ing* (+ object / complement)	**Subject + *be* + Negative + Verb-*ing* (+ object / complement)**
Present Progressive	He **is playing** the guitar.	He **is not** (isn't) **playing** the guitar.
	We **are working** in the garden.	We **are not** (aren't) **working** in the garden.
Past Progressive	I **was listening** to music.	I **was not** (wasn't) **listening** to music.
	They **were waiting** for their friends.	They **were not** (weren't) **waiting** for their friends.

- We use the verb *be* to form the progressive tenses, so we have to follow the rules for *be*.
- Place *not* after *be* to form negatives. Never use the auxiliary *do, does,* or *did* with the verb *be*.

Future with *Will* and *Be Going To*

Review the formation charts for the simple future and *be + going to* in Chapter 9 (pages 151 and 154).

	Positive	Negative
	Subject + Auxiliary + Verb (+ object / complement)	**Subject + Auxiliary + Negative + Verb (+ object / complement)**
will	I **will** go.	I **will not** (won't) go.
	Juan **will** take the dog for a walk.	Juan **will not** (won't) take the dog for a walk.
	They **will** try to catch the next bus.	They **will not** (won't) try to catch the next bus.
	Subject + *be* + *going to* + Verb (+ object / complement)	**Subject + *be* + Negative + *going to* + Verb (+ object / complement)**
be going to	I **am going to** do that tomorrow.	I **am not** (I'm not) **going** to do that tomorrow.
	She **is going to** look for it.	She **is not** (isn't) **going** to look for it.
	We **are going to** celebrate tonight.	We **are not** (aren't) **going** to celebrate tonight.

- When there are two or more verb words, *not* comes immediately after the first word of the verb (*will* or *be*) to form the negative.
- *Not* always appears immediately after *be* to form negatives.

Modals

Review the formation charts for modals in Chapter 10 (pages 166–167, 168, 170, and 172).

Positive	Negative
Subject + Modal + Verb **(+ object / complement)**	**Subject + Modal + Negative + Verb** **(+ object / complement)**
I **can** speak Spanish.	I **cannot** (can't) speak Spanish.
They **must** leave early.	They **must not** (mustn't) leave early.

- *Not* comes immediately after the modal to form the negative.
- Remember that *can* and *not* form one word: *cannot.*

Present and Past with *Have to*

Positive	Negative
Subject + *have / has / had to* + Verb **(+ object / complement)**	**Subject + Auxiliary + Negative + *have to* + Verb** **(+ object / complement)**
I **have to** go home.	I **do not** (don't) **have to** go home.
He **has to** ask for permission.	He **does not** (doesn't) **have to** ask for permission.
They **had to** buy food.	They **did not** (didn't) **have to** buy food.

- *Have to* must follow the structure rules for the verb *have*. Use *do, does,* and *did* to make negative sentences.
- Never use the auxiliary *do, does, or did* with the other modal verbs.

Exercise 3

Change each of the following positive sentences into the negative.

Eli can play basketball very well. → Eli **cannot (can't) play** basketball very well.

1. The children were playing in the park.

   _____

2. She should exercise more.

   _____

3. We drove to Montreal on Friday.

   _____

4. Eric is always late for class.

   _____

5. Some of the employees will organize the company party.

   _____

6. I had to do a lot of cleaning on the weekend.

   _____

7. Those students eat lunch in the cafeteria.

   _____

8. The dog broke the flower vase.

   _____

9. Yan is going to take a trip to Spain next year.

   _____

10. He wants to be a doctor.

   _____

Speaking Activity 5
Change and Exchange

Work in pairs. Your teacher will dictate six positive sentences. Each of you will write them on a separate sheet of paper. Compare your sentences with your partner's. Correct any errors. Next, rewrite the positive sentences as negative sentences. Compare and revise the negative sentences. Raise your hand as soon as you finish. The first pair to finish with the correct sentences wins.

Short Answers

To create a short answer to a Yes/No question, use only the first word of the verb—the auxiliary, the modal, or *be*:

>   *Yes* + subject + auxiliary / modal / *be*

>   *or*

>   *No* + subject + auxiliary / modal / *be* + *not*

In negative short answers, the verb and *not* have to be contracted.

Warm-Up

Work in pairs. Read the dialogue out loud.

>   **Partner A:** Did you go to Tran's party on Saturday?
>   **Partner B:** No, I didn't. I had to work. Were there a lot of our friends at the party?
>   **Partner A:** Yes, there were. It was a lot of fun.
>   **Partner B:** It's Fidel's birthday next week. Is he going to have a party?

Partner A: Yes, he is. Are you going to be able to come to that one?

Partner B: Yes, I am. I'm going to ask my boss for the day off.

Partner A: Does he usually let you have time off?

Partner B: Yes, he does. Well, sometimes he doesn't.

Partner A: Well, I hope he does this time.

Read the dialogue again. <u>Underline</u> all the verbs. What do you notice about the verbs used in the short answers?

Formation

Yes/No Question	Short Answer	
Do you like to watch sports?	Yes, I **do**.	No, I **don't**.
Does he work on Saturdays?	Yes, he **does**.	No, he **doesn't**.
Did they arrive in time?	Yes, they **did**.	No, they **didn't**.
Are you cold?	Yes, I **am**.	No, I'm **not**.
Am I late?	Yes, you **are**.	No, you **aren't**.
Is she from Singapore?	Yes, she **is**.	No, she **isn't**.
Were you and Sam at the concert?	Yes, we **were**.	No, we **weren't**.
Was the boy riding his bike?	Yes, he **was**.	No, he **wasn't**.
Is it going to rain tomorrow?	Yes, it **is**.	No, it **isn't**.
Will the train leave on time?	Yes, it **will**.	No, it **won't**.
Can she speak Russian?	Yes, she **can**.	No, she **can't**.
Would you like some tea?	Yes, I **would**.	No, I **wouldn't**.
Does he have to work tonight?	Yes, he **does**.	No, he **doesn't**.

- The first word—the auxiliary, the modal, or *be*—in the Yes/No question is the only part of the verb that appears in the short answer.
- The only form that changes is the verb *be* when the question is about *you* or *I*.
- Remember that *am* and *not* cannot form a contraction. I am not. → I'm not.

Exercise 4

Answer the following questions using short answers in the positive and the negative.

Did you go to visit your family last weekend?	Yes, I **did**.	No, I **didn't**.
Is Amalia cooking dinner?	Yes, she **is**.	No, she **isn't**.

1. Could your uncle play soccer when he was young?

   Yes, _____   No, _____

2. Do you have any brothers or sisters?

   Yes, _____   No, _____

3. Were you sleeping when I called?

   Yes, _____   No, _____

4. Do we have to write a composition today?

Yes, _____   No, _____

5. Will the students study in the library tomorrow?

Yes, _____   No, _____

6. Should we buy the tickets today?

Yes, _____   No, _____

7. Are you from El Salvador?

Yes, _____   No, _____

8. Did Tran and his sister move into their new apartment on Saturday?

Yes, _____   No, _____

9. Are the friends going to take a trip during the vacation?

Yes, _____   No, _____

10. Did you eat the last piece of cake?

Yes, _____   No, _____

11. Would you like cream in your coffee?

Yes, _____   No, _____

12. Can we get there on the bus?

Yes, _____   No, _____

13. Do the winners get a cash prize?

Yes, _____   No, _____

14. Is it difficult to earn a scholarship?

Yes, _____   No, _____

Bringing It All Together

Speaking Activity 6
Scrambled Parts

Work in teams. Your teacher will give each team five sets of cards. Each set has all the parts of a negative sentence or a question on separate cards. Put the parts of each sentence or question together in the correct order. The first team to finish with the correct answers wins.

Reading

Read the passage and answer the questions that follow.

As you read, pay attention to these vocabulary words in the passage: *assume*, *analyze*, *security*, *transfer*, *credit*, *research*, *document*, and *estimate*.

Buyer Beware

Whether you are buying new or used products online or buying a used car, you should do your homework. "Buyer beware" is an expression that means that you should be cautious when making a purchase. You shouldn't assume that everything is completely as it seems. If the price of something seems too good to be true, it is very possible that it is just that—too good to be true.

If you like to shop online, be careful. Read all the details very carefully. **Analyze** all the information the seller provides. There may be hidden charges for shipping, warranty services, or airport surcharges on travel packages. Compare the product with other online or in-store products. Also, check the **security** of the site if you are paying online. Make sure it's safe before you **transfer** any money. You don't want to put your **credit** card or bank account at risk.

If you are buying a used car, you need to do your **research**. Make sure you get a copy of the vehicle history. That **document** tells you how many owners there were and, more importantly, if the vehicle was involved in any accidents. Always get a mechanic you trust to check out the vehicle before you hand over any money. If the advertisement says "as is," that usually means there are things that need to be fixed and the owner doesn't want to fix them. The phrase "as is" makes you think that the car is not worth fixing. Make sure you know the real cost of buying a vehicle before you buy it. Get an **estimate** from your mechanic for the cost of any repairs that need to be done.

Buying online or in person can be tricky. Do your homework, ask lots of questions, consult some experts, and buyer beware.

Comprehension

Read the passage again. Write five questions (Yes/No or Wh- questions) about the reading passage. Exchange your questions with another student and answer each other's questions.

1. _____?

2. _____?

3. _____?

4. _____?

5. _____?

Discussion

Do you buy products online, from newspaper ads, or from online used article sites? Do you like the convenience of buying things that way? Are you careful? Do you have any advice for others?

Apartment for Rent

Listen to the audio, which is a telephone conversation. The caller is inquiring about an apartment for rent.

Comprehension

Answer the following questions.

1. Which apartment is the caller asking about? _____

2. Where is the bus stop? _____

3. How much is the rent? _____

4. What is included in the rent? _____

5. What must the renter pay on top of the rent? _____

6. What floor is the apartment on? _____

7. Where is the laundry room? _____

8. How much is the security deposit? _____

9. What is the caller's phone number? _____

10. When will the caller go to see the apartment? _____

Writing

Choose a famous person, living or dead. Write a brief description of that person. Write five questions you would like to ask that individual, if you could, and explain why you would like to ask those questions. The composition should be approximately 150 words.

Vocabulary

Read the following sentences. The words in **bold** are from the Reading activity. Use the context to help you understand what the words in bold mean. Then match each word with its correct definition, synonym, or antonym. Finally, write your own sentence using the word.

1. We want to renovate our kitchen. We decided to ask three different contractors for an **estimate** so we would know around how much it would cost.
   Synonym: a) a fixed amount   b) an educated guess   c) exact amount

   Your sentence: _____

2. The investigators say they need to **analyze** all the information and factors involved before they can determine the cause of the accident.
Definition: a) to study all the facts to come to a conclusion
     b) to draw a conclusion without examining the facts
     c) to make something easy to understand

Your sentence: _____

3. Myoko likes to shop online. When she does, she always uses her **credit** card.
Definition: a) describing the amount of money you have to pay
     b) describing the amount of money you can spend and pay later
     c) describing the amount of money you pay every month

Your sentence: _____

4. Check the facts. Don't **assume** that everything you read online is completely or even partially true.
Antonym: a) to know
     b) to guess
     c) to doubt

Your sentence: _____

5. When I fly to Ottawa, I have to **transfer** to another plane when it lands in Toronto.
Synonym: a) to hold
     b) to wait
     c) to move

Your sentence: _____

6. Because officials expect large numbers of people to attend the free concert, they are putting measures in place to provide more **security** for the audience and the performers.
Antonym: a) danger
     b) certainty
     c) safety

Your sentence: _____

7. The main identification **document** you need to board an international flight in Canada is a passport.
Definition: a) a written agreement to transfer money
     b) a written presentation of official, detailed information
     c) an oral agreement to complete a job

Your sentence: _____

8. When you have a project to do for school, do your **research**. First, find out as much information as possible about the subject. Then sort it out and organize what you need.
Synonym: a) an examination
     b) a guess
     c) an estimate based on facts

Your sentence: _____

Chapter Review

Summary

- In Yes/No and Wh- question formation, the first word of the verb—the auxiliary, the modal, or *be*—comes before the subject: **auxiliary / modal / *be* + subject + verb**.
- If the main verb in the statement form is only one word, you must use an auxiliary verb. The main verb *be* is the exception.
- *Be* always changes its position with the subject to change statements into questions. Never use the auxiliary *do, does,* or *did* with the verb *be*.
- Wh- question words ask about a specific piece of information in a sentence. The question formation—**question word + auxiliary / modal / *be* + subject + verb**—remains the same as in Yes/No questions, except when the question word replaces the subject.
- In negative sentence formation, if the main verb is only one word, it needs an auxiliary. The exception is the main verb *be*. *Not* goes after the first word of the verb: **subject + auxiliary / modal / *be* + *not* + verb**.
- The first word—the auxiliary, the modal, or *be*—in a Yes/No question is the only part of the verb that appears in a short answer.

Exercise 5

Change each of the following sentences into a Yes/No question.

John should go to the doctor. → Should John go to the doctor?

1. The referee skated onto the ice. _____?

2. We were playing cards when he called. _____?

3. Sam has to work on Saturday. _____?

4. The flight is going to be late. _____?

5. I would like another cup of coffee. _____?

Exercise 6

Change each the following statements into a Wh- question. The information you want to ask about is in **bold**.

They have **enough** time to get there. → **How much time** do they have to get there?

1. Mohammed **plays the piano** really well.

   _____?

2. **Francine** is the new office manager.

    _____?

3. There are **six** apartments in the building.

    _____?

4. I left school early **because I wasn't feeling well.**

    _____?

5. He put the food **in the refrigerator.**

    _____?

Exercise 7

Answer the following questions. Use short answers.

    Can you play the guitar? → Yes, I can.   *or*   No, I can't.

1. Do you have a favourite restaurant?   Yes, _____

2. Should we tell Marco about the problem?   No, _____

3. Are you going to the film festival next week?   Yes, _____

4. Did you see what they were doing?   No, _____

5. Are the students studying for the test?   Yes, _____

12 Sentence Structure

Overview

In this chapter, you will learn more about sentence structure in English, about sentence types, and, finally, about some common sentence problems and solutions.

- Understanding the proper sentence structure makes your writing and speaking grammatically correct.

- Using different sentence types, both simple and compound, helps your writing to be more interesting and effective.

- Knowing what sentence problems look like helps you avoid errors and know how to correct them.

Warm-Up

Work in pairs. Look at the jigsaw pieces. Determine into what sequence you have to put them to create the picture.

What did you have to do to find the right sequence?
When making a puzzle, what usually happens if you put the puzzle pieces in the wrong way?

Sentence Structure

In English, every sentence has to have specific parts that are linked together so that the sentence can be complete, make sense, and be grammatically correct. Those specific parts are the "parts of speech" you learned about in Chapter 1. It is also important that the parts are in the proper order.

Warm-Up

Read the following sentences. Check if the words are in the correct order. If not, try to correct them.

1. Debora and Dawn are friends good.

2. They go to school together.

3. Like they their teacher.

Formation

For a sentence to be complete and correct, all parts of it must be in the correct order.

 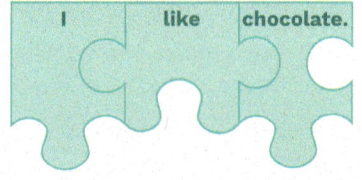

Exercise 1

Unscramble the following words and make them into sentences.

car / is / new / This / a → This is a new car.

1. beautiful / Life / is

   _____

2. them / visit / tomorrow / will / We

   _____

3. must / They / for / study / exam / their

   _____

4. brother / bought / last / My / a / year / house

   _____

5. needs / bread / Melissa / to / some / buy

   _____

 **Speaking Activity 1**
Game—Make a Sentence!

Work in two teams. Your teacher will write several words on the board. The teams will take turns making complete sentences with the words on the board and saying them out loud. If a team can't give a correct response in 30 seconds, the other team gets a chance to make a sentence and score a point. After several turns, the team with the highest score wins.

Sentence Types

You will learn about two sentence types here: simple and compound. Using a variety of sentence types will help make your writing more interesting.

Warm-Up

Read the following two passages.

Passage 1

I am a simple person. I like simple living. Last year, my family and I decided to move to the countryside. Now I have a healthier lifestyle. I also have more time for my family. I really enjoy living away from the city. Sometimes it is difficult. In the future, we will buy a dairy farm. Our other option is to buy land to grow crops. I encourage everyone to try to live his or her life simply. You can do it by moving to the countryside. You can also do it by living simply in the city.

Passage 2

I am a simple person. I like simple living, so last year my family and I decided to move to the countryside. Now I have a healthier lifestyle, and I also have more time for my family. I really enjoy living away from the city, but sometimes it is difficult. In the future, we will buy a dairy farm or a piece of land to grow crops. I encourage everyone to try to live his or her life simply. You can do it by moving to the countryside, or you can also do it by living simply in the city.

Both passages contain the same information. Which passage sounds better? Why do you think so?

Formation

A **simple sentence** has the most basic sentence structure. It contains a single independent statement called a clause. A clause has a subject and a verb, and sometimes includes an object/complement. The subject tells the reader *who* or *what* the sentence is about; the verb indicates what the subject *does* or *is* (action or state).

> **She reads. (independent clause)**
> subject verb

> **She reads many books per month. (independent clause)**
> subject verb   object/complement

A **compound sentence** contains two independent statements or clauses. These clauses are joined by a coordinating conjunction. Some of the coordinating conjunctions are *and*, *but*, *so*, and *or*. When making a compound sentence, use a comma before the coordinating conjunction.

Use *and* to join clauses that have **similar ideas**.

> My husband doesn't play hockey. (independent clause)

> My daughter doesn't play hockey. (independent clause)

> My husband doesn't play hockey, **and** my daughter doesn't play hockey. (compound sentence)

Use *but* to link clauses that express **opposite ideas**.

> I don't like horror movies. (independent clause)
>
> I like comedies. (independent clause)
>
> I don't like horror movies, **but** I like comedies. (compound sentence)

Use *so* to show a **consequence**.

> Aaron was sick last week. (independent clause)
>
> He didn't come to class. (independent clause)
>
> Aaron was sick last week, **so** he didn't come to class. (compound sentence)

Use *or* to indicate **options**.

> We can go to the movies. (independent clause)
>
> We can stream a movie. (independent clause)
>
> We can go to the movies, **or** we can stream a movie. (compound sentence)

Exercise 2

Identify the following sentences as simple or compound.

> Monique has to appraise the house. _____simple_____
>
> Monique has to appraise the house, and she needs to list it on the market. _____compound_____

1. Brittney called Shawn, but he wasn't home. _____

2. I can play the piano, and I can play the violin. _____

3. The bank opens at nine o'clock. _____

4. They don't have enough money, so they can't go to Mexico this summer. _____

5. Jakub is smart and handsome. _____

Exercise 3

Fill in the blanks with the correct coordinating conjunction: *and, but, so,* or *or*.

> Our neighbours are farmers, _____so_____ they have to wake up early every morning.

1. Grace likes to draw, _____ her sister likes to draw too.

2. It was a rainy day yesterday, _____ I stayed home.

3. They went to the party, _____ they didn't like it.

4. My friend needs a new car. He will get a part-time job, _____ he will borrow some money from his parents.

5. The students studied hard for the test, _____ they all passed it.

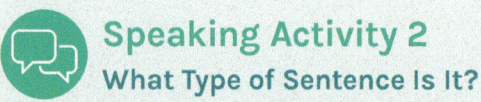

Work in pairs. In the following paragraph, underline all the simple sentences with a <u>single line</u> and all the compound sentences with a <u>double line</u>. (Circle) all the conjunctions. Together, discuss your choices and the reasons you think the sentences are either simple or compound.

Some people actually like having complex lives and constant drama in their lives. It's their personality, so they wouldn't enjoy simple living. Instead, they prefer to be on the go or to meet with people, and they often like to work a lot too. The ongoing activity keeps them motivated and happy. It might be hard to believe, but such people can still find time to stop and rest in their busy lives.

Sentence Problems

Sentences that are incomplete or joined in the wrong way are incorrect. They make reading confusing. If readers can understand your sentences and follow your ideas, they can understand what you are writing in your paragraphs, essays, emails, and anything you write. To write well, you need to know what sentence problems look like and how to correct them. The two main types are fragments and run-on sentences.

Warm-Up

Your teacher will write several sentences on paper strips and cut them into individual words. You will receive one word. Find the classmates whose words can combine with yours to create a complete sentence. Write your sentence on the board.

Formation

Fragments are incomplete sentences. They are missing an important part, or they just finish without a complete idea.

Fragment	Sentence
I like.	I like English.
She driving.	She is driving.
Because he is tired.	He stayed home because he is tired.

To avoid a fragment, test the sentence by asking these questions:

- Does it include a verb?
- Does it have a subject?
- Does the sentence express a complete idea?

Run-on sentences are composed of two sentences that use the wrong punctuation mark or are not joined with a conjunction.

Run-on	We like our teacher, she is very sympathetic.
Correct	We like our teacher. **S**he is very sympathetic. *or* We like our teacher; she is very sympathetic.
Run-on	He missed the bus, he still got to class on time.
Correct	He missed the bus, **but** he still got to class on time.

To fix run-on sentences, do any of the following:

- Place a period (.) between the two complete sentences.
- Place a semicolon (;) between the two complete sentences.
- Place a comma (,) and a conjunction between the two complete sentences.

Exercise 4

Read the following sentences. Next to each sentence, write C if the sentence is correct. If the sentence is incorrect, identify whether it is a fragment (F) or a run-on sentence (RO), and then correct it.

Adam has. _____F_____ → Correction Adam has a great sense of humour.

1. I can't help you I am busy. _____

2. She would like to travel around the world. _____

3. My professor nice. _____

4. Talk to me after class. _____

5. They will check the answers, then they will correct their mistakes.

   _____

6. If you want to succeed. _____

7. We took a lot of photos during our trip to Netherlands.

   _____

8. It belongs to her, it's not yours. _____

9. He likes Japanese cars. For example, Toyotas. _____

10. Nadia doesn't have to work tonight, so she'll go out with her friends.

   _____

Speaking Activity 3
Newspaper Headlines

Newspaper headlines are often written as fragments and not complete sentences. Work in pairs. Read the following newspaper headlines, and together try to guess what the complete sentence might be.

- The gold medal for Canada in women's 100 metres
- The neighbourhood restored
- Brave teenager
- All because of his talent
- Waiting for help

Bringing It All Together

Speaking Activity 4
Game—Join the Sentences

Work in teams of two. The teacher will give you and your partner paper strips with different sentences. You will have five minutes to talk with your partner and combine your sentences using the correct conjunctions. Write the sentences in the space provided. The team with the highest number of correctly combined sentences wins.

_____

_____

_____

_____

Speaking Activity 5
Role-Play

Work in pairs. Prepare a role-play for the following situations. Then perform them in front of the class.

Situation A: Your best friend has a problem. He or she wants to visit a cousin in another province but doesn't have a car. Offer him or her different options. Use conjunctions to link your sentences.

Situation B: Your co-worker asks you for help. There are things that you can help him or her with. However, you also believe that there are things that are his or her responsibility and not yours. State your opinion. Use simple and compound sentences.

Speaking Activity 6
Mini Oral Presentation

Work in pairs. Make four sentences that describe your and your partner's abilities. For each sentence, use a different conjunction. Then you and your partner will present the sentences to the rest of the class.

_____

_____

_____

_____

Speaking Activity 7
Quotations

Work in pairs. Read the following quotations. Identify whether each quotation is written using a simple sentence (S) or a compound sentence (C). Circle the correct letter. Then discuss the quotations.

Sometimes good things fall apart, so better things can fall together. **S C**

—Unknown

Ships in harbour are safe, but that's not what ships are built for. **S C**

—John Shedd

The grand essentials of happiness are something to do, something to love, and something to hope for. **S C**

—Allan K. Chalmers

Happiness is not the absence of problems; it's the ability to deal with them. **S C**
—Steve Maraboli

Life can only be understood backwards, but it has to be lived forwards. **S C**
—Soren Kierkegaard

Ability can take you to the top, but it takes character to keep you there. **S C**
—Unknown

Life's a marathon, not a sprint. **S C**

—Unknown

Each moment spent on this bright blue planet is precious, so use it carefully. **S C**
—Unknown

We need no language to laugh. **S C**
—Unknown

Reading

Read the passage and answer the questions that follow.

Jigsaw Puzzles

As you read, pay attention to these vocabulary words in the passage: *outcome*, *appropriate*, *primarily*, *normally*, *computer*, and *community*.

A jigsaw puzzle is a puzzle, and as with every puzzle, you need a solution to it. The solution or **outcome** of a jigsaw puzzle is to make a complete picture by <u>reassembling</u> its many small pieces. Often, these puzzle pieces are of different shapes, but each piece usually has a part of a picture on it. That makes it easier to determine what pieces go together. When all the pieces are in their **appropriate** spots, a jigsaw puzzle is complete and <u>reveals</u> the entire picture.

The origins of jigsaw puzzles go back to around 1760. People created these puzzles by painting a picture on a flat piece of wood, and then cutting that picture into small pieces with a special wood cutting <u>tool</u> called a jigsaw. These days, jigsaw puzzles are made **primarily** on cardboard. That way, they are easier and cheaper to produce.

Jigsaw puzzles **normally** come in many sizes, ranging from 100 to 1000 pieces. Children's puzzles are usually smaller. There are also family puzzles, three-dimensional jigsaw puzzles, and even **computer** versions of jigsaw puzzles. You can find all <u>sorts</u> of images on jigsaw puzzles. The most typical ones are nature scenes, animals, and buildings. However, you can even turn your photos into puzzles. Some people, after completing a puzzle, glue it to another <u>surface</u> and hang it on the wall to serve as a decoration.

Doing puzzles is a great pastime activity and educational tool not only for kids but for adults too. You can use them to help your child to develop spatial skills. You can also introduce puzzles at cultural and seniors' centres in your **community**, work <u>retreats</u>, family reunions, or parties as a way to make a group of people work as a team. Doing puzzles can even help people relieve stress, learn how to concentrate, and keep their brain active.

Next time you are looking for an activity to do by yourself or as a group, try out a jigsaw puzzle. It's lots of fun!

Comprehension

Answer the questions. Write complete sentences.

1. What happens when you put all the jigsaw puzzle pieces together?

   _____

2. At first, what material did people use to make jigsaw puzzles?

   _____

3. What tool did people use to cut a picture into small pieces?

   _____

4. What do we make jigsaw puzzles from today? Why is this material used?

   _____

5. What images do we usually find on jigsaw puzzles?

_____

6. How big can jigsaw puzzles be?

_____

7. According to the text, what are some benefits of doing jigsaw puzzles?

_____

_____

Discussion

- Do you remember doing puzzles when you were young? Do you do puzzles these days?
- The text gives you some benefits of doing jigsaw puzzles. Do you think there could be some disadvantages of doing puzzles too? Give examples.

Listening

Audio 19 🔊

The Art of Broken Vases

Listen to the audio and answer the following questions.

Comprehension

(Circle) the best answer to each question.

1. Melodie was absent from school yesterday because
    a) she was sick   b) she was moving   c) she was helping Liam move

2. She is excited about yesterday's event.
    a) True   b) False

3. She feels that way because
    a) the movers stole something precious of hers   b) she fell   c) something broke

4. The vases were originally her grandmother's.
    a) True   b) False

5. The subject of the lesson in the last art class was about
    a) mosaics   b) recyclable materials   c) interior design

As you listen, pay attention to the vocabulary words **partners** and **technique** and the context in which they are used.

6. Melodie is happy with Liam's solution to her problem.

    a) True

    b) False

7. The end of the semester art project can be done

    a) individually

    b) in pairs

    c) in small groups

Writing

Write a short composition (maximum 150 words) describing one of the following:

- a location that is special to you
- your favourite pet
- your best friend
- your car or the car of your dream

In your description, use different types of sentences: simple and compound. Make sure to use conjunctions too. Proofread your text for fragments or run-on sentences, and then correct them.

Vocabulary

1. Read the following sentences. The words in **bold** are from the Reading and Listening activities. Use the context to help you understand what the words in bold mean.
   a) It **normally** takes about 30 minutes to change oil in a car, but due to some **computer** problems, the mechanic had to use a specific **technique**, so it took him two hours to do it.
   b) Ariella applied to college a month ago. They usually process applications in June, so she should know the **outcome** of her application soon.
   c) When buying a house, consider the type of **community** that is most **appropriate** for your needs and preferences.
   d) Tom and Bill became business **partners primarily** because they have a very similar vision on what they want to accomplish in their company.

2. Match each word with its correct definition. Use a dictionary to find another form of the word such as an adjective, a noun, a verb, or an adverb. Write the additional forms in the column on the right. The first one provides an example.

Word	Definition	Adjective / Noun / Verb / Adverb
1. appropriate _b_	a) most importantly or in the first position of importance; mainly	appropriately (adj.), appropriate (v.)
2. community ___	b) something that is suitable, right, or correct	
3. computer ___	c) two or more people who work together toward a common goal	

4. normally ___	d) the way something turns out; a result of something; a consequence
5. outcome ___	e) a group of people with common characteristics or interests who usually live in the same area and care about each other
6. partners ___	f) a method or way of doing something in a particular manner
7. primarily ___	g) usually; typically
8. technique ___	h) something describing, pertaining to, or having to do with a programmable electronic device that can store, retrieve, and process data

3. Rewrite the following sentences using the word in parentheses.

   a) **(appropriate)** Do you think it's all right to wear jeans to a job interview?

   _____

   b) **(community)** The people in this area are really friendly.

   _____

   c) **(computer)** Please turn off all the electronic devices when you are ready to leave.

   _____

   d) **(normally)** You should generally think about what you say before you say it.

   _____

   e) **(outcome)** The result of this year's election will be announced at 7 PM.

   _____

   f) **(partners)** Can you and I be a team and work on this project together?

   _____

   g) **(primarily)** What will the teacher mainly consider when marking this assignment?

   _____

   h) **(technique)** The judge evaluated the contestant's method and creativity.

   _____

Chapter Review

Summary

- The proper sentence structure makes your writing complete, grammatically correct, and therefore easy for the reader to follow.
- If you want your writing to be more effective, use both simple and compound sentences.
- A simple sentence contains one clause with a subject, a verb, and sometimes an object or a complement.
- A compound sentence contains two clauses that are joined together with a conjunction.
- The four main conjunctions are *and*, *but*, *or*, and *so*.
- To avoid sentence fragments or run-on sentences, check that your sentences are complete and connected by the correct conjunction or separated by the correct punctuation mark.

Exercise 5

Match the numbered first part of each sentence in Column A with the lettered second part of the sentence in Column B.

Column A	Column B
1. Howard likes to dance, _____	a) but she wasn't there.
2. The movie was _____	b) we have lots of homework to do.
3. My roommate forgot his key, _____	c) and Libby likes to dance too.
4. Clara and Felix _____	d) his dog.
5. I called my friend, _____	e) were very tasty.
6. You can give it to me, _____	f) will move to Vancouver next year.
7. We need to leave now; _____	g) but I was home.
8. He takes good care of _____	h) is looking for a job.
9. The cookies _____	i) or you can leave it with her.
10. Jinny _____	j) really good.

Exercise 6

The following paragraph uses simple sentences. In the space provided, rewrite the text. Use compound sentences whenever possible. Don't forget the correct conjunctions and punctuation marks.

We link individual words to make a sentence. Similarly, we connect two or more links to make a chain. Chain was invented in 225 BCE. People used it to draw a water bucket from a well. Back then, they made chain with metal rings. These days, we also use other materials to make chains. Presently, we use the concept of a chain for many articles. We use it in tools, such as chainsaws. We also use it in bicycles. We even use it in jewellery, such as necklaces and bracelets.

_____

_____

_____

_____

_____

_____

_____

Exercise 7

There are five errors with sentence structure in the following passage. They are <u>underlined</u> for you. Correct them.

Some people think technology can simplify your life. <u>and</u> others think it can make life even more complex. Many of us use technology on an everyday <u>basis but</u> this might not mean it's always good for us. For example, we might benefit greatly when it comes to cars, cellphones, and <u>computers, they</u> save us a great amount of time, <u>or</u> at the same time, they can sometimes be "stealing" our precious time. Some of us also have to admit that we are addicted to technology, and we can't live without it. <u>It a</u> controversial topic.

Exercise 8

Circle the letter of the correct word or phrase to complete the sentences or to provide the correct answer.

1. Eddie got an A on the test, _____ he was very happy.
   a) and   b) but   c) so

2. Nicole grows her own vegetables, _____ she eats them every day.
   a) and   b) but   c) or

3. She is always in a hurry, _____ she loves it.
   a) or   b) but   c) so

4. I like to sit in front of a fireplace and to look at the flames.

   This is an example of a _____.
   a) simple sentence   b) compound sentence

5. Because it's relaxing.

   This is an example of a _____.

   a) fragment   b) run-on sentence

REVIEW
Self-Study

Overview

The self-assessments in this unit give you a chance to review and reinforce the grammar points from Part 3 (chapters 9–12).

Check your knowledge and if you find areas that need more attention, go back to the appropriate chapter and review the material.

Exercise 1

Unscramble the following words and make them into sentences or questions.

this / am / I / work / going to / summer → I am going to work this summer.

1. must / early / I / tomorrow / get up

_____.

2. after / going to / you / What / do / dinner/ are

_____?

3. have / Identical / do / twins / identical / not / fingerprints

_____.

4. a / Can / change / tire/ you

_____?

5. poisonous / Avocados / to / are / birds

_____.

6. , but / The / was / she / difficult / it / test / passed

_____.

7. sunny / It / be / this / will / weekend

_____.

8. taking / Were / the / notes / students

_____?

9. our / learn / We / from / should / mistakes

_____.

10. you / Why / have / now / to / do / leave

_____?

Exercise 2

Change the following positive sentences into the negative.

Positive   Martin Cooper **was** the first person to make a cellphone call, on April 3, 1973.

Negative   Martin Cooper **was not (wasn't)** the first person to make a cellphone call, on April 3, 1973.

1. You should have an annual medical checkup.

_____

2. A blue whale's heart is the size of a Volkswagen Beetle.

_____

3. During your lifetime, you'll eat about 27 000 kilograms of food.

_____

4. Ancient Egyptians slept on pillows made of stone.

_____

5. Forensic scientists can determine a person's sex, age, and race by examining a single strand of hair.

_____

Exercise 3

Change the following sentences into Yes/No questions. Then give a short answer to each question in the positive and in the negative.

Statement   People are about one centimetre taller in the morning than in the evening.
Question   Are people about one centimetre taller in the morning than in the evening?
Short answers Yes, they are.   No, they aren't.

1. We have to protect our environment.

_____?

Yes, _____.   No, _____.

2. Space tourism will be common in the near future.

_____?

Yes, _____.   No, _____.

3. Timothy was working when it happened.

_____?

Yes, _____.   No, _____.

4. You can make change for a dollar in 293 ways.

_____?

Yes, _____.   No, _____.

5. Women's hearts beat faster than men's.

_____?

Yes, _____.   No, _____.

Exercise 4

Change the following statements into Wh- questions. The information you want to ask about is in **bold**.

Statement	Ontario contains over **250 thousand** lakes.
Wh- question	**How many** lakes does Ontario contain?

1. People **in parts of Western China** put salt in their tea instead of sugar.

   _____?

2. Persia changed its name to Iran **in 1935.**

   _____?

3. **Linen** is actually stronger when wet.

   _____?

4. You have to be **16 years old** to get a driver's licence in Canada.

   _____?

5. In the future, we will communicate **by reading each other's minds.**

   _____?

Exercise 5

Correct the errors in the following sentences. The errors are <u>underlined</u>.

1. I did not <u>came</u> to Canada in 1991.

2. To be a successful student, you <u>might</u> study hard.

3. It's very windy<u>,</u> the storm is coming.

4. <u>Is</u> Grace and Hannah going to the summer camp next year?

5. How often does she <u>talks</u> with her mom?

6. I <u>should</u> like some tea, please.

7. The soup was too spicy, <u>and</u> I did not eat it.

8. Monarch butterflies <u>can to</u> travel up to 8000 kilometres per year.

9. <u>Have</u> strawberries more vitamin C than oranges?

10. I <u>wont</u> be here tomorrow.

Exercise 6

Fill in the blanks with the correct form of the words in parentheses. Use correct verb tenses (simple present, simple past, past progressive, future), modals, and short answers.

Ten years ago, while I 1 _____ **(do)** my master's degree, I 2 _____ **(learn)** a lot about myself. In particular, I remember one class on adult learning. One day, our professor 3 _____ **(say)**, "In this class, you 4 _____ **(have, negative)** a final exam. Instead, you 5 _____ **(write)** an essay: an autobiography. To write it, you 6 _____ **(modal, advice)** reflect on your life and your learning style. You 7 _____ **(modal, possibility)** also use various textbooks and other scholars' theories. Your essay 8 _____ **(modal, lack of permission)** be longer than 30 pages. You 9 _____ **(modal, obligation)** submit it by the end of the semester. 10 _____ you _____ **(have)** any questions?"

Some of the students asked, "11 _____ **(modal, permission)** we keep it afterward?"

He answered, "Yes, you 12 _____ **(modal, permission)**."

When I look back, I have to say it 13 _____ **(be, negative)** an easy project, but I really 14 _____ **(enjoy)** it. These days, I 15 _____ **(read)** my autobiography at least once a year. It's so good that I often 16 _____ **(ask)** myself, "17 _____ I really _____ **(write)** it?" I proudly reply, "Yes, I 18 _____ **(do)**."

In the future, I 19 _____ **(give)** it to my daughters so that they 20 _____ **(modal, possibility)** read it and learn more about their mother. I think everyone 21 _____ **(modal, advice)** write his or her autobiography once in their lifetime. It 22 _____ **(be)** a great tool to realize who you really 23 _____ **(be)** in the past, who you 24 _____ **(be)** now, and who you 25 _____ **(modal, possibility)** become in the future.

Exercise 7

Find and (circle) all the words in the word search below. The words "or" and "so" are already done for you. Copy the remaining letters from the word search into the spaces below it to find what the message says.

adjective	can	intelligence	plan	sentences
adverb	combine	modal	prediction	simple
advice	comma	mosaics	puzzle	~~so~~
agenda	complex	must	question	technology
and	conjunctions	negative	request	yearbook
but	goal	~~or~~	resolution	

P	C	C	O	T	C	N	C	O	M	M	A	G	R	A	T
L	U	A	L	E	R	O	M	O	S	A	I	C	S	A	T
A	P	Y	N	C	I	E	M	O	I	A	G	E	N	D	A
N	U	E	P	H	N	O	S	B	D	N	S	Y	O	C	N
U	Z	A	R	N	T	A	F	O	I	A	I	N	I	O	D
S	Z	R	E	O	E	D	H	S	L	N	L	E	D	M	N
L	L	B	D	L	L	J	R	E	Q	U	E	S	T	P	E
A	E	O	I	O	L	E	E	N	U	S	T	V	E	L	G
D	L	O	C	G	I	C	O	T	E	A	I	I	N	E	A
V	E	K	T	Y	G	T	A	E	S	D	R	M	O	X	T
I	S	G	I	E	E	I	Y	N	T	V	O	U	P	N	I
C	O	O	O	R	N	V	E	C	I	E	A	D	B	L	V
E	Y	A	N	F	C	E	O	E	O	R	R	T	U	H	E
E	N	L	E	X	E	T	L	S	N	B	E	V	T	E	L
C	O	N	J	U	N	C	T	I	O	N	S	M	U	S	T

Message

_____!

___ _____ _____ ____!

___ ___ _____ ___ ___

____ _____?

Appendix A

Common Irregular Verbs

Base Form	Simple Past	Base Form	Simple Past	Base Form	Simple Past	Base Form	Simple Past
arise	arose	feel	felt	make	made	speed	sped
be	was, were	fight	fought	mean	meant	spend	spent
beat	beat	find	found	meet	met	spin	spun
become	became	fly	flew	mistake	mistook	split	split
begin	began	forbid	forbade	pay	paid	spread	spread
bend	bent	forget	forgot	put	put	spring	sprang
bet	bet	forgive	forgave	prove	proved	stand	stood
bind	bound	freeze	froze	quit	quit	steal	stole
bite	bit	get	got	read	read	stick	stuck
bleed	bled	give	gave	ride	rode	sting	stung
blow	blew	go	went	ring	rang	stink	stank
break	broke	grind	ground	rise	rose	strike	struck
bring	brought	grow	grew	run	ran	swear	swore
build	built	hang	hung	say	said	sweep	swept
burst	burst	have	had	see	saw	swim	swam
buy	bought	hear	heard	sell	sold	swing	swung
catch	caught	hide	hid	send	sent	take	took
choose	chose	hit	hit	set	set	teach	taught
come	came	hold	held	shake	shook	tear	tore
cost	cost	hurt	hurt	shine	shone	tell	told
cut	cut	keep	kept	shoot	shot	think	thought
deal	dealt	kneel	knelt	show	showed	throw	threw
dig	dug	know	knew	shrink	shrank	understand	understood
do	did	lay	laid	shut	shut	upset	upset
draw	drew	lead	led	sing	sang	wake	woke
drink	drank	leave	left	sink	sank	wear	wore
drive	drove	lend	lent	sit	sat	win	won
eat	ate	let	let	sleep	slept	wind	wound
fall	fell	lie	lay	slide	slid	withdraw	withdrew
feed	fed	lose	lost	speak	spoke	write	wrote

Appendix B

Contractions

Simple Present

We often join the verb *be* or the auxiliary verb with *not* to form contractions or shorter forms. Join the two words together and use an apostrophe (') to replace the letter *o*.

Be + *not*	Auxiliary + *not*
is not → isn't	does not → doesn't
are not → aren't	do not → don't

He is not at home right now. → He isn't at home right now.

We do not take the bus to school. → We don't take the bus to school.

Note: *I am not* is the exception. We make a contraction only with the pronoun *I* because a contraction with *not* is too difficult to pronounce.

I am not a teacher. → I'm not a teacher.

Simple Present—*Be*

The verb *be* doesn't need the auxiliary verb *do* to form the negative. There are three ways of forming contractions or shorter forms with the verb *be*—one in the positive and two with the negative. The apostrophe (') replaces the missing letter.

Positive	Negative—Joining Subject Pronoun with *be*	Negative—Joining *be* with *not*
I am → I'm	I am → I'm not	
he is → he's	he is not → he's not	he is not → he isn't
she is → she's	she is not → she's not	she is not → she isn't
it is → it's	it is not → it's not	it is not → it isn't
we are → we're	we are not → we're not	we are not → we aren't
you are → you're	you are not → you're not	you are not → you aren't
they are → they're	they are not → they're not	they are not → they aren't

I am not hungry. → I'm not hungry.

It is not cold today. → It's not cold today. *or*
　　　　　　　　　　　　　It isn't cold today.

They are not very old. → They're not very old. *or*
　　　　　　　　　　　　　They aren't very old.

Present Progressive

Because we use the present tense of *be* to form the present progressive, follow the same rules for forming contractions as used for the simple present of *be*.

Be + *not* + verb *-ing*
is not going → isn't going
are not starting → aren't starting

It is not raining. → It isn't raining. *or* It's not raining.

We are not studying. → We aren't studying. *or*
　　　　　　　　　　　　　We're not studying.

Simple Past

We contract the verb and *not*.

Be + not	Auxiliary + not
was not → wasn't	did not → didn't
were not → weren't	

It was not late. → It wasn't late.

You were not alone. → You weren't alone.

I did not go there. → I didn't go there.

Note: There is no contraction possible with the subject pronoun and the verb *be* in the simple past.

Past Progressive

Because we use the past tense of *be* to form the past progressive, there is **no** contraction possible with the subject pronoun and the verb *be* in the past progressive.

Be + not + verb –ing
was not watching → wasn't watching
were not doing → weren't doing

I was not dreaming. → I wasn't dreaming.

They were not driving. → They weren't driving.

Simple Future with *Will*

Will can form a contraction with *not*. *Will* can also form a contraction with the subject pronouns.

Subject Pronoun + will	Subject Pronoun + will + not
I will go → I'll go	I will not go → I won't go

I will do it. → I'll do it.

I will not do it. → I won't do it.

She will leave at 9:00. → She'll leave at 9:00.

She will not leave at 9:00. → She won't leave at 9:00.

Simple Future with *Be Going To*

Because we use the present tense of *be* to form the future with *be + going to*, follow the same rules for forming contractions as we do for forming the simple present of *be*.

Positive	Negative	
Be + going to	**Be + not + going to**	
he is going to → he's going to	he is not going to → he's not going to	
they are going to → they're going to	they are not going to → they're not going to	

Note: *I am not* is the exception. We make a contraction only with the pronoun *I* because a contraction with *not* is too difficult to pronounce.

I am not going to study. → I'm not going to study.

He is going to study. → He's going to study.

He is not going to study. → He isn't going to study. *or*
He's not going to study.

Modals

We can form contractions with these modals and *not*.

can	cannot swim → can't swim
could	could not swim → couldn't swim
must	must not go → mustn't go
should	should not leave → shouldn't leave
would	would not like → wouldn't like

May not is the exception. We cannot make a contraction with *may* and *not* because the contraction is difficult to pronounce.

> You may use this computer. → You may not use this computer.

Use the auxiliary *do* with the modal *have to* in a negative sentence in the present or past, to make a contraction with *not* and the auxiliary.

do + Negative + *have to*
does not have to → doesn't have to
do not have to → don't have to
did not have to → didn't have to

She does not have to work today. → She doesn't have to work today.

We do not have to write the test. → We don't have to write the test.

They did not have to do that. → They didn't have to do that.

Would can form a contraction with the subject pronouns but usually only in positive statements.

Subject Pronoun + *would*
he would like → he'd like

I would like to go to the concert. → I'd like to go to the concert.

Appendix C

Modals

Modal	Meaning and Use	Example Sentences
can	present ability	Johan can speak several languages.
	polite request (most informal)	Can I help you?
	permission (most informal)	You can use this computer station.
could	past ability	As a young man, he could run long distances.
	polite request (informal)	Could you pass the salt please?
	permission (informal)	You could do that later.
has to / have to	present and past necessity	I have to study tonight.
		He has to go to work.
		We had to leave early.
	present and past lack of necessity	You don't have to pay extra.
		He doesn't have to take lessons.
		They didn't have to attend the lecture.
may	request (most polite)	May I help you?
	permission	You may leave when you finish the assignment.
must	present necessity	I must leave by 9:30.
	present lack of permission	You mustn't drive the wrong way on a one-way street.
should	advice	You should think before you speak.
would	polite request (normal)	Would you collect all the books for me?
would like	offer	Would you like another cup of coffee?
would like to	desire	I would like to travel this summer.

Glossary

Words from Academic Word List (AWL) sublists 1 to 3 featured in bold in the Readings are **bold** in the glossary. These words are key high-frequency vocabulary that students should pay attention to.

Word or Term	AWL Sublist	Definition	Chapter	Page
accommodate (v.)		to make the way things happen match the needs of the people who are doing them	10	174
accomplishment (n.)		an act or objective successfully completed or achieved	2	34
accurate (adj.)		exact, precise	8	137
achieve (v.)	2	to succeed in something that you set out to do; to reach a goal; to accomplish something	9	160
acquire (v.)	2	to buy, obtain, or receive something that becomes your own	10	174
adapting (v.)		changing to suit or to help succeed in a new situation	6	101
adopting (v.)		taking something as your own	8	137
affect (v.)	2	to cause, influence, or produce a reaction or a change to something or someone	10	175
analyze (v.)	1	to examine or study all the facts or aspects of a thing or a situation in detail in order to draw a conclusion	11	196
approach (n.)	1	a considered or thought-out way of doing something or thinking about something	8	137
appropriate (adj.)	2	something that is suitable, right, or correct	12	210
areas (n.)	1	places or specific locations or parts of it	5	86
aspects (n.)	2	specific parts, characteristics, or features of something	8	137
assess (v.)	1	to evaluate or judge the merits or value of something	2	35
assistant (n.)	2	a person who helps with a task, usually at a lower rank than the person who is in charge of the task; a helper	9	161
assume (v.)	1	to accept information to be accurate as is, without question, doubt, or evidence to the contrary	11	196
at risk (prep. phrase)		in danger; not safe	11	196
available (adj.)	1	describes something that anyone can get, find, or have; not busy	2	35
become familiar with (phrasal verb)		to get to know or recognize an area, an activity, or a person	1	16
benefits (n.)	1	advantages or profits gained from something	4	66
beware (v.)		to be careful	11	196
campus (n.)		the area and buildings of an institution, educational or business	1	16
cautious (adj.)		careful or aware that there might be problems	11	196
challenge (n.)		a difficulty; something requiring you to work hard to achieve it	9	160

Word or Term	AWL Sublist	Definition	Chapter	Page
colonization (n.)		the act of having new people come to live and control a new area	8	137
commit (v.)		to decide to do something completely, until it is finished	9	160
community (n.)	2	a group of people with common characteristics or interests who usually live in the same area and care about each other	12	210
complex (adj.)	2	not straightforward, but rather difficult or complicated	7	119
computer (adj.)	2	describing the use of a programmable electronic device that can store, retrieve, and process data	12	210
confusing (adj.)		not clear; possible to misunderstand	1	16
conquered (v.)		took control over someone by force	8	137
consequently (adv.)	2	as a result; as a consequence of something; therefore	6	100
considerable (adj.)	3	quite large, significant	8	137
constantly (adv.)	3	without stopping or change; continuously	8	137
contribute (v.)	3	to give something in order to help achieve something	3	52
contemporary (adj.)		in the present time; at the same time as something or someone else	6	101
coordinate (v.)	3	to bring together, match, or organize different elements so that they work together well	10	174
create (v.)	1	to make something new from other material or objects, or to make something happen	2	34
credit (adj.)	2	describing the amount of money available to use for buying something and to actually pay for it later	11	196
crowded (adj.)		not having much space; a lot of people or things in the same space	5	86
crucial (adj.)		really important or necessary	4	66
cruise (n.)		a short, organized trip, usually on a boat	5	86
decades (n.)		groups of 10 years	10	174
define (v.)	1	to provide a clear explanation of the meaning of something	6	100
definitely (adv.)		certainly; without a doubt	1	16
derives (v.)	1	has its origins in; comes from	6	100
design (v.)	2	to create or to plan something usually by the means of drawing it	7	119
determine (v.)		to decide or choose	4	67
display (v.)		to show or demonstrate	7	119
document (n.)	3	a written, printed, or digital presentation of detailed information, often official, such as proving ownership of something or a passport	11	196
domination (n.)	3	having control over someone or something; supremacy	8	137
efficiently (adv.)		in an economic and effective way	7	119
embellished (adj.)		has additional or exaggerated details	6	101
enhances (v.)		makes better; improves	4	66
ensure (v.)	3	to make sure or certain	3	52
entertainment (n.)		an activity produced by someone for the enjoyment of others	5	86
entire (adj.)		whole, complete	3	52
environment (n.)	1	the situation or conditions around you; surroundings	6	100
errands (n.)		small tasks that you need to do outside of your home, such as shopping or going to the bank	3	52

Word or Term	AWL Sublist	Definition	Chapter	Page
establish (v.)	1	to begin or create something with a set or specific plan so that it will succeed	9	160
estimate (n.)	1	an initial calculation of the cost, value, or time required to complete an activity or pay for something; an educated guess	11	196
evaluate (v.)	2	to examine something; to assess its advantages and disadvantages; to determine the value, quality, or importance of something	9	160
evident (adj.)	1	clear; obvious; easily understood	5	86
evolved (v.)		changed or developed over time	6	100
expand (v.)		to grow larger	8	137
expensive (adj.)		costs a lot of money	10	174
experts (n.)		people who have highly specialized knowledge and skills in a particular field	8	137
extend (v.)		to give an opportunity or reach out to someone	3	53
feature (n.)	2	an important or notable part or aspect of something; an important characteristic	1	17
fees (n.)		charges or costs; the amount of money you have to pay for the courses, activities, or services you want	1	16
finally (adv.)	2	emphasizing that something is complete after a long time or delay; at last	1	17
financial (adj.)	1	relating to finances; involving money	9	160
fireworks (n.)		minor explosives set off to produce bright lights and sounds in the sky for the entertainment of others	5	86
focused (adj.)	2	concentrating on, directly looking at, or paying attention to something specific	2	35
gain (v.)		to get, achieve, or add to something	10	174
generation (n.)		an age group living in the same period of time; your grandparents, your parents, you, and your children are examples of four generations	6	100
giving up (phrasal verb)		stopping doing something because it is too difficult	9	160
grand finale (n.)		the final part or end of a show that impresses the audience even more than the earlier parts	5	86
guidelines (n.)		a list of instructions or ideas to follow	4	66
hidden (adj.)		not clear or not easily seen, possibly on purpose or intentionally	11	196
hiring (n.)		the act of selecting and giving someone a job	2	34
identify (v.)	1	to find; to spot; to recognize	7	119
illustrate (v.)	3	to create a picture or a physical or mental image of something in order to explain it more clearly	6	101
immigrants (n.)	3	people who move, usually permanently, from one area or country to another	6	100
impact (v.)	2	to affect; to have an effect on something	7	119
incidents (n.)		things that happen and perhaps are unexpected; potentially unhappy events	6	101
income (n.)	1	money earned or obtained through employment or investment	10	174
incorporating (v.)		bringing different things together to become one	7	119

Word or Term	AWL Sublist	Definition	Chapter	Page
individuals (n.)	1	distinct persons; identified as singular humans and not part of a group	10	174
influences (n.)		the things, ideas, or people that make you decide to do certain things	8	137
initially (adv.)	3	originally; at the beginning; at first	5	86
inspire (v.)		to make you want to do the same thing and make you believe you can	9	160
instead of (prep.)		the opposite of what was just mentioned; in place of; or not	3	52
interact (v.)	3	to talk with, communicate, or do things together with other people	3	52
investments (n.)	2	actions of investing money to gain profit; financial dealings	9	160
involved (v.)	1	to be or take part in something	3	52
issues (n.)	1	topics or subjects of discussion	7	119
items (n.)	2	objects; articles; things	5	86
kinesthetic (adj.)		referring to your body's movement and ability to move	7	119
legal (adj.)	1	connected or related to law or lawful activity	9	161
lineups (n.)		lines of people waiting for their turn to get or do something; queue	1	16
link (n.)	3	a connection between things or something in common with others	6	101
loaded (adj.)		full of; containing a lot of	2	35
locate (v.)	3	to find the precise place or location of someone or something	1	16
look forward to (phrasal verb)		to be very interested in what is going to happen in the future; to anticipate	3	52
major (adj.)	1	important, significant	8	137
negative (adj.)	3	the opposite of positive	7	122
normally (adv.)	2	usually; typically	12	210
obesity (n.)		the effect of being very overweight or weighing more than you should	4	66
outcome (n.)	3	the way something turns out; a result of something; a consequence	12	210
participation (n.)	2	the action of taking part in something	3	52
partners (n.)	2	two or more people who work together toward a common goal	12	211
percent (n.)	1	one part in 100	4	66
periods (n.)	1	extended or specific lengths of time	8	137
persist (v.)		to continue to do something until it's finished, even if it is difficult	9	160
physical (adj.)	3	relating to the body	4	66
play dates (n.)		times set aside for children to get together to play and socialize	3	52
positive (adj.)	2	describing something that has a good, optimistic quality	5	86
potentially (adv.)	2	describing a possible outcome in the future; possibly; not yet, but possible	2	35
predominantly (adv.)		in the majority; mainly	7	120
primarily (adv.)	2	most importantly or in the first position of importance	12	210
proceed (v.)	1	to continue	9	160
process (n.)	1	a series of actions or steps a person takes to achieve a particular end or result	3	52
professional (n.)		someone with special training or education to do a specific job	2	161
projects (n.)		planned activities or work with a specific purpose or expected result	2	34

Word or Term	AWL Sublist	Definition	Chapter	Page
purchase (v.)	2	to buy; to pay to obtain something	5	86
quality time (n.)		time that is valuable or good for the people who spend it together	3	52
quit (v.)		to stop doing something	9	160
range (n.)	2	variety; available selection	5	86
reassembling (v.)		putting something back together or in the order it is meant to be	12	210
register (v.)	3	to put your name on an official list in order to qualify to do something; enroll; sign up	1	16
relevant (adj.)	2	connected to what is being talked about	7	122
rely on (phrasal verb)	3	to be certain of; depend on; count on	2	35
renovate (v.)		to change something in a house or building to make it more up-to-date or more modern	2	34
requires (v.)	1	makes necessary; specifies as necessary; needs	1	16
research (n.)	1	the careful, detailed examination or study of a subject to find out more information and draw conclusions	11	196
restricts (v.)	2	limits; creates boundaries or limitations on activities or individuals	10	174
retreats (n.)		activities away from the normal environment to work on new ideas or to get together with friends	12	210
reveals (v.)		shows something that wasn't easily seen before	12	210
role (n.)	1	the position, function, or purpose that someone or something has	4	67
roots (n.)		beginnings or origins of something; sources	8	137
savings (n.)		money that you set aside or do not use so that you can use it for a future purpose	10	174
schedule (n.)		a plan or list of things or activities you need to do, often including times and places; a timetable	1	16
sector (n.)	1	a specific area (physical, economic, or referring to an activity)	10	174
security (n.)	2	the state of feeling safe or providing protection and safe surroundings	11	196
sedentary (adj.)		staying in one place; not physically active	4	66
seek (v.)	2	to attempt to find or get something; search for	4	67
select (v.)	2	to choose something from a number of options; to pick	1	16
self-esteem (n.)		how you feel about yourself	4	66
service industry (n.)		an area of business that serves the public, such as restaurants, hotels, entertainment, and so on	10	174
shift (n.)	3	regular period of time of work, such as day, evening, or night shift	10	175
significant (adj.)	1	something that is important, special, or meaningful	4	67
similar (adj.)	1	having a lot of characteristics in common but not completely the same	6	101
sites (n.)	2	specific places or locations, in this case, on the Internet	2	35
sorts (n.)		kinds or types	12	210
sources (n.)	1	the original places where you find information	2	35
souvenirs (n.)		objects to remind you of a place or an event	5	86
spatial (adj.)		involving space and things within that space	7	119
specific (adj.)	1	exact; particular; definite; precise	1	16

Word or Term	AWL Sublist	Definition	Chapter	Page
stalls (n.)		partially enclosed or divided areas for displaying or containing objects, such as a vegetable stall (where one sells vegetables) or a horse stall (where a horse is contained within a building)	5	86
strategy (n.)	2	a plan or method of action designed to bring a desired result; a plan	1	16
structure (n.)	1	the organization or patterns of the many parts of something	8	137
stuff (n.)		an informal word for things or objects in general	1	16
suffers (v.)		experiences the bad effects of something, such as a disease	4	66
sufficient (adj.)	3	enough; the amount that is needed to satisfy a need	4	66
support (v.)		to help or give strength to something or someone	9	160
surface (n.)		the top area of a thing	12	210
surveys (n.)	2	research studies, examinations of something; tools or methods to collect data to gain information on a certain topic	4	66
task (n.)	3	an activity, a piece of work to do	3	52
technique (n.)	3	a method or way of doing something in a particular manner	12	211
theories (n.)	1	principles, ideas, or speculations used to explain something, usually created by researchers or scientists	7	119
tool (n.)		an object, instrument, or device that is used to perform a task	12	210
traditions (n.)	2	customs or beliefs passed from generation to generation	3	52
transfer (v.)	2	to move something or someone from one place to another, such as money or ownership from one account or person to another	11	196
trend (n.)		the direction people are viewing and going along with; something such as a fashion trend or a way of thinking	2	35
tricky (adj.)		difficult or challenging; not easy to do	11	196
trust (v.)		to have confidence in something or someone; to have the feeling that someone is not going to hurt you	11	196
unrelated (adj.)		having no connection with a known thing	10	174
varied (v.)	1	differed; changed; offered a choice or selection	5	86
vendors (n.)		people who sell things	5	86
visualize (v.)		to bring an image to mind; to be able to see something in your mind	7	119
warranty (n.)		a guarantee or an assurance that something will do what it's supposed to do for a certain amount of time	11	196
worth (n.)		the value of something; to be worth something means it is a good idea to do and there will be a benefit	11	196

Credits

Chapter 1

Photo

2 Wanwalit Tongted/Shutterstock
9 top © Jesús Arias | Dreamstime.com
9 centre Jeny Che/Shutterstock
9 bottom Song_about_summer/Shutterstock
8 © Andreykr | Dreamstime.com
7 Lokichen/Shutterstock
4 © Dip2000 | Dreamstime.com
12 © Michel Bussieres | Dreamstime.com
16 Chunumunu/Dreamstime.com/GetStock
17 © Katarzyna Bialasiewicz | Dreamstime.com

Chapter 2

Photo

22 Photo by Rémi Boyer on Unsplash
24 Poomipat/Shutterstock
27 Mark Bowden/iStockphoto
31 amana images/Thinkstock
34 Manu Padilla/Shutterstock
35 DuxX/Shutterstock
36 Rawpixel.com/Shutterstock
37 © Tyler Olson | Dreamstime.com

Chapter 3

Literary

52 Adapted from "Make breakfast a family affair" by Ottawa Family Living Magazine http://www .ottawafamilyliving.com/make_breakfast_a_ family_affair

Photo

42 bottom © Elizabeth Salomons
42 centre bottom Prostock-studio/Shutterstock
42 centre top © Ahilfoto1 | Dreamstime.com
42 top © John Blanton | Dreamstime.com
44 bottom Chayantorn Tongmorn/Shutterstock
44 top Marina Zlochin/Thinkstock
47 Photo by Ben Weber on Unsplash

49 Gustavo Frazao/Shutterstock
52 © Mehmet Doruk Taşcı | Dreamstime.com
54 Shift Drive/Shutterstock

Chapter 4

Literary

66 Based on: 1. http://www.cbc.ca/news/ yourcommunity/2012/05/whats-keeping-kids-from-being-more-active.html 2. Active Healthy Kids Canada (2012). Is Active Play Extinct? The Active Healthy Kids Canada 2012 Report Card on Physical Activity for Children and Youth. Toronto: Active Healthy Kids Canada. OR Summary: www.activehealthykids.ca 3. http://www.csep.ca/ guidelines"
68 TOM'S DINER, Words and Music by SUZANNE VEGA © 1987 WB MUSIC CORP. and WAIFER-SONGS LTD. All Rights Administered by WB MUSIC CORP. All Rights Reserved. Used By Permission of ALFRED MUSIC

Audio

68 TOM'S DINER, Words and Music by SUZANNE VEGA © 1987 WB MUSIC CORP. and WAIFER-SONGS LTD. All Rights Administered by WB MUSIC CORP. All Rights Reserved. Used By Permission of ALFRED MUSIC

Photo

60 © Joni Hanebutt | Dreamstime.com
62 top CandyRetriever/Shutterstock
64 oliveromg/Shutterstock
66 ESB Professional/Shutterstock
68 Brendt A Petersen/Shutterstock
70 Jacob Lund/Shutterstock

Chapter 5

Photo

78 left © Elizabeth Salomons
78 right © Elizabeth Salomons
79 top © Morganeborzee | Dreamstime.com